WRITERS
IN THE
CLASSROOM

WRITERS IN THE CLASSROOM

Edited by

RUTH NATHAN

Christopher-Gordon Publishers, Inc.
Norwood, MA

FOR LARRY NATHAN

Christopher-Gordon Publishers, Inc.
480 Washington Street
Norwood, MA 02062

Printed in the United States of America

10 9 8 7 6 5 4 3 2 1   96 95 94 93 92 91

ISBN: 0-026842-05-6

SHORT TABLE OF CONTENTS

TABLE OF CONTENTS

CREDITS FOR *WRITERS IN THE CLASSROOM*

Chapter 2

Topic lists used by permission of Emily Brown, Julie Hamann, and Kris Klann. Topic sheet and cat story used with permission of Nicole Kosiba.

Chapter 4

"First Kiss" used with permission of Helen Sasinowski-Paull.
Response to "The Drummer Boy of Shiloh," by Ray Bradbury, used with permission of Rachel Anderson.
"My Favorite Childhood Toy" used with permission of Amy Hoggard.
"First Grade Teacher" and "Dear Millie" used with permission of Laurie Wentzel.
"An Embarrassing Situation" used with permission of Patricia M. Salvador.
"Bad Habit" used with permission of Cheryl Lyn Bart.
"Dialogue" used with permission of Barbara J. Bird.

Chapter 6

Excerpt from material by Scott Charles Ford used with permission.

Chapter 7

Excerpts from the song "Shrimp Boats," by Paul Mason Howard and Paul Weston, are used with permission of Hanover Music Corporation.
Excerpt from short story "The Peanut Butter Kid" are used with permission of David Ramsey.
Excerpt from "The Great Escape" used by permission of Nicole May.
Excerpt from "Down South" used with permission of John Pitts.
Excerpt from "My Only Home Boy" used with permission of Dezmon Faulkner.

Chapter 9

Excerpts from *Changes in Latitudes* (1988) and *Bearstone*, (1989), by Will Hobbs, are reprinted with permission of Atheneum Publishers, an imprint of Macmillan Publishing Company. Copyright © 1988 and © 1989 by Will Hobbs.

Chapter 10

Excerpts from *My Blue Jay* are used with permission of Jessida Faigle.
Excerpt from *Big Bear* used with permission of Eric Rothfeder.
Excerpt from *Clones* used with permission of Terry Strother.
Excerpt from *One Mystery is Tough Enough* used with permission of Jonathan Dalin.

PREFACE

This book began in a flash, on Highway M115, around Mesick. It was late June of '89, still early summertime when teachers can have grandiose plans and take themselves seriously. I was headed home after a week at the Traverse Bay Writing and Reading Workshops where about ten teacher/writers led half-day writing sessions, followed by half-day sessions on pedagogy or writing-lab work. The workshop leaders' areas of expertise varies from summer to summer. This particular year we had had writers of fiction, plays, poetry, non-fiction, news, editorials, and feature articles. Undoubtedly, this variability is what lead to "the flash." Why not, I thought, edit a book where these writer/teachers, and perhaps other I know, would share their writing as they had with their students all morning in Traverse, and then talk about teaching in individual chapters varying by genre or topic. In other words, I wanted these writers to put themselves on the line *first*, talk about teaching, *second*.

That's how *Writers in the Classroom* began. It's just a little over a year, and here you have it: nineteen chapters and an epilogue by teachers who *write* and often, but not always, *publish* their work. Each chapter is divided into two parts, A and B, just as I'd dreamed. In Part A, you meet the authors as writers through uninterrupted segments of the type of writing they enjoy and do best. In Part B, you meet the authors as classroom teachers, most (not all) full-time, where they share how they teach their students to write—classrooms where teachers write with their students and share their evolving drafts. Each author has attempted to abstract some principles related to the teaching of writing from their experiences as actual writer/teachers, and to demonstrate these principles in the context of real classrooms from the primary grades through college. What a joy to read their work, and what a relief not to be *told* what to do, but to be *shown*.

How Writers In The Classroom Is Organized

Writers in the Classroom is divided into three parts. Part I, Starting with What You Know, includes entrees into finding good topics (Steinberg, Wilkins, and Smith), discovering new genres through other genres (Deen and Weber), and revising from the vantage point of what you know best (Monkmeyer).

Part II, Working Beyond What You Know, offers revsion (re-seeing) or rewriting (re-wording) strategies the writers in this section have found helpful. The Hobbs and Clark chapters both deal with precision and style. My chapter covers one aspect of improving story dialogue by helping readers envision the scene and empathize with the characters through a process of adding on, while Juliana Janosz shows us how to write story leads that engage. Most of these strategies would be labeled "rewriting" because they're rewording of ideas already set forth. Gloria Nixon-John and Terry Blackhawk, on the other hand, deal with revision in the true sense of the word. That is, while writing rough draft, or rewriting it, these authors believe writers may stumble upon new approaches, alternative points-of-view, or entirely different topics altogether. While Terry Blackhawk approaches revision through story writing and Gloria Nixon-John through poetry, both these teacher/writers are similar in their willingness to let go of one idea, approach, or even genre, in favor of another.

Part III, Working Within Specific Genres, does exactly what it says: Writer/teachers work with children and popular genres from the starting point through development, in some cases (Temple, Asher, Hayes), or from the starting point through polishing, in others (Hilla, Steele, Roop, Oomen). The Epilogue, also in Part III, is a poetic piece by Sheila Cowing about the importance of publishing children's work.

WAYS TO APPROACH THIS BOOK

There are several ways readers might approach *Writers in the Classroom*. One way is by **genre**. For example, those interested in writing short stories will want to read the Steinberg and Wilkins or Weber chapter first (finding topics), followed by Hilla's chapter, then Blackhawk's, Monkmeyer's, Nathan's, Asher's, Hobb's and Clark's.

A unit or class in poetry might have the reader beginning with Nixon-John's, Steinberg's, Smith's, Weber's or Wilkins's chapters (finding topics and revising), followed by Oomen's chapter on writing and publishing collaboratively.

If the reader is interested in essay writing, Rosemary Deen's chapter is a must, as is Larry Hayes's. These are both extraordinarily accomplished essayists who begin with the known, or with what's of extreme, personal interest, and gently prod students along, offering strategies which are eminently helpful.

Another way to approach *Writers in the Classroom* is by **objective**. That is, let's say the reader/teacher is interested in students combining content knowledge with their imaginations to produce high quality work. I'd suggest reading the Roops' chapter and Frances Temple's first, followed by Hobbs's and Clark's. The first two chapters will give the reader ideas for approaching the objective, the last two, for polishing. Of course, where stories have been written, the Monkmeyer chapter on adding detail, and mine, on dialogue, also might be of interest. In my opinion, the Asher chapter is crucial, as well: Acting out is a powerful form of prewriting.

If the reader's objective is **rewriting**, then the Hobbs, Clark, and Monkmeyer chapters will be helpful, as is the Janosz, and Hayes chapters. If the objective is **getting started**, all of the chapters in Part I were useful along with Blackhawk's, Nixon-John's, and Oomen's. The question of **how to structure a story** would send me to Steele, Asher, and Clark. **Publication issues** are discussed by Hilla (the effect computers had), Oomen (effect of collaboration), Hobbs (effect, period!) and Sheila Cowing's Epilogue.

Another approach to *Writers in the Classroom* is by **grade level**. Chapters most suited to elementary teachers are by Wilkins, Weber, Monkmeyer, Nathan, Clark, Hobbs, Janosz, Asher, Steele, the Roops, Temple, Oomen, and Cowing. Middle school teachers might start by reading Steinberg, Weber, Monkmeyer, Hobbs, Nathan, Clark, Janosz, Asher, Steele, Oomen, and Cowing, and later pick up Deen, Hayes, Smith, then the rest. High School and college teachers might try Steinberg, Weber, Deen, Smith, Nixon-John, Blackhawk, Clark, Hobbs, Janosz, Hilla, Steele, the Roops, Temple, Cowing and Oomen, first, followed by all the rest.

Lastly, a fourth entreé into *Writers in the Classroom* is my way, reading all the Part A's, followed by all the Part B's. That's how I'd do it now that I've read, reread, and *enjoyed* all the chapters.

Enjoy, please, and write me c/o Christopher-Gordon Publishers, Inc. if you like this collection. I'd love to edit a second volume—I have the writers lined up!

FOREWORD

For some reason, I always get a little nervous when someone hands me a new book about teaching writing. I like to have all the newest writing books up on my shelves, because my students think I'm smart and well-read. "Oh, I see you have the new Ruth Nathan book." I like to hand them out to other teachers, "Here you need to read what Don Murray says." But when I sit down to read new writing books, I'm always a little apprehensive. Maybe it's because I'm afraid I'll find ideas that conflict with my own teacher instincts. Maybe I'm afraid I'll find out somebody is already doing what I'm doing and has better names for it. Maybe it's because I'm afraid I'll read about some hotshot teacher who is doing wonderful things in her own class, things I should be doing: "using editing groups to improve revising" and "building ownership through publishing" and "rhetorical strategies to enhance critical thinking" and "making the essay easy." I think I'm a fairly decent writing teacher, but hearing other teachers' accounts of wonderful things happening in their classrooms sometimes leaves me feeling inadequate, diminished somehow. I'm not sure why, but reading new books on writing generally leaves me a little queasy.

Maybe all writing teachers are like I am, secretly. Maybe even the ones who sound so confident and knowledgeable in books and presentations feel the same insecurity I feel when they read about other writing classes. I think all teachers who take any risks at all are plagued by uncertainty and doubts, doubts that lurk just beyond the faint circle of light of their own knowledge. For me, as a writing teacher, the light of certainty is a flickering one. I find it difficult to stand up in front of people and say, "This is what I do in my class. It works." I always want to qualify that statement, "It worked last week or it worked with certain kids or it didn't work but I know how to fix it." I'd rather say, "This is what I'm trying to do right now. These are the things I'm working on as a writer and these are the things I'm working on as a teacher." Sometimes new books about teaching writing make me nervous. I order them from Heinemann and Christopher-Gordon and then just let them sit around on my desk until I get the courage to open them up and steal a peek.

I let this book sit around awhile. I was reluctant to plunge into it. *Writers in the Classroom*. I liked the title, but I knew the authors were published writers and I was nervous. Sometimes writers say really stupid things about learning to write: "study grammar; take Latin; read Aristotle." These writers might tell me they learned to write by copying passages from Thomas Wolfe or some other chilling testimonial. I thumbed the book a few times thinking; "Who are these people and what do they know that I don't?" I was relieved not to find anything stupid or pretentious in this book. This is a book of stories, stories about teacher struggles to become good writers and teachers. The stories they tell of their teaching sound honest and sincere. Reading the book made me want to begin writing my own stories again.

I put the book aside and went directly to my Macintosh to begin thinking about books I still want to write. That's another mark of a good book on writing: It makes you want to write your own book. I made a list of books I should write: an excrutiatingly honest book about how challenging it is to teach writing in real schools with real kids, but it sounds like these authors have already done that; a book about my own struggles as a writer with some of my own pieces, but that's in here too. How about a book that helps us sort through the relationship of process and product? Someone needs to help us think through the current preoccupation with processs. I'm nervous about the potential misuse of the term and the proliferation of some "writing activities" in the name of process. I'm worried that many teachers who want to teach about process don't understand the importance of building rich contexts in which students read and write and learn.

As a writer, I know that the process/product schism we've manufactured is mainly artificial, your basic "straw binary" as Janet Emig would say. "We emphasize process in this class rather than product." Impossible! Process and product are inseparable. Concerns about them oscillate and hum in a working writer's mind like a spinning gyro. Some writer know about processes, at least their own; some writers are even willing to talk about processes and reflect on them; but all writers are obsessed with product. What was it Annie Dillard said in *The Writing Life*? "Process is nothing; erase your tracks. The path is not the work." Is she right about that? I'm not sure, but I'm trying to set my classroom up in such a way that students can develop unique and individual approaches to writing tasks. The stuff kids write in my class is product, and I want it to be good, and I want them to like it and work on it for months and feel it's their very own. Maybe I'm not ready to write a book about process yet.

For the past two years, I've been trying to run my writing classes like a studio, an art studio or an architecture studio or. . . a writing studio. I got the first visions of such a class from reading Donald Schon's *Educating the Reflective Practitioner*. Awkward title; wonderful book. Makes me ache to get in the classroom every time I pick it up. Maybe that's the definition of a good book on teaching writing. It makes you want to teach kids while you're reading it. Schon talks about his observations in an architectural studio where the master designer is trying to help the fledgling architects get started. He creates this scenario where the master says to the beginners, "I can tell you there is something you need to know and with my help you may be able to learn it. But I cannot tell you what it is in a way you can now understand. I can only arrange for you to have the right sorts of experiences for yourself." Great stuff. For the writer who teaches writing, it is always the same. I know stuff I have learned from my own experimentation, but it will do you absolutely no good to hear about it frome. You have to learn that stuff for yourself. Who originated the notion that people can learn complex and difficult things by listening to someone else tell them how to do it? My challenge as a writing teacher is to create an environment that promotes work, to put writers to work and do anything I can to keep them at work until they begin to understand a writer's work for themselves. The authors of this book talk about work and model writers at work. I like writing books that talk about work.

I began trying to organize my class like a working studio in 1989 in the English department of the University of California at Santa Barbara. UCSB was a great place to hang out, and learn things. I was a Visiting Professor. Great job: no committees, no advisees, no phone calls, and I could ignore the departmental memos. That year was pure teaching, razor clean and scary. I was teaching freshman composition for the first time in 20 years and an upper division writing course for students of all academic majors. My classroom space didn't look much like a studio. No skylights. No wonderful tables or easels or sinks or paint splashes on the floor. No smocks. It wasn't interior decorating I was after. It was the values of a studio I was trying to effect. In the studio classroom, repeated practice and experimentation are the norm. Students don't expect to get it right the first time. Getting it right may not be important at all; individual visions and versions are what's important. And writers come to those versions by experimenting, by trying out ideas. That's always tough to get students to buy. They keep saying, "We don't know what you want." You keep saying, "I want you to read and write and think." It was a battle of wills at the outset. The teacher's role in the studio is to stay out of the kids' way, but not too far out of the way. Studio teachers are highly selective with their instruction which for me means only telling kids things when they absolutely have to know it. I found myself responding to student questions like, "What do you want?" with "I want to see your version of this." And to "Does this look right?" with comments like, "What do you think?" Brilliant teacher answers. Most of the stuff I used to "teach" kids they can learn for themselves by working as writers in the studio.

I finally screwed up my courage and gave this book a thorough reading. Read the thing from cover to cover, and it was a good read. I felt like I had found some colleagues, some colleagues who struggle with the same things I struggle with. They sound like writers who know about teaching. I'll have to admit I was impressed by the courage of these authors. They put pieces of their own writing on display right up front in their chapters. I'm not sure I'd be brave enough to do that. The ideas in this book are grounded in classroom practice; the authors sound surefooted, comfortable. They have a sense of what works and what doesn't work. It's the unique combination of "How I work as a writer" talk interspersed with the "What I do in my class" talk. I like that best about the book. I didn't feel queasy at all after I read it. I wanted to find a classroom and start teaching.

Dan Kirby
The University of Central Florida

Mike Steinberg says everyone has a story to tell. He believes it, just like he believes everyone will be famous for fifteen minutes. Because Steinberg values those "fifteen minutes" like no other person I know, he's one of the most delightful writing instructors you'll ever meet. He's what I imagine Raymond Carver must have been like, the man whose famed, most critical comment was, "It's good you got that story behind you." Steinberg's chapter is a rush, a rush into taking yourself seriously from the start. Reading him is like reading a Jim Dodge novel; he doesn't stop. In this chapter Steinberg guides us through using personal narrative in an attempt to show us how students, given the opportunity, engage with one another, help each other out, and finally come to trust that they will "eventually take ownership of the writing." To "take ownership" is a serious step, the place writers must start if they are to go anywhere. In a very real sense, his chapter is most like Heidi Wilkins's. Though Mike works with college students and Heidi with first graders, there's more in common than not.

CHAPTER 1
PERSONAL NARRATIVES: TEACHING AND LEARNING WRITING FROM THE INSIDE OUT

By Michael Steinberg

PART A: MOVING ON

Why don't I care about basketball anymore?

Several good reasons, maybe. I'm pushing 50 and I don't play competitive ball anymore. The players, even the pros, are two and three decades younger than me. Or—the game's changed so much since I grew up in the 50s. Reasonable reasons, but they don't seem like enough. Not for someone who used to be on fire for the sport.

Already an aficionado at 13, I read everything I could find about the game—from Clair Bee's romanticized Chip Hilton novels to the *Sporting News*'s weekly gossip and stats. There was nothing I didn't know about basketball: rosters, team records, even jersey numbers.

As much as I enjoyed studying basketball, I loved to play. Cold winter afternoons would find me scaling schoolyard fences to play three-man pick-up ball with the older guys. Weekends, I hung around the playgrounds to watch the City "legends": Bed-Sty's Connie Hawkins, who had the swoop of a majestic eagle; the ballet-graceful Manhattan giant, Lou Alcindor (aka Kareem Abdul Jabbar);

1

the Bronx's 5 foot 3 wizard, Frankie Townsend, who from a standing leap could dunk two basketballs at once. I knew that if I stayed late enough at the playground, I'd get chosen into a pick-up game; but usually my team of short, slow white guys was back on the sidelines faster than you could say "swish." Still I could boast that I played ball with "the Hawk" or "Big Lew" or "Frankie T."

And then there was "The Garden." I was 13 when my dad took me to my first college double-header. The moment we surfaced from the 8th Avenue subway station and passed under Madison Square Garden's glittering marquee, I felt like I'd stepped into another dimension: I couldn't take my eyes off the shiny, yellow hardwood floor. During the layup drills, I got caught up in the pregame glitz: Acrobatic players in satin warm-up suits hung in mid-air gracefully curling lay-ups against the glass backboards while pep bands blared out fight songs; NYU cheerleaders shouted, "Let's go Violet, Violet let's go;" and the two guys in the seats next to us handicapped the game. "It's Villanova in a walk," said one, and the other countered with. "No way José, gimme NYU. Lay me ten big ones on the spread and you're on."

As soon as I was old enough to go to the city on my own, I made weekly pilgrimages—traveling 50 miles on the bus and subway—from my home in Rockaway to the Garden. On Thursdays, it was college basketball double-headers; Tuesdays, the Knicks. Each game, I went through the same ritual: cruised the lobby; eavesdropped on the bookies and touts, trying to pick up inside tips; sat in my usual seat—mezzanine, section 215—dead mid-court; kept score; and devised my own strategies—loudly coaching players to "go back door" or "set a screen" or "cut to the hoop."

Over the years I kept running into a group of other "Garden rats": In time we formed our own coterie. For ten years, we met regularly before double-headers at Nedicks' on 49th and Eighth—where we'd gab about our heroes, set up betting pools, and gulp down the latest stats.

The high points of our winter were two major tournaments—the Holiday Festival at Christmas and the National Invitational Tournament in March. The tournaments paired the best local teams—St. John's, NYU, Manhattan, CCNY, LIU—against national powers like North Carolina, UCLA, Kentucky, Kansas, Notre Dame, so tickets were hard to come by. The night before the Garden box office opened, we'd camp outside, huddling in blankets, noshing on cold franks and swigging warm beer while we doped out the tournament pairings and took cat-naps in shifts.

In those days, my mind was a highlight film of Garden tournament games: Bill Russell and K.C. Jones's national champs from San Francisco barely beating Tommy Heinsohn's outmanned Holy Cross team; Providence's Jimmy Walker tossing in 50 points to set a Festival scoring record; Lew Alcindor's triumphant homecoming; the yearly NIT upsets engineered by Joe Lapchick's scrappy St. John's city kids; and the performance I'll never forget: In the last Holiday Festival at the old Garden, Bill Bradley scored 44 points against Michigan, only to foul out with four minutes left and see his team lose—on a Cazzie Russell jumper at the buzzer.

In 1964, the old Garden was razed to make room for a parking lot and the arena was moved downtown to 34th Street. That same year, I finished college and went to Michigan State for graduate school. As soon as I arrived in East Lansing, I purchased a season basketball ticket and signed up to play on two intramural league teams and one city rec team. On my nights off, I played pick-up with the other gym rats.

For the next 15 years, at Christmas and in mid-March, I made my semi-annual pilgrimage back for the Holiday Festival and the NIT. But by the late 60s the Garden kept changing: The mezzanine had become a corporate "sky box;" you charged your tickets on a credit card and took what the "Ticketron" computer sent you; the scalpers were 12-year-olds who wore Mohawk "do's" and sold drugs on the street; and the New York teams I used to root for—NYU, Fordham, Manhattan, CCNY, LIU—no longer played there. By the mid-70s, only St. John's was left and most of its best players were recruited from junior colleges somewhere in Texas or Oklahoma.

My life was changing too. In 1974, when I got my Ph.D. and an offer to teach English at Michigan State, it began to register that the athletes I watched were the same age as the students I played intramural ball with.

On television, the games seemed boring, irritating. The networks covered basketball coast-to-coast, so you couldn't tell one style of play from another: Iowa farmboys had the same moves as playground guys from Brooklyn. In the interviews, instead of "back door picks," and "boxing out," 20-year-old players boasted of multi-year contracts and agent's fees.

In 1979, I missed my first NIT.

I didn't mean to. I was reading a new lit anthology for next term's class, and it seemed more urgent than the tournament. But then, I was still half-disappointed that the airline was booked up when I called in a day before the first double-header.

A year later, I quit playing intramural ball, tired of getting banged around by 19-year-old kamikazes.

Next year, I skipped the Holiday Festival: I was busy writing a book.

This past spring I got involved in a teaching project in the schools and forgot to keep track of the NIT, even though Michigan State got to the semi-finals.

Now, doom hovers.

I'm a step away from turning into an aging midwestern college professor.

So maybe that's why—even though I know I'll be skiing in Northern Michigan—I booked a Christmas week flight to New York, to meet the old Garden gang for a 30-year reunion.

Just in case.

Just in case I need to feel young.

Just in case I need to love basketball again.

PART B: WHY WRITE NARRATIVE?

My immediate goal in any writing class—middle school through graduate—is to help students become more active, engaged, writers. The simplest way, I've found, is to start them off with a personal narrative. The narrative's form invites students to use their imagination, experience, and their own voices, and it encourages them to write about themselves and the world they live in. When writers of any age accept that invitation, it is much easier to coach them along, to encourage them to help each other, and finally, to trust that they will eventually take ownership of the writing.

Moreover, in working with narrative I've discovered that students who can compose them freely often have more success when they begin to write in other prescribed forms—whether creative, academic, or "real-world" genres. That's because writing is an "inside-out" activity. If you can compose fluently in one form, you can learn to compose competently in others. Since good narrative often contains elements of exposition, argument, and analysis, students who can write it can, given adequate time and instruction, learn to master exposition, argument, and analysis better than those who have written exclusively in those school-sponsored forms.

Those are not the only good reasons to use personal narrative in the classroom. Other benefits include the following:

- Personal essays encourage self-discovery and self-insight: They offer us the gift of surprise and wonder.
- They allow us to indulge in the sheer joy of tracking an insight or idea, and of letting it unfold at its natural pace and length.
- They offer us the freedom of our moods: We can be meditative, serious, critical, outrageous, sarcastic, empathetic, and so forth.
- They encourage us to follow the sometimes illogical twists and turns of our "monkey" minds.
- They allow us to discover and present our best, our worst, our most eccentric and idiosyncratic selves.
- They encourage us to make sense of our lives, to better understand who we are.
- And most important, narrative writing offers us opportunities to explore and come to terms with our own shared humanness.

Those of us who write personal essays know that they are fun to compose; and in a writing workshop, they're natural ice-breakers. Most everyone has a story (or stories) to tell. And when students are swapping stories, responding to stories, the writing classroom becomes a lively and dynamic workplace. Many of my most memorable (and productive) classes have been personal narrative workshops.

In this chapter, I'd like to demonstrate how I use the workshop approach to teach personal essay writing in two different settings—first with teenagers and then with experienced English teachers. In addition, I will talk about how conducting a series of writing workshops with both groups helped me compose one of my own narratives, "Moving On" (see Part A).

TEACHING AND WRITING NARRATIVE WITH TEENAGERS

First, let me recount my experience in a recent high school in-service.

I set the workshop up as a three-day-a-week, one month unit on "Growing Up." Our main activities were to read and respond to a variety of personal essays and to write our own pieces. To break the ice on the first day, we did some freewriting and talking about our experience as readers and writers—how we learned, who taught us, what books we liked, disliked, teachers we loved and hated, why, and so forth.

When students read their freewrites back to one another the discussions were animated and lively: They told stories about how their mothers and fathers read them kid books like *Dr. Seuss* and *Winnie the Pooh* before bed; some talked about the stories and books they wrote as pre-schoolers and in early elementary grades; others went on about their favorite and most hated teachers.

Next, we read and responded to selected personal narratives about childhood and adolescence. Dick Gregory's "Shame," for example, was about a childhood classroom incident which publicly humiliated Gregory and still had a profound influence on him twenty years later; in Langston Hughes's "Salvation," the author wrote about how the pressure of conformity forced him—at age thirteen—to lie about his faith; Jean Sheperd's "The Endless Streetcar Ride into the Night and the Tinfoil Noose" was about a devastating yet comic turning point in a young boy's life; Nora Ephron's "Shaping Up Absurd" told of a woman's lifelong struggle to come to terms with the adolescent stigma of having small breasts; Gloria Naylor's "Mommy, What Does Nigger Mean?," was a moving story about how a young black girl learns that insults can have a powerful effect on how we see ourselves; Harry Crews's "The Car" showed how the author became obsessed with automobiles—and how that obsession, for a time, controlled his life; and finally, Terry Gallway's "I'm Listening As Hard As I Can," told how a physical affliction can deeply affect a child's self-concept.

These readings were on-going assignments that lasted for the duration of the workshop. I chose them because they all deal in one way or another with the pressures and joys of growing up; because they represented a range and variety of topics and approaches; and because they were well-written.

Before tackling each essay, we discussed things like "firsts,"—first date, first kiss, and so forth—embarrassing moments, crucial decisions, peer pressure, personal obsessions, and the like.

As we read these narratives, we also did some prereading, during reading, and post-reading activities—things like predicting, speculating, and question-forming. For example, when we read Dick Gregory's "Shame," I asked the class to begin by reading only the date, title, and first page of the piece. Then we wrote a prediction scenario, shared those in groups, and finally read the entire piece. Once we finished reading, we did some focused freewriting and journal writing on our responses to the activity, I asked students to tell me what kinds of strategies they used when they were reading; and if they felt their scenario was more satisfying than Gregory's and why. These questions and others like them helped encourage the students to make personal connections with the readings.

In additional journal writings, I asked students first to respond personally and/or expressively to the essays. Some wrote letters to the author, or prequels and sequels; others did editorials about their likes and dislikes, while some simply wrote about issues or experiences that helped them to relate themselves to the writer's world.

The journal's intent was to urge students to read not only for self-discovery and personal meaning but also to help them examine the texts to see how writers shaped their work for an audience. For example, I had students discuss in their journals how effectively or ineffectively they thought these writers told their stories—how they set up their main points, how they used supporting examples and details, how effective/ineffective their leads and endings were, and how organized their pieces were.

Combining expressive and analytical writing gave the students the opportunity first to discover their ideas and personal connections with the essays and then to examine and discuss those same pieces from the perspective of how they were written and constructed—a process similar to the one they would soon experience in writing their own essays.

As we read and responded to the assigned essays, we began composing our own personal narratives. First, we all brainstormed a host of subjects related to "growing up"—things like childhood, school, family, sports, to list a few. Then as we narrowed our subjects down to topics, the students and I began writing about first dates, embarrassing moments at school, conflicts with friends and family, leaving home, moving, and so forth.

Next, we all did some freewriting on our topics. As I wrote along with them, I began following the trail of an idea that had been sitting somewhere back in my unconscious for a while. I'd gotten the idea from an "About Men" column in *The New York Times Sunday Magazine*. The piece was a childhood recollection about a time when the writer and his father attended a baseball game together. Consequently, when I began brainstorming in class the first thing that came to mind was my memory of watching my first basketball game at Madison Square Garden with my dad when I was 12 years old.

That image became the start of my piece.

The next day we shared our brainstorming in groups and talked about what happened—what discoveries we made, what problems we ran into, what successes we had, what surprises occurred, what worked, and what didn't. Jason, a student who has trouble getting started, said he wrote five different stories before he hit on the one he liked; Tina said she found her story in less than five minutes of brainstorming; Martin expressed surprise that his story came to him so easily; Kristen started writing about her father's drinking problem and ended up with an essay about her first day of school.

At this point, I shared my own brainstorming and explained how I discovered my story.

First, I talked about how I got started. I showed them some of the problems I ran into and those I solved. For example, I hit a dead end in my brainstorming when I couldn't decide whether to make the piece a childhood memoir or extend the narrative into my adult years. When I decided to move the story forward into adulthood, I discovered that I was writing a piece about letting go of old habits. After my explanation, we all shared our brainstorming with one another in small groups: Martin found out he'd already written a rough draft, while Tina discovered that her story about a hurdles race she ran in high school stil needed an ending. Others were struggling to find their topics.

By sharing their brainstorming, students began to see that each of us has a different composing process and that there is more than one way to find and develop a topic.

As we moved through the writing process, I used my own developing piece to help me conduct a series of demonstration mini-workshops. For example, I modelled how I wrote my rough draft, how to give and receive feedback in response groups, and how to work with conference partners. I also demonstrated how I revised my draft, I shared some of my own most effective revision strategies, and I showed them how to work in proofreading and editing groups. Finally, I worked with them on polishing final drafts.

As our pieces began to take shape, I went back to the readings to model how writers support their points and organize their essays. I showed the class how Dick Gregory, Langston Hughes, and Nora Ephron all used a variety of strategies to drive their points home. Gregory came right out and told us how bitter and unhappy he became as a result of being humiliated in class; Hughes's story built up to a climactic moment where he learned that he had to lie in order to go along with the majority; and Ephron's point about how she struggled to come to terms with being a social outcast was a running theme throughout her piece.

I also used the readings to demonstrate how writers devise effective and interesting leads—"grabbers:" I asked the students to go back over the essays they had read, pick the three best introductions, and explain why they chose them. Then we all rewrote our leads.

At each stage of the process, we wrote about and discussed our struggles and successes. Mid-way through the process, I asked students to write me a short "how it's going'' letter telling me about their drafts, feedback groups, revisions, editing—their overall progress. In his letter, Martin wrote: "I need to change the first paragraph because my group was confused about Jaimie and Gary. Nobody knew who Gary was, so they didn't care about him. I think I need to describe him and what a neat guy he is. I also need to tell where I am and who I'm talking about in the first part of the story, Christy Heller, not the other Christy."

Jason switched subjects and then found it easier to write on his new idea. "When I first started writing," he said, "I had another essay altogether different. It was about my first fight with a bully, but I couldn't get it to work, so I changed my topic and wrote about the break-up between me and my girlfriend and how badly I felt. Once I started writing, I couldn't believe how it all came out so quickly. I couldn't stop writing."

Mark discovered the value of sharing his draft when he wrote, "I learned not to be afraid to show my work to other people in the class. I was afraid at first they wouldn't like it, but once they began telling me the things they thought were working, I felt like I'd gotten my point across."

Kristin saw the need to consider her readers: "I thought there wasn't a single problem in the essay," she wrote. "It wasn't that I was arrogant, just real confident, a feeling I usually don't have after writing an essay for a class. But after my group partner read it over in class, I was shocked to find so many places where it didn't make sense. I guess a lot of things that make sense to me need to be explained to a reader. The thing I have to work on when I revise is not to write my essay as if the reader knows what's going on, but to use examples and details which let him see what I do."

Lisa found that she had to set her draft aside from time to time. "When I write my rough draft," Lisa said, "I start out with all these expansive, vague ideas and then nail things down slowly but surely. I can really tell that by looking at my drafts. I can see the weak, vague spots easier if I come back and look at the writing after being away from it a day or so. Doing it a little at a time makes the writing seem easier."

Brian had loosened up and became less of a word squeezer. "One thing I've noticed," he wrote "is that I don't dread writing so much anymore because I've realized that what I write down isn't written in stone. I can change it on the next draft, or make it better, or scrap it completely. Also, I tend to write kind of formally, and I'm learning to loosen up I think."

And finally, Tara discovered for herself that "this writing process will help me when I do my essays for history and social science and even when I have to write my autobiography for my college application."

By reflecting on their composing processes, many of the sutdents began to discover the kinds of successes and struggles that most practicing writers experience regularly. For example, by brainstorming some students learned that there are plenty more words where those came from; others found out how to let their subjects choose them; a few, like Lisa, learned how to set their drafts down and come back to them; alert students like Kristin discovered that even when you think a piece is done, there's still more work to do; and a few, like Tara, found that writing first in this genre makes it easier to compose in more prescribed forms for other occasions.

When the unit ended, I asked each student to type up his/her piece and submit it for publication in our class anthology.

Meanwhile, I saw that it would be a while until I'd be able to complete my own piece—at least to my own satisfaction. So, I submitted my working draft for publication in the class anthology and promised myself I'd pick the writing up again in my summer workshop.

TEACHING AND WRITING NARRATIVE WITH ADULTS

Every summer, I coordinate a week-long, three-credit writing workshop for K through college teachers. Last June, over one hundred of us met in a retreat setting where we wrote, shared, played, ate, drank, and essentially lived together as a community of writers. The teachers who attend can elect to write in a single genre all day or they can write in that genre in the morning and participate in pedagogy workshops in the afternoon. The morning writing workshop I facilitated was called "About Women, About Men: Personal Narratives That Run Deep."

I decided to center the workshop around narratives which said something about ourselves as men and women growing up in the 40s, 50s, and 60s. Our subjects would inevitably be: childhood, adolescence, dating, school, family, marriage, parenting, career choices, aging and looking back, and so forth. When we finished our pieces, those who chose could submit them either to the "About Men" or "Hers" columns of *The New York Times Sunday Magazine* or to any other publication they thought was an appropriate forum.

I had only a week with the teachers, so I had to move much faster than I did with my high school students. Although these 15 teachers had elected this workshop, initially they were every bit as frightened and tentative as my high school students—perhaps even more so. One reason for this is that they felt the pressure of expectations; English teachers, especially, are self-conscious about not being expert "creative" writers, when in fact most have never written expressively, save for personal letters and perhaps an occasional poem—and very few have written personal narrative. In fact, the majority of teachers I've worked with have little or no experience as writers except for the analytical/critical essay-writing they did in school or the kind of writing they do regularly on the job. As a result, all but the most experienced and confident teachers in any writing group are disenfranchised writers. Like the students they teach, they've never been encouraged to write for self-discovery or self-exploration.

As a formerly disenfranchised writer myself, I decided that it would be more appropriate for me to try and create a safe haven for tentative adult writers rather than teach and model the kinds of "how to" strategies that I did with the high school students. Therefore, I approached the session as a self-enrichment workshop—an opportunity to write, to take some risks, and share freely. I also had a selfish reason for being so non-directive: I wanted time to resume my own piece and I wanted to participate in the sharing.

On the first day, I gave a brief overview of personal narrative writing, talked a bit about the "About Men, About Women" theme, and then asked the teachers to introduce themselves to one another.

I laid out two long tables and placed on them folders full of personal narratives, some of which were my own, and many of which were clipped from various columns, newspapers, and magazines. I also set out several essay collections: Anna Quindlen's *Living Out Loud* (a collection of her popular "Life in the 30s" column which ran in *The New York Times* for several years); Donald Murray's "Over Sixty" columns from the *Boston Globe*; Barbara Lazear Ascher's *Playing After Dark*; Susan Allen Toth's *Blooming: A Small Town Girlhood* and *Ivy Days*, both autobiographical books on growing up female in the 50s and 60s; Joseph Epstein's *The Middle of My Tether*, and Phillip Lopate's, *Against Joie De Vivre*.

In addition, I displayed such "self-help" books as *Inventing the Truth*: *The Art and Craft of Memoir*; *Writing Down the Bones*; *On Becoming a Writer*; and *The Craft of Writing*—all of which deal with matters of getting personal writing started and keeping it going.

Everyone was free to browse through the "class library" and take anything he/she wanted. Those few who had already come with ideas for writing could work independently, and for those who needed a prompt to get started, I offered an exercise which went like this: Two partners brainstorm three ideas for a story and each reads the three ideas to his/her partner. Each partner then picks one of the ideas for the writer. Then both write a rough draft, exchange drafts for feedback, make some revisions, and write a final draft. What's nice about this exercise is that by helping each other choose topics to write about, each writer invests in the other's piece. It's a quick and dirty way to develop a small support community inside a 10 person or more workshop.

Whatever activity they chose—browsing in the library, writing alone, working in pairs on my story prompt—everyone had to come back a half hour before the daily session ended to share his/her writing and tell us what happened to him/her during the composing process.

About half-way into the first session, I found I had time to work on my own piece. It had been almost half a year since I began it, so I simply read it over and made some preliminary notes for revisions. Because I'd had so much time away from it, I could see all the holes in my writing, so I redrafted an outline.

When we reconvened, as expected, the most experienced writers were eager to share. I tried however, to nudge some of the more tentative people as well. Nancy, at first reluctant to talk, told us how she'd tried to encourage a disturbed student who ultimately ended up committing suicide. Nancy's problem was how to dramatize her feelings about the boy: Should she write about herself as the subject or about him? How should she arrange the narrative?

As people jumped in with suggestions, Nancy began relax. In fact that night she approached me in the dorm and spent an hour working over her draft while I offered suggestions.

Other people were at different stages in their composing. Debby was reluctant to share her thoughts just yet, but she was willing to listen to others read their drafts; Janet was reading around in the class library and hunting for a topic; Shirley simply couldn't write, she felt that this might be too difficult for her; Jeannie already had a draft going; so she took off to write under a tree; Mary was ready for small group feedback; and by working with two partners, Pat was discovering that he was writing something that was potentially powerful and moving.

By having the full group reconvene at the end of each session, we all benefited from finding out the different ways each of us composes. Moreover, the sharing session (or processing) was a way of getting the group to hear about each other's struggles and successes. And it showed them that it was okay to help each other along.

On the second day, we met as a whole group for an hour and talked about our progress. After everyone reported in, I asked each one what kind of feedback he/she would prefer. Janet wanted to work alone; Debby was still reluctant to go into a group, so she worked with Pat; Jeannie kept writing on her own; Shirley did the same; Mary conferenced with me; Nancy sought out a group of three others who wanted to read their drafts aloud; and because he was writing from a female point of view, Dave wanted a group of women to listen to his draft.

Once again, I asked that everyone return for the last half hour, this time to share some of the drafts in progress with the whole group. And again, I found that I had some free time to work on my own piece. By now, I was more comfortable with my writing. I liked the main body of the essay, but I knew I needed more work on my intro and ending. So I began to rework my beginning.

On Wednesday, I announced that we all had to have a clean, typed draft ready by Friday for our group anthology. We also had to have our drafts ready so that everyone could show his/her work during the workshop's final day sharing session. (It's a tradition that on the last day—Friday—all 100 plus teachers from the morning workshops—poets, children's writers, playwrights, nature writers, and so forth—convene to present/display the week's writing).

At first, my group felt a little uneasy about this deadline, but when I explained that our pieces could still be viewed as works in progress, my people breathed a bit easier.

We continued to work as we had the previous two days, but I noticed that most of the teachers were beginning to open up to each other and enjoy the writing. Debby had joined a group and was sharing her piece; Jeannie now needed feedback, so she sought me out for a conference; Janet began her piece and was working with two others in a group; Pat was almost ready to put the finishing touches on his; and Shirley, unfortunately decided not to continue writing her piece.

Inevitably what happens when adults—especially English teachers—get together to share and to talk about writing is that (unlike younger students) they give each other very specific kinds of feedback: They talk about good leads, main points, using examples, organization, focus, voice, and so on.

So by mid-week, many of the pieces began to take shape. My own, in fact, was coming together. Mainly on the strength of advice I'd gotten from two of the other workshop leaders, I'd settled on a new beginning and ending. I could see where I still had a decision to make: How much of the piece was going to be a childhood reminiscence and how much of it would be about the adult who changed from a fanatical basketball junkie to the rehabilitated middle-aged teacher/writer.

On Thursday, we wrote, shared, and polished our pieces to ready them for the anthology and for Friday's display. Some, like Pat's and Mary's were finished pieces already. Pat was reflecting back on the funeral of a friend and some of the writing was so beautifully evocative and controlled that I asked him to share with the whole group. Reluctantly he read. Here's a short excerpt:

> This is not what I expected. This is not a class reunion. We have not just run into each other at an airport. Al, you are standing with your back to your dead father and your sorrowful mother, Al where did you get that suit? You're dressed like Gordon Gecko. What the hell do you do out there in California? How do you get so thin? You're tan. Your shirt collar isn't showing behind the knot in your tie— how do you do that? You look like this all the time, don't you? Do you remember how mad your dad got when watermelons grew behind your front evergreens because we spit the seeds there the summer before? Do you remember how you stole Pee Wee Seeley's new catcher's mitt and I got blamed?

Like Pat's, Mary's piece about a childhood spitting contest was funny and authentic; others like Nancy's and Jeannie's still needed more polishing; some like Janet, Dave, and Debby were just getting their pieces to shape up.

By the end of the week, 13 of the 14 participants—myself among them— displayed their writing and submitted pieces for the workshop anthology. When the workshop ended, I revised mine for two weeks and sent it to *The New York Times*. Even though it was recently rejected and I'm reworking it once again, I felt I'd accomplished what I'd set out to do: I finished the piece and in the bargain learned a few things about my writing process, about teaching adults, and about why I no longer love basketball.

WHY PERSONAL NARRATIVE HAS VALUE

What made both workshops succeed was the enthusiasm of the writers for their subjects, their willingness to work on their writing, and the initiative they took in helping each other out. They learned the value of sharing and of developing a writing community. They also worked through their fears and inhibitions; they took risks, and they brought their own experiences to bear on a piece of writing. Finally, they learned how to shape their ideas for an audience—and eventually for publication. In short, they wrote from the inside out.

As for me, by facilitating and participating in both workshops, I not only had some fun composing my own piece, but I also confirmed a long-standing suspicion: Writing narratives have important value for tentative or inexperienced writers. By working through the composing process, both the students and teachers recognized that this genre made the same demands and required the same kinds of composing strategies as any piece of school or real world writing—exposition, argument, criticism, report writing, business letters, and so forth. After completing their personal narratives, most of them felt more confident and prepared to write in other, more prescribed forms.

For most students and adults, the personal essay can be a comfortable form of expression, one that offers opportunities for discovery, for personal growth, and for initial success. As such, it's an important step toward becoming an active, life-long writer. Those are reasons enough for me to continue to write narratives and to include them in any writing class I teach.

REFERENCES

Murray, D.M. (1989) *Expecting the unexpected: Teaching myself and others to read and write.* Portsmouth, N.H.: Boynton/Cook.

Murray's advice on "planning for discovery and surprise," and "listening to the text" is invaluable for inexperienced writers young and old.

Zinsser, W. (1987). (Ed.), *Inventing the truth: The art and craft of memoir.* Boston: Houghton Mifflin.

A fine collection of essays by pros like Russell Baker, Annie Dillard, Toni Morrison, and others who offer advice on the pleasures and problems of memoir writing.

Goldberg, N. (1986). *Writing down the bones: Freeing the writer within.* Boston and London: Shambhala.

Not directly related to narrative writing but a relaxed, enthusiastic "Zen" approach to discovery writing—for writers who have trouble getting started.

*Heidi Wilkins likes an audience. Most writers do but what singles Heidi out is that she never forgets this in the classroom. Routinely, she lets children choose their own topics because, I believe, she loves seeing her children read their work to their friends. In fact, her first graders often choose topics **because** of their audience. When first grader Vanessa reads, "It started talking to me," the children respond. Vanessa **waits** for the response. This IS audience. In addition to topics that run off the tops of her children's heads, Heidi, as does Leonora Smith, pulls at times. She uses children's literature, and sparks new interests not though of as yet, but known.*

CHAPTER 2
TOPIC GENERATION WITH ELEMENTARY CHILDREN

By Heidi Wilkins

PART A: RECALCITRANT RETRIEVER

"He's the one. He's so cute."

I loved this puppy.

We were ready for a dog. Endlessly we had discussed size and breed. No unanimous choice here.

"How about a cocker spaniel?"

"No short dog!" my husband responded firmly. "I don't want a dog I have to bend over to pet." No stooping for this man.

At the next dog show I asked, "Where are the tall dogs?" En route to the Rotweilers, I saw them. Chesapeake Bay Retrievers. I liked the looks of this breed. Short wavy fur, full chested, sturdy dogs with alert golden eyes and expressive faces. These were dogs with a history; a true American breed, and they were tall. Unfortunately, not a single puppy was available. Numerous phone calls throughout the U.S. led us to a kennel in our own state and a three month old male puppy. Driving to the kennel my husband warned me. "These dogs aren't easy to handle. I've heard you need a baseball bat to train them."

But seeing this puppy running through a field, ears flapping, chasing and returning sticks, his warning lost all meaning. A few puppy licks and I was totally enchanted. He was mine.

Max quickly made himself at home. Nose prints covered the doors and walls, occasional wet spots appeared on the carpet, childproof closers were installed to keep the garbage where it belonged. The breeder's explanation had let me know that Max was not the average "Chessie." Chesapeakes are known to be aggressive, fiercely loyal, and skilled retrievers. Max was shy. He had been passed over by those who usually owned these determined hunting dogs. Max's shyness, however, did not keep him from demonstrating his ability as a retriever. He would bring tissues, pencils, newspapers, magazines, towels, anything left on the floor or within his mouth's reach and drop them near me. Shoes and socks were his favorites.

Repeatedly, I explained to Max that I disapproved of his habit. Our daughter's room became his favorite retrieving ground. He hunted her stuffed animals and deftly cleared the dollhouse of chairs, tables, and people. Then his retrieving took a new turn. Object in his mouth, darting into the room, eyebrows up, he'd stand and wait. No longer content to just "bring," catch me if you can was the game. I'd reach; he'd back away.

"He's making me crazy," I'd complain.

"He's a retriever. He'll grow out of it," said my husband.

"He better do it soon," I thought.

I couldn't wait. I decided I needed expert help. I enrolled both of us in a dog obedience class. Max learned the meaning of "NO!" Long hours of practice taught him the importance of bringing things to his owner. A firm verbal command and Max would come, sit, and gently deposit any object into an outstretched hand. The fun gone, he soon gave up most of his indoor retrieving.

One Saturday I had planned a small party. Max followed me while I dusted, vacuumed, and fluffed cushions. He watched as I prepared food and set the table. Our guests arrived. Max shyly greeted everyone with wagging tail and friendly barks while safely standing in another room.

After some conversation, the guests were seated. As we began our meal, I heard Max trotting down the stairs. I turned. There was Max—my husband's dirty underwear hanging from his mouth.

"Max, bring it!" I screamed, glaring at my husband.

He, along with our guests, had started to laugh. Max just stood there. I tried again, softening my tone.

"Bring it, Max."

Delivering underwear was not what Max had in mind. Here was a game worth playing. Three months of dog obedience behind me, I knew just how to deal with his disgraceful behavior. Show him who's in charge. I stood up. He bent over, front paws down, underwear still hanging from his mouth. I stepped forward. He bounced sideways. Laughter surrounded me. Embarrassment began to cloud my thinking. I hissed at my husband. "Do something!"

Max's shyness had totally vanished. Parading the underwear like spoils from a victory, he visited each person at the table. Me, following Max around the table; he, always a step ahead. My husband, struggling to control his laughter said, "Come on, boy, bring it." Max looked up. Perhaps his master's voice brought him to his senses. Max turned, walked to the head of the table, sat, and offered his prize. "Good boy, Max," my husband said, and Max proudly walked away.

PART B: TOPIC GENERATION WITH ELEMENTARY CHILDREN

Often as I talk with other teachers about my classroom they are amazed that my first graders write at least three times a week. "How do you think of topics for them to write about?" they ask. "I don't," I answer. For many years I struggled to find interesting and meaningful topics for my students, making writing a teacher-directed activity. Through reading, reflecting on my own writing, and listening to other teacher-writers, I discovered that writers write best when they select their topics. First graders can choose topics, and then, with some talk and some work, they can bring their writing to an audience.

As a writer I enjoy having an audience. I share my work with the children and often use my own writing to introduce the idea of self-selected topics. Writing time in my classroom begins by having the children sit close to me. I show them a photograph of my dog, Max. Then I say,

> "Max is my dog. He's a Chesapeake Bay Retriever. He climbs into the bathtub and licks the tub. Or if there's a bar of soap, he eats it. I think he's funny. Sometimes I write about Max. I write about him because I know him. I have a draft about him. I'd like to read it to you. Is that alright?" The children nod and encourage me to read.

Max's antics has my audience giggling. My lesson continues.

"Does my draft remind you of something that has happened to you and an animal?"

Immediately the responses come.

"I have a Golden Retriever, he picks up stuff."

"My dog runs around in circles."

"I have a cat, she's crazy."

"Why do you say she's crazy?" I ask.

"She bounces off the wall."

There is laughter and the conversation continues. This is what I've been planning. Topic lessons need involvement. Discussions about dogs, cats, birds, hamsters, and other pets are going on, and we are on the verge of great drafts.

Sharing my own writing is a strategy I often use with emerging writers. The first graders listen to my draft and know that I write about ordinary events. I ask them to tap into their own lives for topics. Topic generation becomes an opportunity to reflect. Young writers become convinced that they have something to write about. I also use a number of other strategies that allow children (Grades 1–6) to select and record their own topics. The remainder of this chapter is a description of those strategies.

Being An Expert

Often after I've read my own work to a class, I lead into what Donald Graves (Graves, 1983) calls "expert" topics. I meet with my class and remind them of my Max story and tell them I know so much about Max that I consider myself an expert. Using a marker, I make the number "1" on a large sheet of chart paper. I write "Max" and briefly tell another Max adventure.

I then make the number "2" and beside it draw a flower. With young students I ask them to help me write the word in "invented spelling." With older students I write the word flower. I begin,

> "My mother loved flowers. When I was little, she took me outside with her while she weeded. She taught me the names of the flowers surrounding our house. There were clematis, calendula, snapdragons, and many more. Whenever we went anywhere, she would point out flowers, name them, and tell me where they would grow best. Now I'm almost an expert. My friends call me and ask me what flowers will grow well in the shade or in the sun, and I can tell them."

I put number "3" on the chart and write "Linda." "Linda is my friend. I've known her for 15 years." I talk about our friendship. "We like to give each other little surprise presents. Once she hid a Snickers, my favorite candy bar, under my pillow." They respond to the topic eagerly. They tell about their own friends. "I ride my bike with my friend." "My friend and I have a secret fort we built by ourselves."

Next to number "4" I write "potato." I talk about how potatoes are planted, how they grow. The fact that you can lift the plant and remove some of the crop early has always intrigued me. "I love the taste of potatoes. Potatoes are my favorite food. I have a cookbook that has only potato recipes."

By now the children are bursting with ideas of their own. I give my fifth topic, golf. "I like to play golf. Once I hit a tree with my golf ball and the ball ricocheted hitting me in the ear." We groan together, me remembering, the children imagining, the pain.

I put away my marker, the modeling completed.

"Is there something where you're an expert?" I ask.

First graders easily see themselves as experts at Nintendo, their pets, families, rainbows, and the universe. For older students, a favorite trip or place often emerges as a topic. The invitation to share orally allows children to hear each other. Topics become acknowledged and the author is recognized as an expert. The children then record their topics on a Topic Sheet (Nathan, 1989), single words if possible, as a reference for future writing times.

My own listing of topics as a model may seem lengthy. Because I keep my explanation animated and allow for questions from the students, the children seem comfortable waiting until the end of the lesson to record their own ideas. Another option would be to pass out topic sheets at the beginning of the lesson so that students record their own topics while the teacher models.

Lucy Calkins (1986) points out: "Children write about what is alive and real for them—The content of the writing workshop is the content of real life, for the workshop begins with what each student thinks, feels, and experiences and with the human urge to articulate and understand experience." These self-selected topics, areas where we as writers feel real and alive, allow us to relate our perceptions. The authenticity of our writing depends on how well we choose our topics.

Young writers can experience their world and record potential topics (see Figures 2.1 and 2.2).

FIGURE 2.1

TOPICS

Julie

1
2

I LK to
Go
stM

ILK FrGs

3
4

I LK PoePL

I LK PLMS

FIGURE 2.2

Nicole knows her area of expertise. Her topic sheet indicates she knows about cats (see Figure 2.3). The audience responds with laughter when she reads her draft. They want to know more. She is successful (see Figure 2.4).

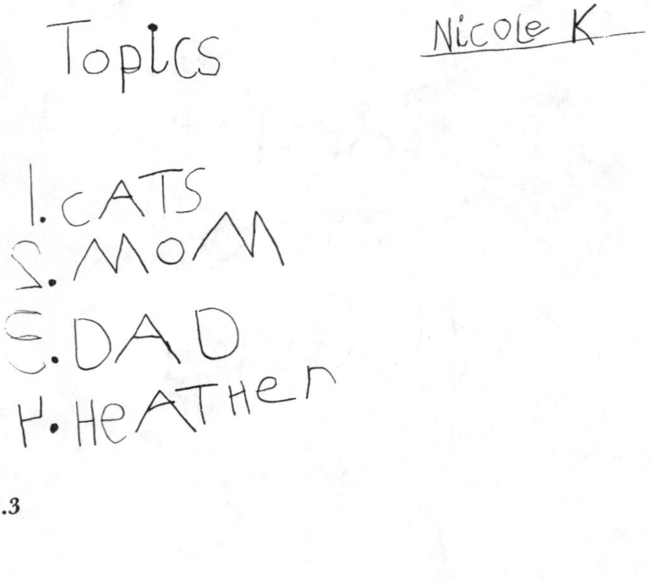

Topics

Nicole K

1. CATS
2. MOM
3. DAD
4. HeATHer

FIGURE 2.3

My Cat Bs ^bounces Off
the Wall. She is krs. ^crazy

Nicole K

FIGURE 2.4

USING LIKES AND DISLIKES TO FIND A TOPIC

I use the likes and dislikes strategy with older students. I ask them to think about things they like. Folding a piece of paper, I tell them to write the word "Like" at the top. Modeling on the chalkboard or overhead, I start my own list: my husband, new shoes, dogs, earrings. I ask the students to make their own list. I limit the time to two minutes; this adds a sense of urgency and they write quickly. When the time is up, I ask for volunteers to share their lists. Hands pop up and "Me! Pick me" fills the air. I choose one student and invite the rest to listen carefully and record any idea they may have forgotten. After several students share, I ask them to reread their own lists and circle two items. By circling two items, they are forced to narrow their focus and establish an area of interest.

The lesson continues; I write "Dislike" on the board. The students chorus "yes" when washing dishes heads my list. Checking papers elicits giggles, and anchovies receives loud "yucks." I direct them to write their own lists within the two minute limit. Although they approach this task enthusiastically, young writers are often surprised that they can only name a few dislikes. One problem with this lesson occurs when students place the names of people on the dislike list. A solution came from my colleague, Julie Janosz. She suggests that writers need to focus on behaviors of those persons, such as: rude people, unfair people, people who call me names.

The dislike list is shared with great enthusiasm: "home work," "cleaning my room." As the lists are shared, I remind the students that all of their suggestions are possible topics for drafts (see Figure 2.5).

Again I ask them to circle the two items of most interest. These authors now have at least four starts for future writing times.

For the last two years I've kept my own lists generated in classrooms. I am delighted by the wealth of ideas I've gathered from these lists and use them for my own writing.

Using Literature To Generate Topics

This is a delightful approach for topic selection using trade books (Nathan, 1989). I choose a book. After reading *Thunderstorm* by Mary Szilagyi (1985) to the class, we discuss her craft.

> "What would you say to the author if she were here?" I ask.
> "I like your words."
> "I liked the part where the birds talk."
> "I liked it when dog goes under the couch. My dog does that."

We discuss the wonderful illustrations. The author lets us see and feel the storm.
"What was the author writing about?" I ask.
Her topic, a thunderstorm, is quickly identified.
"How do you think she got the idea to write about this topic?"
They speculate. Perhaps the author is afraid of storms? Maybe she has a little girl who is afraid of storms? We consider all the possibilities. Again we look through the book concentrating on how much the author tells us about her topic. I show the children another book titled *Thunderstorm* written by one of last year's first graders. Steven's construction paper covered "book" receives the same attentiveness as

Kris K Lann

204
11-2²

Like	Dislike
cat	(school)
(fast cars)	orders
motersiacels	(making my Bed)
four weelers	(cleaning my room)
bikes	washing dishes
baseballe	barbies
football	waiting in line
soccer	going shoping with
sailboats	my mom
(moterboats)	work
tennies	
dogs	
chocolate cake	
swimming	
cedier point	
days of school	
Nintendo	
T.V.	
movies	
cookies	
ice cream	
food	
eggs	
clness	

FIGURE 2.5

Mary Szilagyi's book. Steven's words capture his audience. His characters converse, find their way through problems. The benefit of using literature becomes clear as young writers try out their own sense of story.

"Wow, I liked it when they rode their bikes when it was lightning."

"Is this a true story?" they ask.

I rely on the skills of authors whose work I enjoy to show students how to create pieces of fiction. Whenever possible, I show the writers in my classroom that they are choosing the same topics as published authors.

USING JOURNALS AND DAY BOOKS FOR TOPICS

Journals provide another source of potential topics. Casual observations about daily events may lead into a draft. Nicole's teacher uses prompts to begin journal writing. One such prompt was "Tell about hiding places." The prompt is only given five minutes of writing time. Later Nicole expands her quick write into a delightful account of how she scares her sisters.

> . . . I scare my sisters by sneaking up behind them and touching them, grabbing them, yelling at them, grabbing their legs as they walk by or holding my hands over my mouth and making scary noises. I scare my sisters because I need to laugh at something funny and it is.

She continues this draft as she talks about the consequences of her acts.

Another prompt, "Choose something in your backyard that comes alive," held a seed for fiction writing. Vanessa writes in her journal,

> In my backyard my big tree came to life. It started talking to me. It said hi! My name is tree and I want to be your friend. Can you do me a favor? Yes what is it? Can you tell your brother and his friends not to climb me? OK!

Later Vanessa extended her journal write into a fiction piece about a talking tree that included her younger brother as one of the characters.

Topic selection lessons are an opportunity for elementary children to explore areas of their own experience. Selecting their own topics, they learn to trust themselves as authors. They become writers who choose genres and know what an audience expects. They can allow themselves to abandon a draft knowing they have the opportunity to select again and again and again.

REFERENCES:

Calkins, L.M. (1986). *The art of teaching writing.* Portsmouth, NH: Heinemann Educational Books.

Graves, D.H. (1983). *Writing: Teachers and children at work.* Portsmouth, NH: Heinemann Educational Books.

Nathan, R., Temple, F., Juntunen, K. and Temple, C. (1989). *Classroom strategies that work: An elementary teacher's guide to process writing.* Portsmouth, NH: Heinemann Educational Books.

Szilagyi, M. (1985). *Thunderstorm.* New York: Bradbury Press.

SELECTED BIBLIOGRAPHY

Calkins, L.M. (1986).*The art of teaching writing.* Portsmouth, NH: Heinemann Educational Books.

Lucy Calkins's book is filled with practical ideas for beginning and managing a student-oriented writing classroom.

Nathan, R., Temple, F., Juntunen, K. and Temple, C. (1989). *Classroom strategies that work: An elementary teacher's guide to process writing.* Portsmouth, NH: Heinemann Educational Books.

The authors of this book offer wonderful lessons and strategies that support the writing process in the classroom.

Murray, D.M. (1989). *Expecting the unexpected: Teaching myself and others to read and write.* Portsmouth, NH: Boynton/Cook.

Donald Murray explores the issues of being a writer and also how to teach writing. He celebrates the surprises that occur in writing. As a teacher he gives lessons, and as a writer he reveals his craft.

*As a writer, **Leonora Smith** reminds me most of Sharon Olds: her attention to details that matter, the surprise of ordinary language butting itself up against "a paisley of motion." In her own approach to invention, presented here, she asks the reader to do what she does on occasion—what I've come to know many writers do—pull disparate parts of one's life and world together and see what happens. All art is viewed through the prism of experience. Convinced of this, Leonora wants us to try our hand at poetry, her way. Each author in Part I of* Writers in the Classroom *offers ways into our world that pry and tug and pull. For Leonora, what she will see tomorrow remains the mystery she yearns to uncover, so the prying and pulling and tugging become her tools, and ours.*

CHAPTER 3
IMAGINATIVE WRITING TECHNIQUES: GATHERING STRENGTH FROM THE UNIVERSE

By Leonora Smith

PART A: FISH, SPRING, WINDOWS

"If I could look at him long enough, I should see his dreams."
—Ouspensky, *In Search of the Miraculous*
(quoted by Colin Wilson in *The Occult*)

These students, dopey with spring—their heads
bob over the text like droopy mums.
Behind their wavering eyelids, there's more to see—

as glancing out your window you might see
a cloud of sparrows flitter between trees, or even a veldt
where zebras prance in tall grass, instead of Cincinnatti—

something real or imagined snatching your attention
like a moment when you are not exactly first in love
but just after that, when you suddenly can't believe your luck,

or like the moment I woke up after my son was born, his head
pointy from forceps—no matter how flat his forehead was,
he was so *beautiful*. Or my my husband watched the fish

dart and flash in his aquarium—the African Cichlids who evolved
their own near-marine colors sequestered in the underwater Galapagos,
of the rift lakes, Tanganyika and Malawi.

He overcrowds them, so there's no room
for territoriality. Still they bump one another with their snouts
when they cross paths, who is big enough or mean enough

to eat whom mapping the space they take, a paisley
of motion, a pattern you can almost see—if you know it's there—
in the near-invisible water. The way I see bits of the student's dreams

as bright flashings over their bored-looking heads—
all of us improbably jammed together against nature—
like flickers of tiny Northern lights, in cardinal,

gold and turquoise colors—the Red Empress, the Peacock, the Electric
Blue—run-amuck auras, some more than a little cannibal,
but all shimmery as aquarium·fish, or the rainbow halos of circus angels.

PART B: ENCOURAGING INVENTION AND INSPIRATION

Rag-tag bits of dreams, snippets of conversation, oddments from garage sales (like zebra-foot lamps and World War II clothes), queer passages of text—that's what my poems and stories are built from. Sometimes, of course, a writer comes to the page with "something to say" and a sense of how it should be said. Often, though—more often than advice to beginning writers might suggest—we come groping, trying to discover our material, and the shape it might take: Rummage cannot be organized in advance of finding it, and I am not quite sure that what I expect will be a poem will not veer off into story or essay, or that the story will not compress itself into a poem, or that the essay's one voice will not become many voices, demanding to speak for themselves in a play

At such times, it is helpful to turn our attention outward, to the rich gifts of the world, and their power to engage our memories and our imaginations. I have developed working methods which prompt me to engage with the world in a playful, exploratory way; which stimulate my memory and my imagination; and which serve as a charm against that writers' nightmare of coming up empty. These methods employ "found images" and "found sentences" much in the way visual artists may use found objects in sculpture or collage. I have used these methods to write stories, poems and essays myself, and, over the years, have found that various versions of them can serve as stimulating teaching devices.

The basic principle is this: Take something which does not belong to you—a bit of text, an unrecognizable sound from the street, a woman in the mall saying, "I'm always waiting," the sight of a cat stalking a bird outside your window. This something is a gift from the world, meant for you because it *captures* your attention. And focusing on something outside yourself has another advantage—it frees you from the confines of your immediate experience. Much current advice to writers suggests that autobiography is the only fit subject for poetry and fiction: "write what you know." But this literary fashion has its limitations. As Robert Bly says of what is called confessional poetry, "concentrating on anger" may cause us to "lose [our] thirst for mountains" (Bly, p. 126).

Take **one** such thing, outside yourself, and see what in you responds to it—it will be something you do not expect, something you do not already know, something you will discover or invent: It is your own Rorschach, allowing your full self to respond without the self-consciousness of knowing you are writing about yourself (as, of course, you always are) without the worry that someone will think badly of you (if they can, they will; all writers come to expect it). Faulkner's complex novel, *The Sound and the Fury* derived from a single image—a girl in muddy underdrawers, climbing a tree (Cowley, p. 130).

Take **two** such things and try to connect them, even if they have nothing to do with one another—say, the sound of a car exhaust starting on a winter day, and the divorce papers you have just been served, or the wiggle of egg custard and moonlight. The two things form 'poles' of your mental and emotional battery and between them—when you are lucky—a electric spark will jump. Some theorists suggest that the "joining together of different and apparently irrelevant elements" is the key to all creative activity (Gordon, p. 3). Write "between" these things, generating as many ideas as you can to connect them: eating egg custard by moonlight, the word "shimmer"—there, that feels right. Now we are started up.

Take **three** such things, and you create a triangle. There is something special about three—trio, triangle, trinity—because while two points make a line, three create a space. When you create this space, you create a piece of imaginative geography in which new worlds of imagination and discovery can come into being, in which what you know but don't know you know will form itself, in which the knowing and experience of things which seem to be "in the air" will take a shape you could not have predicted. Write yourself—or something, whatever comes into your mind—into this space. Prepare to surprise yourself.

You are entering the realm of mystery. As the French writer George Simenon said, when asked if he outlined his novels in advance, "I know nothing whatever about the events which will occur. . .otherwise, it would not be interesting to me," (Cowley, p. 13).

In the same way we make constellations—figures with stories behind them—from groups of stars, we project patterns and shapes onto bits of the world, and behind these patterns and shapes are stories and metaphors which send out threads for us to pull, or trails to follow like fairy tale trails of breadcrumbs. I call the process I use in my writing and teaching process triangulation, not only after the number three, but also after the use of the word in surveying, as method of finding an unknown position from points that are given.

Watch and listen as the ideas and images and objects come together. This is not a gimmick, but more like a magic trick—a way of launching yourself out into space, beyond the confines of your autobiography, the ordinary conditions of 'now,' and what you already know (or at least, know that you know). When you make yourself receptive in this way, you are no longer at service of a narrow "self-expression," you are at service of gifts the world has given you, and it becomes your hope, responsibility and honor to do them justice.

As Colin Wilson says in the bit of text I chose for an epigraph my poetry series, *Faculty X*, from which "Fish/Spring/Window" is taken, we become more intensely alive when we focus our concentrated attention on the world outside ourselves, when we allow ourselves to become" . . .overwhelmed with a sense of the infinite *interestingness* of things" (Wilson, p. 28).

STIMULATING THE MIND TO PRODUCTIVE WORK

How do I use these methods that are so important to my own work, in my teaching? In general, I follow this principle: I never ask another human being, no mater how young, to do something I would not do myself. My recent story, "Garnet and the Eastern Mole," in *Alaska Quarterly Review* tells the story of a World War II veteran who is besieged by moles invading his lawn, condescended to by his son, and haunted by recurring images of the Japanese soldiers he burned out of their underground hide-outs during the final U.S. sweep of the Pacific.

The story originated with three images: the (numerous) mole runs in my lawn; a story I heard on the radio about killing moles by putting human hair in their runs—it catches in their soft fur, and they kill themselves trying to rub it off; and a new Oldsmobile. I selected these images, not because I had story to tell, not because I had a main character in mind, but because I wanted to see what would happen.

By exploring the space created when I put these three elements together, I invented (discovered?) Garnet, who then took on a life of his own. It now seems to me inevitable that the person driving the shiny, candy-apple red Oldsmobile is Garnet, and that he employs it as a strategic but fair weapon in his war against moles, because, having burned people in World War II, he will not stoop to such low tactics as flame throwers—or hair in mole runs.

The real challenge for me, and for any writer, at any age, in any genre, is to find a way to stimulate the mind to productive work. As a teacher of writing, I feel my responsibility is to help my students, no matter what age or what they are studying, to find a variety of ways to set the mind off—creating, making connections, finding patters—so that they can bring these methods into play when they need them. And what has worked for me often works for them.

TWO LISTS OF PEOPLE AND ONE OF OBJECTS

In workshops using material from movies and TV to stimulate writing, we set this process to work by creating three lists—two lists of people and one list of objects—lists salvaged from the students' brains. People: Charlie Manson, Snoopy, Harriet Tubman, a wise old man, Dollie Parton, and Pope John XXIII (often someone from the class appears on the list, too.) Objects: a favorite lasagne, a nude photo, a bundle of pencils, size 12 sneakers, a locket. . .whatever comes to our minds.

We then divide into groups, with each group choosing three items, for example: Snoopy, Dollie Parton, and a pair of size 12 sneakers. (Already, you begin to imagine the possibilities.) From these three items, the group constructs an event. The only rule for the story is that something must happen. Since no one has a particular personal investment in these objects, there is none of the hesitation here we usually see when we ask people to "make something up," nor any of the self-conscious attachment to an individual story that "must be told." It is pure and simple mind play, and the fact that it is play makes us free to invent.

Each group then uses the event it has created in that triangle marked out by the two people and the object as the basis for a movie. (I provide a sample of screenplay format.) After redrafting and revision, we read the scenes aloud. In short order, usually parts of three class periods, we learn how to stimulate our imaginations, practice working in groups, and almost as if by magic, my students learn the rudiments of screen play format—understanding how writing functions as map for visual media—without any direct instruction.

On the course evaluations, many students say this activity is their favorite part of the course: "I never knew I could be so creative." "All kinds of new ideas kept coming into my mind." "I hadn't made stories up like this since I was a little kid."

THREE NAMES, THREE KEY WORDS

In teaching content, the same principle applies: Put together non-contemporaries—Harriet Tubman, Nero, and Ronald Reagan; or people from literature who might have fascinating conversations if they met—Huck Finn, Holden Caulfied, and Heidi, or people who share ethnicity or gender—Mrs. Haversham, Gloria Steinem, and Susan B. Anthony. Writing these people into the same tale helps the student identify patterns and make connections that expand their mental maps of the world, in a context of playful discovery that makes learning (and teaching) a pleasure. As we create dialogues and new situations, we develop our abilities to write both with and beyond our personal experience, engaging the crucial skills of speculation, projection, and imagination—indispensable writerly skills too often neglected in schools.

Or, before reading a text, we select three key words—preferably three words with emotional force—and write a paragraph using all three of them, such as "black power," integration, and "whitey" before reading *The Autobiography of Malcolm X*. The three words form a shape and into this shape the students pour their own knowledge and predictions about the test, engaging them beforehand in what they are to read. When students write themselves into the subject matter in this way, they learn it from the inside out, manipulate it, engage with it, come to know it in an intimate way. And they learn the real skills professional writers have—to make full use of what is at hand.

In a workshop for gifted high school students, The Olivet Institute for the Gifted and Talented, sponsored by the Michigan State Board of Education, we go to even greater lengths at salvage. I have prepared a box of my oddments—a loud red plaid sport coat, a pair of zig-zag tongs, a plastic device for shaping Chinese-style dumplings, several net dresses, a sari, a disgusting tie with what appears to be an airplane crash on it, as well as several noise-making instruments such as a whistle and a bottle filled with dried beans. Many of the objects are, to their virtue for this purpose, unidentifiable—are they cooking implements or weapons?

We break into groups, and each group selects three objects. Practically speaking, these objects overcome the initial problem in group writing—coming to agreement on what subject to choose. In the same way that a form can be the starting place for a poem, our three found objects provide an initial structure, a jumping-off point, from which the students—with a facility that always amazes me—create a skit. In less than half an hour, they return with stories of murder and intrigue, wise men holding forth, often hilariously funny but always well constructed, because when given an opportunity to tell a story, human beings—thank heavens—will.

We then perfom these for one another. Not only do we see our own ability to create stories "out of nothing," and our ability to engage and entertain others with them, we also establish a basis for skill-oriented discussions of plot and structure: How many elements can a writer profitably use in a story? (Gordon Lish, former fiction editor at *Esquire*, once claimed that the short story writer can "ride," at most, "three horses.") How does the introduction of a new element alter a tale? How is an object transmuted into an image, and what does this mean? Most importantly, though, is the power we see to *make* art from what is at hand, to take the surprising meaning we can find in objects which at first glance seem ordinary and disconnected—as our own lives may seem, at times—and to use our imaginations to transform them into gifts we give back to the world.

At the same workshop, in line with my endless fascination with salvage, I have asked students to create accumulations about something that obsesses them. In the room, each of us has a sheet of paper pasted to the wall, with our obsession written on it: Each other person is to contribute to this obsession by adding words, phrases, found object. Sometimes poems and stories arise, as the phoenix from ashes, from these accumulations.

SHARING DREAMS

The most full-blown application I've made of the method of triangulation in teaching was in a dream workshop at a recent Traverse Bay Writers' conference, where the students are high school and college teachers. Why dreams? Dreams are never banal. The images in dreams are truly original, a product of an individual's most creative powers at work, out of the control of rationality. For self-doubters, dreams are proof absolute of their ability to create.

Think of this—ask ten friends to tell you the story of their divorces. Odds are, you'll get nine versions of the same story, with, perhaps, one off-key—like the story of my student who superglued all her husband's car doors closed. Mostly it will be misery. Then ask the same women to tell you a *dream* they had about (or during) their divorces. You will have similar themes, but no repeats—unusual and eccentric images such as talking frogs and elephants raining down from the sky, and scuttering of claws, gifts from mysterious dream figures, conversations with bears, constellations of feeling, that connect the familiar with the unfamiliar.

I asked each student at the dream workshop to come prepared to dicsuss a dream. First, to flesh the dreams out, we did word associations, recalling sounds, images, locations, colors, persons connected to each dream; then, we spent the first day discussing the dreams, until we devised our assignment: I came ready to use three of *something* because of my love of triangulation, because I knew three made a space. Linda D., who studied with Stephen Dunning, refined the suggestion on the basis of work she had done in an earlier workshop.

Our assignment became to choose three images—one from our own dream, one from another person's dream, and one from our surroundings. We could write in any form—poetry, fiction, essay, or whatever—drawing on the images that we had projected: Linda S's description of a water hyacinth floating out to the sea, and herself by the bayou, singing aloud made-up hymns; Connie's seascape and mixed-up day and night; Grace's retreat with her horse, and her Tom Mix belt buckle; Lori's dream meeting with the Piston's Chuck Daly, and the trashy-flashy comedienne they watched; Karen's mysterious black box and her "vanilla sort of person" and Linda D's dream of waking in a room to the slap slap of distant running bare feet, coming ever closer, and the dream way she "furnished the room" so "she would know where she was."

The idea of using an image from someone else's dream seems a little like thievery, but in this case, it was a gift, a gift which was reciprocated, since we not only took but gave. A new constellation of energy and imagination arose where before we could only say what happened to us and what we already knew. Karen's vanilla man became the main character in Connie's sea-side story; Linda S. took Karen's black box for her story "Rabbit Heart" while I used Linda's image of the water hyacinth floating down stream—and something I didn't realize I was using, an image of a delta—for my poem, still in progress, titled, "Gone."

The hymns appeared everywhere, snatches of hummed melodies in the air. Sometimes things transformed themselves: Linda S's home town Thibedeux, became the name of the main character in Lori's story. On it went, the stories and poems gaining their own momentum until we had a hard time recalling which image had come from whose dream, or whether the images we were using had come from a dream or from real life. They came in the form of poems, short stories —were they literary stories? mysteries? science fiction? We were still discovering.

There is a special kind of sharing which goes on in working this way—not only a constellation of images but a constellation of human beings focusing on the same, unknown material. Once this sharing begins, it takes on a force and power in which everything seems to fit together, in which meaning is enhanced, a process which gains its own momentum, one which Jung called synchronicity.

Linda S. told a story about a difficult day at school, in which, worn out, she was driven to stop in the hall and look to the heavens, her palms turned upward as if in supplication.

"What are you doing?" one of her students asked.

Her reply came from somewhere she could not explain: "I'm gathering strength from the universe."

In the end, this is the point of the method I present here, to give students ways to write that allow them not only to explore their own immediate histories, their own self-interests, their own conscious experiences, but also, ''to gather strength from the universe.''

The poem which begins this section, ''Fish/Spring/Window'' is a constellation of three images: my students (and myself) scarcely able to keep from nodding into half-sleep on a suddenly sultry spring afternoon; the fish moving in their bright territorial patterns in my husband's fish tank; and a mental image, that mysterious leap the mind sometimes takes when the ordinary is transformed to the miraculous, suggested by the random bit of text from Colin Wilson's *The Occult* which became the poem's epigraph: ''If I could look at him long enough, I should see his dreams.''

The 'should' is used, in the original British sense meaning ''could,'' but it also seemed to me to carry a teacherly obligation—to see students not only as they *are*, but as what *they can be*, not only to help them follow rules of writing and understand genre-based conventions and play to audiences, but also to help their minds function in imaginative and visionary ways like those I have described here, to, as the poem says, ''see bits of my students' dreams/as bright flashings over their bored looking heads—/. . . shimmery as aquarium fish, or the rainbow halos of circus angels.''

If you try this method, be ready for mystery. To me, everything is more the same than different, and teaching is like composing a text: You must leave open spaces for the unexpected to happen, for the poem to become a story or the story to become a play. If everything is specified and pinned down, if there is no space, all the life and mystery will be squeezed out of it, and there will be no room for dreams.

REFERENCES

Bly, Robert *News of the Universe*. Sierra Club (San Francisco: 1980).

Cowley, Malcolm, ed. *Writers at Work* (First Series). Viking (New York: 1959).

Gordon, William J. *Synetics*: The Development of Creative Capacity. Collier (New York: 1961).

Smith, Leonora. ''Fish/Spring/Window.'' *College Composition and Communication*. (December: 1989).

Smith, Leonora. ''Garnet and the Eastern Mole.'' *Alaska Quarterly Review* (Fall/Winter: 1988).

Wilson, Colin. *The Occult*. Vintage (New York: 1973).

SELECTED BIBLIOGRAPHY

Four types of books—in additon to what is obviously most important, reading good poetry and fiction, as much of it as I can—have been useful to me in my writing:

I. Books which do not focus directly on writing, but which stimulate the imagination or use of the senses. I have found methods of divination, such as the *I Ching* and Tarot helpful in this respect. A recent book useful in fleshing out dream images—though it is written with an eye toward self-development rather than aesthetics,—is:

Gendlin, Eugene T. *Let your Body Interpret Your Dreams.* Chiron Wilmette, 1986.

II. Advice for writers. The best tell you how to think about what you do, rather than how-to. But don't believe everything you read.

Brande, Dorothea. *Becoming a Writer.* Tarcher New York, 1981. (Originally published by Harcourt Brace in 1934). ·
Gardner, John. *On Becoming a Novelist.* Harper & Row New York, 1983.
Gardner, John. *The Art of Fiction.* Vintage New York, 1985.

III. Interviews with the self-reports of writers on their working processes. These are most useful as gossip, and for psychological confirmation of the oddities of writers' working habits, the habits of the famous being no more peculiar than your own. The most famous are the Paris Review Interview Series, volumes three through eight, edited by George Plimpton.

IV. Women writers on writing. Women still being at a considerable disadvantage in the publishing world, I have found writing about women's experiences as writers valuable in maintaining my sanity. For the sad realities, I particulary recommend:

Russ, Joanna. *How to Suppress Women's Writing.* University of Texas Austin, 1983.

*If you're a camper and **Alan Weber's** reflections don't make you cringe, I'm not sure what will. The tire in the mud, Freeze-dried food. A sudden storm. What else could go wrong? Based on his own experiences writing to his nephew, Weber discovered the power of writing: its ability in the doing, to lead you into knowing what you wouldn't have known. He speaks of writing's ability, when it's expressive writing, to enable connections. James Britton has said this for years, as has Toby Fulwiler, but each of us must come to this understanding alone, with pen in hand. In his chapter, Weber offers strategies that have worked for him: prompts that get students off square one and into exploring what they know. The chapter is filled with student examples, which makes it as refreshing as it is helpful.*

CHAPTER 4
FOCUSED REFLECTIONS: TAPPING INTO LIFE EXPERIENCE

By Alan Weber

PART A: SMOKEY

When I was in grade school, I remember watching Smokey the Bear commercials on TV. They were mini-lectures on camping and forestry etiquette. Small, cute animals would gather around Smokey as he delivered sermons on picking up campsite trash or respecting the territory of furry creatures. I never dreamed as I packed for my first real camping adventure that Smokey would personally deliver a message to me.

With the accepted draft of my doctoral dissertation still being typed, my wife and I fled westward from the cornfields of central Illinois. We had planned a three month extravaganza which would take us through the Black Hills of South Dakota toward the Cascades of Oregon. We then would head down Highway 1 on California's coast to San Diego where a left turn would point us toward Big Bend National Park and eventually New Orleans. We hoped to arrive in Chicago to take a "real" shower and celebrate Thanksgiving with my parents.

Since camping was a new interest, we quickly learned what not to do in Smokey's wonderful wild. Ravens ate our unattended lunch in the Badlands. Bears devoured a week's worth of suppers in the Grand Tetons when we left a well-stocked cooler on a picnic table while we slept. (Luckily, we didn't bring our unfinished desserts into the tent.) The most memorable experience, however, occurred near Craig, Colorado.

The air was fresh and crisp as we drove into the hilly terrain west of the Rockies. Against the gray bark of the aspen trees, the yellow leaves fluttered in the swirling breeze like excited monarch butterflies.

We searched for a suitable place to pitch the tent and found a dry campsite on top of one of the foothills. The area was desolate, ten miles from the main highway and five miles from the nearest paved road. A gust of wind ripped a flurry of leaves from the branches and scattered them along the ground. The fall air pricked our skin with notions of winter. We built the perfect campfire after a macaroni and cheese-onion soup-potato chip-apple dinner. The green wood on the campfire hissed; we sipped the then exotic Coors beer. We felt content, alone, and together. We went to bed as rain pattered on the tent's stretched canvas and hissed on the fading embers.

As I peeked out of our tent in the morning, a Dr. Zhivago wonderland stunned me. No leaved dangled from the aspens. No golden colors brushed the landscape. Now, pillows of snow hugged the dark tree trunks and nestled in the boughes. Snow-coated branches turned the trees into fantastic creatures. A light fog blanketed the campsite.

We solemnly packed our gear as the snow creatures wilted in the warming sun. We hopped into our Plymouth Duster, destined for new sights. Unfortunately, as I accelerated the engine, we merely spun our wheels in a foot of mud. Unknowingly, we had parked off the gravel drive in what had become a quagmire. We pushed and shoved, swore and pleaded, argued and conferred. Still, the brown beast didn't budge. After an hour, we admitted we were stuck.

There was not a soul in the campgrounds. In fact, we had not seen anyone since yesterday noon at Andy's diner off the main highway. We stashed our parkas with fruit and candy and headed down the narrow road for help. While we sought isolation during most of the trip, we now prayed to hear the voices of others. Two snorting steers frightened us as we hoofed around a blind curve. The bull stared at us, lowered his head, and grunted. Fortunately, he meandered by our rigid bodies.

An hour later we had sloshed half way down the mountain where the road turned to blacktop. Still five miles from the highway, we grew tired and wet. The snow had turned to puddles of water at this lower elevation and our anxieties into a numbing fear. Then, we heard a distant noise. As it grew louder, we shifted gears from a slow amble to a quick walk. Around a low arching curve, we saw salvation. A grey national park jeep crammed with three rangers purred toward us.

When they stopped, we told them our plight. They appeared almost happy at our dilemma, as if we were the object of their professional fantasies. They beamed like boy scouts eager to earn another merit badge.

When we arrived at our car, the three rangers mulled around brainstorming ways to free our Duster. They looked immaculate in their freshly laundered pants, starched shirts, and pleated jackets. The brims of their mountie hats lay directly perpendicular to their jaws. Their polished boots reflected a professional attitude.

They attempted to push the car from its muddy captor, with no success. After a brief conference, the rangers got a chain from the back of their jeep. As one rather plump ranger who sported a bushy moustache was about to plop himself on the ground, I pleaded that I was already dirty and could crawl under the car and hook the chain myself. The rotund officer wouldn't hear of it. He and his buddy slid onto the ground and like carefree eight-year-olds, caked the backs of their trousers and jackets with mud. They seemed to revel in the muck as they hooked the chain and eventually pulled the Duster to safety.

I wanted to show these men my gratitude and knew that offering them money might be taken in the wrong way. So, I asked if we could treat them to breakfast. The heavy set ranger looked at me with the comforting eyes of a cartoon character and politely declined. A piece of dried mud stuck to the rim of his hat and moisture clung to his furry moustache.

"How long will you be camping," he quizzed. I said for another two months.

Like the gentle teddy bear I knew from TV, he put his arm around my shoulder and in the caring voice of a sage said, "Do us one favor on your trip and you'll make our efforts worth it."

"Sure," I said.

With the innocence and compassion of a small child, he looked at me with big, sad eyes and simply said, "Be nice to the animals."

It was at this moment that I knew why all the forest creatures gathered around Smokey.

PART B: FOCUSED REFLECTIONS AND LIFE EXPERIENCE

When I was in graduate school, I enjoyed the times I wrote to my 12-year-old nephew, David. These letters offered welcomed relief from the highly structured, scholarly writing required in my academic courses. I had an opportunity to tap into my own ideas and feelings, rather than reiterate, compare, or apply someone else's. In one letter I recaptured the embarrassing moment of finding myself in the wrong bathroom at the campus pub. Another time I shared a lucky encounter I had with Duke Ellington. The anecdote that begins this chapter is a longer version of a letter sent to David about a memorable time spent in Colorado.

I realize now that these letters helped me externalize my thinking and draw personal connections to my academic readings, lectures, and writing. They allowed me to sift through my experience and talk on paper, to get ideas out where I could see them. I remember telling David about some of my high school teaching experiences, that I subsequently included in a graduate paper about literary response.

This chapter details how K–12 teachers can create focused writing situations in which students find ideas and toss them around in their minds, much like I did when writing David. It also suggests ways that teachers might design writing prompts that help their students think more creatively and critically in all content areas.

THE CHARACTERISTICS OF FOCUSED REFLECTIONS

Before discussing ways of using reflective journals in content area or writing classrooms, I want to explain what focused reflections are and why they are important in language arts and academic classrooms. Toby Fulwiler (1987) and James Britton (1975) both have described expressive and journal writing at length. Focused reflections are expressive accounts that allow students to recall, speculate, or reflect upon real situations, fictitious occurrences, or acquired knowledge. In language arts classes, they allow students to think aloud on paper about what they enthusiastically chatter about in the hallways, individually brood about in their bedrooms, and dreamingly wish while at their desks. In social studies and math classes, focused reflections give students a way to link textbook concepts to their own life experiences. They help students predict, clarify, and discover content area concepts.

Focused reflections are short eight to ten minute writings usually done in class. They are written for the trusted audience of writers in the classroom. It is exploratory writing that is shared in pairs, in small groups or with the entire class. These reflections differ from private journals and diaries not meant for others to read. They serve as points of departure for classroom interaction, talk, and discovery. Students are encouraged to take risks in their thinking, so the writing often is quick and inventive, punctuated by mechanical errors (no puns intended), run-on sentences and fragments. If spelling is a big problem, students are instructed to leave a blank space for the word or to spell it phonetically.

Because these writings are shared in pairs or groups soon after they are written, teachers do not have to collect and read every student entry. The writing is evaluated usually for "doneness" since making personal connections is the main objective. Students are simply asked to write as much as possible during a set length of time (on occasion, a minimum number of lines) and make their writing legible. An important by-product, of course, is writing fluency which is often a prerequisite for academic success.

RATIONALE FOR FOCUSED REFLECTIONS

There are three major reasons why focused reflections are a powerful tool in the classroom: First, focused reflections allow students to perceive or see what they are thinking. If you stand too close to an impressionist painting, it is difficult to see any identifiable forms. Your eye merely recognizes blotches of paint. However, when you stand back from the painting, you gain perspective and the blotches blend into an intelligible picture. Writing allows students to step back and perceive their thoughts in context. It helps students make sense out of their experiences. Jean Paul Sartre stopped writing when he went blind because he couldn't see what he was thinking. Focused reflections are intended to keep the students' eyes wide open.

Second, focused reflections help students generate and clarify their ideas. Linguists such as Vygotsky (1962) state that the relationship between thought and language is so symbiotic that after age four it is difficult to determine which is the cause of the other. Which came first? The chicken or the egg; thought or language? Focused reflections enlist a naming response: What shall I call it? How shall I word this? They give experiences and thoughts form and substance and encourage intellectual connections. Notice the associations the following ninth grader made when asked to write down what she knew about the nervous system at the beginning of a unit in biology.

The nervous system is composed of a whole bunch of nerves that meet up the vertebrae to the back of the head. Everything we do is connected. If we want to move a finger, a message is sent down from the brain to that nerve and the finger moves. These messages move up and down so fast that we really don't have to think about moving. There are also nerves that tell when we're hurt. If we didn't have nerves, I could keep hitting myself until eventually I die without feeling pain.

You can see Mary's mind sweep her own experiences to link the general concept of nerves to meaningful associations in her own life—pain.

Third, focused reflections encourage students to play around with language and ideas. When I first started writing on a word processor, I learned the computer by playing around with it. I touched keys not knowing if the computer would shut off, explode or delete a word. Before I got too precise and professional, I needed time to familiarize myself with the machine and program. Focused reflections help students familiarize themselves with new ideas. Alfred North Whitehead (1959, p. 29) stated that those who become highly talented in a field were usually introduced to that field in a playful way, an almost romantic way. Then, you move on to the precision stage. Focused reflections allow students to take thinking risks and toy around with their ideas.

In the example below Cheryl describes a bad habit that she enjoys in a playful manner:

> A bad habit I really enjoy is to eat something and put the empty container back in the refrigerator or cupboard. My favorite thing to do is to finish a bag of chips and leave only the crumbs remaining. There is usually a very angry person in the kitchen when the bag is opened next and someone wants to eat some chips. I think that the reason I enjoy this habit is because it annoys people so much. This bad habit was never really that much of a habit until my mother started telling me how mad she gets when she finds empty things all over the house.

Cheryl takes thinking risks which require no prescribed order or sequence. She finds new ways of connecting ideas.

WRITING A PLAY

There is growing evidence that playfulness of language is more than just a precursor to serious thought. Daiute (1989) has argued that play *is* a form of thought for young elementary writers. She shows that children build writing skills through their playful use of language and asserts that this play engages critical thinking. Two writing prompts that underscore the importance of playfulness are "firsts" and "favorites."

Firsts   One way to nudge students into playfulness is by writing about "firsts." These prompts are easy to create and enjoyable to write. For example, a good topic for younger children is writing about their first school friend or first playground fight. Older students like to write about their first date, the first time away from home, or their first time being grounded. Think about your students' age, previous experiences, and interests when inventing these prompts.

Often my students surprise me by twisting the context of a situation. Notice how Helen creates an unexpected context in her anecdote describing her first kiss.

> I was laying in his arms, all of my defenses down. I didn't know what to do, I wanted to cry and laugh both at the same time. I did not know that he wouldn't hurt me

for anything. He was too gentle and loving. Then, before I knew what was happening, he bent his head down toward mine and kissed me on the cheek and smiled. I couldn't help it, I started to cry. I didn't know what to do and neither did he. So at that point dear old Dad handed me back to Mom and said, ''I don't know what to do when she cries.'' And I started to laugh.

Other ''first'' prompts are listed below:

- Relate the first time that you ever felt guilty. What was the circumstance? Who was present?
- Share the first time that you were punished in school. Describe the person who punished you or the place you were punished.
- Write about your first bicycle, the first Christmas you remember, or first lie you ever told.
- Describe you first family vacation, the first time you realized there was no Easter Bunny or the first time you understood that there was no justice in this world.

Favorites   Writing about favorites encourages sensuousness, silliness, and nostalgia. When I think of my own favorites, I think specifically of wine. It was a 1959 Château Haut Brion, shared with good friends after a veal picante dinner laced with wild rice and truffles. My journal reads: ''The wine attacks the taste buds in smooth, small explosions. Each burst fills the mouth with separate tastes of vanilla, oak, and fruit. The overall effect is that of purple velvet massaging the palate.''

Laurie's focused reflection of her favorite teacher was eventually revised and sent to Miss Guider.

> . . .When I was in first grade my teacher's name was Miss Guider. I thought she was so beautiful. I thought she looked like a Barbie Doll. Her hair was thin and straight but curled under slightly at the botton. She had sandy blond colored hair that was just past shoulder length. . .

Prompts about favorites are endless. Students might write about their favorite athlete, their special hiding place or their pet peeve. Other favorite topics of mine include TV shows, food, especially desserts, colors, moods, heroes, vacation spots, and jokes. Here are some exerpts form Kevin's focused reflection about his toy or plaything:

> ''My favorite toy was a clown. It was about as tall as me when I was 5 years old. Its legs were red and white striped. Its arms were too. Its feet and hands were dark red. . .''

WRITING AS SEEING

We have mentioned that focused reflections help students see their thinking. They do this by forcing students to view their ideas from various perspectives or for diverse audiences. They also encourage students to display their ideas in familiar or novel styles and forms. Empathetic situations, format writing, monologues, and dialogues exemplify four ways for students to perceive their world through different colored lenses.

Empathetic Situations.   One strategy to help students "see" their ideas and experiences is through empathetic situatons. When I was a freshman in high school, I was the class clown. Nothing pleased me more than to disrupt the class routine ever so slightly and make the teacher smile. One day my shenanigans went beyond the bounds of Brother Jones's rules and he blurted at me, "Weber, if you think this is so funny, you teach the class." I'm not totally convinced that my attempts that day at instructing algebra led me to choose teaching as a profession, but I do remember what it felt like to be in charge not knowing what was going on. Brother Jones kept me in that role for the entire period.

Empathetic situatons help students identify with another person or object. The writing prompt puts the student in the "shoes" of someone or something else so they see the world from that new perspective. These situations allow students to participate in the physical sensations, cognitive decisions, intense feelings, and imaginative capers of the object or person from whose point of view they write. Below are a few situations that have worked with my students.

- You are an old bull who roams the fields of the countryside looking for trouble. One morning you awake and discover that you are sensitive to green, not red. How does this situation complicate your life?
- You are a big brother teaching your little sister who just mastered the dog paddle the real "basics" to get her started in diving. What kind of directions will you give her and what points and precautions will you coach?
- Describe your bedroom from the point of view of an object inside it, like a bedspread, sock, or stuffed animal. Try to use "showing" details so readers can discover from what point of view you are writing.

Laurie takes on the persona of an advice columnist in the following exerpt. She responds back to Millie, a woman who can't understand why her husband of twenty years is daily visiting his mother and snacking before dinner.

Obviously your husband really cares for his mother. Maybe he enjoys spending a lot of time with her. If your husband has complained about your cooking before, then you might think it worth your while to take a cooking class. Also, try to make the healthiest and naturally wholesome meals you can. People often equate Mom's cooking with healthy food. On the other hand, if he doesn't complain. . .I think you should talk to his mother and tell her how bad the situation is for you.

Formats   Another way to help students gain perspective on their ideas is by varying formats. If you think back to your own public school writing experiences, you probably wrote in just a few standard forms or formats. Some teachers don't even remember writing at all except for sentence completions, notes and answering the questions at the back of the chapter. The most common forms of writing people mention are the essay or theme, essay tests, letters, poems, research papers, and stories. Steve Tchudi (1980) listed alternative formats that students might compose, including autobiography, memoirs, jokes, confessions, and sermons. While these formats are primarily intended for final draft writing assignments that require some length, they also provide creative ways for structuring shorter expressive writing prompts.

Below are some examples of reflective prompts that ask the student to write in a different format.

- Write a magazine ad that attempts to sell one of the seven deadly sins: lust, avarice, greed, gluttony, envy, sloth, or pride. (See the November, 1987 issue of *Harper's Magazine* for some great examples.)
- Write a telegram to your mother explaining your sudden decision to travel to _____. (Insert the country you have no desire ever to visit.)
- Create a petition which describes a way to abolish what you consider as the most pressing social, environmental, or political injustice.
- Write a newspaper want ad that describes a person that you would like as a friend.

There is no doubt about the kind of friend that Jessica seeks in her Want Ad:

WANTED: A FRIEND

This person must be female, trustworthy, intelligent, fun, and be sort of a tomboy. You may not be a snob, prissy, really tall, lazy or unadventurous. I am blond, short, have freckles, no glasses, and I like to read a lot.

If you are interested, please call 221-2356. Ask for Jessica.

(I would not like myself for a friend because I am a little bossy.)

Monologues and Dialogues   While some formats like brochures, reference manuals, parables, and proposals are too long for expressive pieces of writing, some types of interview formats are easily adapted to pieces written in a short 8–10 minute time span. Two specific formats adapted from James Moffett (1986) are monologues and dialogues.

Monologues are characterized by imitating a person's thoughts (inner monologue) or actual speech (exterior monologue). Possible outer monologue prompts include imitating a father's scolding of a small child, or a literary character's anguish upon discovering a personality flaw. Often students create characters in strange or unfamiliar places whose monologues reflect their inner feelings and emotions. For example, I once had my students create an interior monologue for a teenager who had seen hell for the first time. They related the punishments inflicted upon people guilty of unmentionable crimes and sins.

While extended dialogues are often found in plays and film scripts, you can devise shorter versions in which students select an idea about which they have strong feelings, have studied in a particular subject area, or have researched in the library.

Barbara Bird devised the following dialogue prompt for her high school home economics class. The students were studying a unit on family planning when she asked them to write a dialogue consisting of eight entries (two per speaker) for the following situation:

> Carol and Dave were married right after their high school graduation. Dave has a good job and plans to go to college at night. Carol would like to have a child now so the baby can ''grow up'' with them, but financially they will have to be very careful. Also, Dave admits he is not sure he is mature enough to bring up a child.

The radio dialogue takes a different twist since it asks students to write a radio or TV transcript between a famous interviewer and a notable, historical figure. For example, students are asked to create a dialogue between Barbara Walters and Galileo which explains the discovery that the earth is not the center of the universe.

WRITING AS DISCOVERY

Focused reflections not only help students visualize and play with ideas, they also generate and clarify thinking. These prompts prod students to speculate, predict and reason on higher thinking levels. They also force students to clarify their thinking through problem-solving strategies. Thinking Scenarios and Problematic Situations are two effective prompts for this purpose.

Thinking Scenarios   Thinking scenarios are focused reflections which tap into various critical thinking levels like evaluation, analysis, and application. The easiest way to write these prompts is to focus on the purpose of the writing. Below are four prompts about the same topic which reflect different kinds of thinking. The purpose is underlined and the thinking skill appears in parenthesis.

- After reading three of your classmates embarrassing situations, *judge* which one you think is most embarrassing and why. (Evaluation)
- Read the embarrassing situation on page 45 in your book and write an Ann Landers column *analyzing* what caused the situation to happen. (Analysis)
- Pretend you are a psychiatrist and *interpret* the embarrassing situation that your writing partner has composed. This ''analysis'' can be serious or humorous in tone. (Interpretation)

Patti's description (below) of an embarrassing situation that occurred in eighth grade is not merely an exercise in recall. By putting her experience in her own words, she gains self understanding. (Comprehension)

. . .Two of my girlfriends and I left 7th hour early and headed for our lockers. One of my friends ran ahead of us in order to slide on the floor. However, because her soles were rubber, she stumbled. I thought this was a fun idea so I imitated her. I ran ahead. . .and ended up on the floor. . .I happened to fall right in front of the study hall door. Consequently, everyone in the large room saw me sprawled out on the floor with the reddest of faces.

Problematic Situation   Posing a problem with no obvious solution is an effective way for writers to predict alternative choices and possibilities. The problem can be real or imaginary. The important consideration is that the writers bring their own values, experiences, and prior knowledge to the situation, as is possible in the sample prompts below:

- You have discovered a dragon in your living room. You are unsure about whether it is friendly or mean, but the dragon is filthy. How would you bathe this dragon?
- A prospective employer wants to find out what kind of thinker you are. He gives you a ping pong ball and asks that you describe some of its unusual uses.
- Your twin sister needs a kidney transplant and you are the only suitable donor. The operation could severly limit your ability to take part in sports, your great love. Describe what goes on in your head as you make a decision.

Many problematic situations are designed or keyed to textbook material. They ask the students to predict or invent a solution for a problem discussed in the readings. Judy Mesack from Grayling, Michigan created the next situation for an eighth grade reading class before studying the book, *The Drummer Boy of Shiloh*.

You are 14 years old and have run away from home to join the army and fight for your side in the Civil War. It is April and you are lying on your blankets trying to sleep the night before the big battle. You have never been a drummer boy, nor have you ever been in battle. Explain your thoughts on this night. Tell what you think a drummer boy does during battle and why these actions are necessary.

Rachel Anderson, an eighth grader in Mrs. Mesack's class, responded in the following way:

I am very nervous and trying to muster up some courage, but every time I think about it, my heart flutters. I'm very scared for my life and I don't want to die at 14. I'm not too sure what a drummer boy does, but I think I'm supposed to beat my drums when I see the enemy troops.

Rachel's identification with the main character and prediction of his actions engage her in the reading selection.

CONCLUSION

Some focused reflections serve as the basis for longer, polished reports, stories, or formal essays which are evaluated and graded. In fact, this kind of exploratory writing gives students a choice in developing their ideas into final products which may proceed through the revision and editing stages of the writing process. They can produce "published" writing in a method similar to the way I developed Smokey, where I sifted through a folder of my expressive writings and expanded it into a personal anecdote about life's fragility and human kindness.

Whatever the final outcome of focused reflections, they primarily serve as invitations for students to hook up academic learning to their own experiences. The process enriches both sides of the human coin, making life's encounters valuable on multiple levels, while at the same time personalizing academic studies.

REFERENCES

Britton, J., Burgess, T., Martin, N., McLeod, A., and Rosen, H. (1975). *The development of writing abilities (11–18)*. London: Macmillan.

Daiute, C. (1989). Play as thought: Thinking strategies of young writers." *Harvard Educational Review*, 59, 1–23.

Fulwiler, T. (Ed.) (1987). *The journal book*. Portsmouth, NH: Boynton/Cook.

Tchudi, S. (1980). *The ABC's of literacy: A Guide for parents and educators* New York: Oxford.

Moffett, J. (1986). *Active voices IV*. Upper Montclair, NJ: Boynton/Cook.

Vygotsky, L. (1962). *Thought and language*. (G. Vakar, Trans.). Cambridge, MA: MIT Press.

Whitehead, A.N. (1959). *The aims of education and other essays*. London: Ernest Benn Limited.

SELECTED BIBLIOGRAPHY

Fulwiler, T. (Ed.) (1987). *The journal book*. Portsmouth, NH: Boynton/Cook.

A thorough description of the characteristics and applications of journal writing across the curriculum.

Mayher, J.S., Lester, N. and Pradl, G. (1983). *Learning to write/writing to learn*. Portsmouth, NH: Boynton/Cook.

Discusses the relationship of writing and learning within the context of the writing process.

Botstein, L. (Spring, 1990). Damaged literacy: Illiteracies and American democracy. *Daedalus 119*, 2:55–84.

Explores the historical, political, and cultural consequences of illiteracy. Puts forth the argument that written language is the active instrument of a literate society.

*Most teachers who own **Rosemary Deen's** and Marie Ponsot's text,* Beat Not the Poor Desk *(1982), know what tattered means. My pages hang by thin thread. So useful is their approach to the essay, Anne-Marie Oomen and I teach it throughout our state. We invited both writer/professors to Traverse City last year, where they mesmerized a group of teachers anxious not to do it wrong. "It," essay writing, scares so many. But in this chapter, Deen puts that hovering ghost to rest. She teaches out of the principle that learning is empirical and inductive. "Learning is change; writing is the energizing, perfecting habit we call skill." Deen says the expository essay combines imagined thought with the feeling of intellect. How remarkably similar to Frances Temple's belief that historical fiction invites both, as well.*

CHAPTER 5
WRITING EPOSITORY ESSAYS: DEVELOPING A STRUCTURE

By Rosemary Deen

Note: I wrote the first version of my essay specifically for this book. (This is my usual experience as a writer: I write prose when people ask me to, and poems when I do what I like). Following the steps described in part B, I began with a center, a family story I've told myself over and over. I wrote concretely, without concern for what meanings it might have. Then, thinking about the behavior of the person I take to be the central character, I abstracted an idea from the story and expressed it as a single word, a subject. I wrote to define it, not generally, from a dictionary, but out of my own experience and thinking about the main action. These new first paragraphs made the story into the middle of an essay, the support for the idea I was now asserting. Then I wrote a new ending by returning to the original definition and saying more about it in the light of the story. This gave me in a simple form the expository essay, the essay that supports the idea it asserts.

PART A: RESPONSE-ABILITY

Response is the first way of being responsible. It's giving others the kind of attention they didn't ask for and maybe couldn't ask for. So response is having confidence in someone else without waiting to be justified. It's readiness to take the initiative; it doesn't ask, "What do you want me to do?" It possesses a kind of sympathetic determination. It's staying in tune with someone different from you because your feelings are paying attention. Response is a child knowing what it's like to be a mother cat.

We know that one of the ways little children learn about being human is to imagine their own experience and project it onto the world around them. Sometimes they get it wrong. One of my young children told me, "When *I'm* the mother, *you* are going to go to bed early." Even at that, she was already the mother in letting me know the consequences of my behavior. But when they get it right, even their sympathetic response to their toys or pets helps them experience responsibility.

I'm not talking about the responsibilities parents try to extract from children in exchange for permission to own a pet. I mean the way responsiveness in very young children leads them to take the initiative in gestures of caring for some- one else—the pets they see as "someone." Then the animal becomes human- like, turnes its animal feelings to human feelings and its animal ways to human ways. There are plenty of stories of remarkable animals with apparently human characteristics: the cat who invented for himself a game, a cross between baseball and hockey, or the cat who could baby-sit. What I think is remarkable in these stories is not the animal, but how "human" humans have made an animal. The stories aren't animal lore but human lore. Some people say that animals can trans- cend their nature for us, their human companions. But we don't know what animal nature is. More accurate to say that we teach animals to transcend our stereotype of animal nature because we need to imagine everything around us in a human form.

This idea crystallized for me on the morning Muffin turned up missing. Her new kittens, still in their box at the back of the girls' closet, were mewing and nuzzling each other frantically. Finally we located Muffin, across the street on the flat roof of a town house. She peered over the edge, meowing at us, and we stared up at her. What could make such a good mother leave her young for such heights?

"How did you get up there, Muffin?" we called. What are you doing up there?" There she was, the mindless creature, yelling unreasonably down at us, and there were her kittens back in our house yelling in the girls' closet.

The children were upset, hopping about, excited, going to be late for school if the adventure kept up. The house tenant had already left for work. There was no way to the roof.

"We've got to call the fire department." Catherine, nine, and Mary Stella, seven, agreed.

"Come on down, Muffin!" called John.

"Come on, Muffa-doodle!" That was Barbara.

"Don't we have a ladder that would reach to the roof of their house?" That was Matthew, the oldest.

I was exasperated. Imagine trying to hoist a ladder high enough even for sec- ond story windows! A magic ladder with aluminum hands reaching out to the damn cat! I choked on the impossibility of explaining it all. They all looked at me, their unreasonable mother. Opinion was focusing on the fire department.

"You can't just call the fire department. It's only in kids' books and TV shows that the friendly firemen come down the street and rescue the family cat." Disbelief all around. "It's probably even against the law to call the fire department for a cat." Exasperation all around. "If they come out for a cat, then they won't be in the firehouse when a real, a serious alarm comes in, don't you see?"

"This *is* serious," said Mary Stella, looking up at poor Muffin, who was still meowing way down at us, her sweet face above her snowy bib. She was a small, tender cat, a pearly tiger with a lovely white breast and belly. Drat her.

"Don't worry, Muffin, " called John, who was five and Muffin's favorite. She'd had her kittens on his bed at two in the morning. "Don't worry, Muffin. We'll get you down!"

"I don't see how," I muttered. But John was tuned to Muffin's feelings, not mine.

"How did she get up there, anyway," I asked the kids.

"She climbed a tree," said Barbara.

"She never climbs trees and she'd never leave her kittens to go tree-climbing." The children waited for me to answer my question. "A dog must have chased her up the tree—Mr. Macho's insane German shepherd. Then she went out on that limb over the roof. Then her weight bent the branch down to the roof, and she hopped off. But then the branch snapped back up. She'd have to jump up to get it, and she could never do that. Oh, dear!"

"Call the fire department!" they all yelled.

"You know, you kids are going to be late for school if you don't watch out. Gracious! It's late! Time to get your books and get going." I was doing this all wrong: failing to solve the problem, betraying the cat for the fire department, interrupting the shapely narrative unfolding before our eyes.

The children's father was ready to leave for his classes. He had no interest in narrative. If he put a novel down, he'd never pick it up again. As the movie wound to its supreme tension on the television, he'd say,, "Well, clearly it's not going to get any better," and flick off the set or turn his back on the screen and depart for bed. Pythagoras, yes. Newton, yes. *The Timaeus*, yes. But story, no. He was immune to suspense. He backed the car out of the driveway and waved goodbye to the six of us clustered on the sidewalk. Seven of us, counting Muffin. Eleven of us, counting the kittens in the closet.

I started to herd the children across the street toward their school books. John, in afternoon kindergarten, staying behind to comfort Muffin.

"Come on, Muffin! You can do it! Jump on the branch! Come one, girl!" I hurried across the street to get away from childhood's belief in the impossible.

"I want to stay with Muffin," said Barbara.

"You're not much bigger than Muffin. I think you'd better stay with me." I gathered her hand.

"Are you going to call the fire department now?" Catherine was laying out my program. Instead of keeping quiet, I went through the reasons again why the fire department wouldn't come.

Mary Stella imagined the worst. "If she stays up there all day, the kittens will starve—or maybe Muffin will get so worried she'll jump off the roof and hurt herself!"

"The fire department's only a few blocks away," Catherine pointed out reasonably.

"If we get the ladder up, I could climb up and get her." I pictured 11-year-old Matthew in a small red fireman's hat, mounting the ladder while Muffin waited to leap into his arms. Oh, drat the dumb cat!

"Maybe the fire department will know who you should call." Mary Stella gazed at me firmly, her hand on her books, ready to gather them up when I'd signed the contract.

"The kittens have stopped crying, anyway," Catherine observed. "They're all worn out."

"Well, that's one thing in my favor." I refused the reproach. "Let's not run upstairs to see how they are and wake them up. Off you go!"

And off they went, past John, who looked very small from our window, calling up to Muffin, who looked even smaller. I paced back and forth in front of the telephone after checking on the kittens and looking up the fire department number. I was imagining their probable response: "*Listen*, Lady. . ."

Well, be reasonable. Somebody in New York must know what to do about this. It must happen every day. Maybe the yellow pages have a listing under "Pet Rescue" or something. Maybe some radio station has a pet owner's hot line. Maybe the architect-owner of the building has a key. "Henry, the orkitectur," John called him, fascinated to watch the building go up brick by brick and to know the "orkitectur" personally.

"Here she is!" John walked in and held the screen door for Muffin.

"What happened! How did she get down?" Muffin paused to refresh herself with milk before cutting upstairs, followed by Barbara.

"She jumped up and got the tree branch and came down."

"But she couldn't do that. That branch was high."

"Well, she did."

"How did you get her to do it?"

"I just kept saying, 'You can do it, Muffin! You can do it!' And she jumped up a few times and then she made it."

I remember you, Muffin, and so do the children. We remember the time you saw John in his snow suit up to his knees in the middle of a snowy meadow—how you set off to join him, breasting the drifts like a swimmer, though you hated snow. How, when Leonard was jogging through the woods in the country, he'd spot you darting in and out, after or ahead of him. How when he and I walked down the country road in moonlight or starlight, you were dodging along, into the woods ahead of us, then behind crouching in the ditch, never at our heels like a dog but accompanying us now and then, cat-fashion. "A dog can be penned," said a judge settling a neighborhood dispute, "but a cat may walk where it will." You were the cat of the children's childhood, the free, responsive will.

Though there were plenty of others, you became human more completely, in your cat way.

I got kittens for young children not just because I like little creatures, but so that the children could humanize them. I didn't think they could "take responsibility" for them. Children need pets, I think, when they are too little to be responsible for someone else. I knew I would have to feed, clean up after, train, and arrange services for a cat. I didn't think I could bargain—"Now, if you want this pet, you'll have to promise. . ." Children need the pleasure of creating something—perhaps by raising a young animal—without the burden of contractual responsibility, to imagine their humanness in some other youthful or innocent creature as one way of realizing it. They need to be kind and tender in response to what they can imagine is human in animals. *Re-sponsere* "to promise in return." The root meaning of the word suggests Marianne Moore's "responsive and responsible."

Little children can't normally make tangible things that last—things they can see in the making, brick by brick, things that seem equal to their power of making. As we adults see it, their power is largely potential. We give them scope for it in play, if they're lucky. But actually their power to make is a peak of energy. They are fitting new skills into their repertory of skills, and are newly interested in abstractions like letters and numbers. They are creating ideas through language. Their feelings too are expanding. They can love, in addition to their family, a book or project—even a special teacher. Their power of response is particularly acute and fresh, but often, as the way of the world is, it meets with defeat or confusion. Yet response is the simplest expression of good will, a kind of morality of imagination. It's self-instructing and self-constructing. For the luckiest young humans, if we can help it along, the whole world inside them is unfolding into responsive forms which give them a sense of themselves as active, purposive human beings.

PART B: PARABLE INTO ESSAY

The essay in part A has the elemental structure of the kind of work teachers in content courses want in the more special or elaborate forms of final exam, critical essay, and research paper. There the concrete center is data about the subject the writer has studied, for example, statistics in a sociology course or the *Federalist Papers* in a course on constitutional law. The teacher wants to see what data the student knows, what he or she can assert about it, and whether the evidence really supports the assertion. In what students call "the real world" it is also necessary to know how to specify an assertion so that it can be supported, and have the evidence in order to support it.

The set of assignments I'm about to describe does two things at the same time that are often (unfortunately) divided into two different courses: a thinking course, where learning and organizing data is the point, and early writing courses where teachers depend on narrative structure and imaginative writing to promote pleasure in fluency and prolific power.

But if we work with structure, it's possible to fuse these apparent opposites because structure can be realized concretely or abstractly—or anywhere in between. Or to put it another way, because thought is not separate from pleasure. And if we speak of the function of this structure—assert, define, support—it is apropriate for both beginning and advanced courses. The course was originally designed by my colleague Marie Ponsot for students who cannot pass a minimum competency writing examination. The work fits a beginning writing course because it always works from the concrete and because it's elemental—and I mean "elemental" not in the denigrating sense of "childish" or "remedial," but literally, in the sense that oxygen, hydrogen, nitrogen, and carbon are the elements of organic life. For the same reasons, it's been used for junior high writers. The definitions of young writers are usually more playful and metaphoric. And it suits an advanced course because it's an intellectual structure, however elemental. Whatever is elemental can be developed differently by different persons. It's a handsome structure for any writer.

But why, aside from the beauty of its shape, should it be used with young writers at all? For two reasons. If, as I believe, genuine learning is experiential—that is, if ideas and concepts arise out of the concrete material we know directly or imaginatively—and if thinking is not separable from feeling, then it's never too early to encourage young people to draw concepts out of their actual experience. I realize there's a place in school for memorizing concepts the teacher passes on, but there's an encouragement of passivity and obedience that goes along with this, unfortunately. It's worthwhile helping youngsters to search their real experience for concepts, and test the ideas they are always willing to assert by the concrete data they have already mastered, either in life or from study. Here they can learn that genuine originality springs not from trying to be different from everyone else, but from originating a definition out of what they really know. This little essay structure is a peaceable and pleasurable way to practice the shape of thinking.

The second recommendation for young writers is that it is a two-stage piece of writing. It's true rewriting, not remedial writing to correct mistakes but rewriting to unpack an idea. Most writers get their idea after they've written, and they offer a primitive version of it in one sentence at the end of a paragraph or the essay. Their essays are a series of afterthoughts. It's useful to learn early that you can change afterthought to forethought, can take an idea that occurs to you after you've sketched out your material and put it up front where you stand responsible for it.

I've been asked what the relationship is between my students' writing and mine. My writing is not a model. I enjoy writing with my students, and if they ask me to read my writing along with theirs, I do. I teach structures, and a structure is always embedded in its various versions. We intuit structure only as we see it repeatedly in its infinite variety. We can't learn the sonnet structure even by reading 150 by the same person. Knowing all of Shakespeare's sonnets would not prepare you for the way in which ''Leda and the Swan'' is a sonnet. Structure is generative. Writers imitate a model; they originate their version of a structure. For inexperienced writers, a model is always the Right Answer.

I have a political agenda (the same one everyone else in this book has), a simple idea that a democracy is based on the value of differences. Like everyone else, I believe that can't go beyond lip service until differences count. So I keep working on differences. As a parent and a teacher I'm scared at how much power over others I'm given. I don't want to have to trust my own innocence, so I try to get rid of that kind of power however I can. Others more savvy, more diplomatic and adroit can use their own writing wisely, I'm sure. Luckily for me, young students are naturally self-centered and overwhelmingly interested in their own writing. That's good motivation. I'm as self-centered as they are, of course, but after 35 years of teaching, I'm more conscious of it.

My writing is only one version of the ways the structure can be imagined. The idea this course stands or falls on is that writers can produce models for themselves. The steps described here are small. None of them takes more than 10 minutes of nonstop, can't-do-it-wrong writing. I hope you readers will write directly as you read the ''directions'' segment and see what models you create for yourself. The ''comment'' sections that follow the practice of writing are tiny essays on the principles embedded in the practice. The practice is incremental. We never do anything once, and we move forward without leaving anything behind. What writers can do and have done, they do again. We repeat and transform as we go forward. Practices that began separately integrate. Narrative passes through the crux of definition and becomes expository essay.

In the whole course we work in 14 weeks of two 75-minute sessions. The work of the course is: 6 fables, 4 parables, and 14 essays. Writers read all their work aloud, write and read observations, practice prolific writing, write from generative structures, and rewrite.

We can write so prolifically because we spend all our time writing and reading—no time in introductions and explanations. There's a core of work that writers can't do wrong, so we don't spend time on public correction. We work in what Marie Ponsot calls "a forward rhythm." As she says, "Coherent shapes—sentences, literary forms, and group meetings—are networks for fluent energy." (CS 145-6)

These notes take you through the middle or turning point of the course. Writers have written 6 fables, and we are ready to write the first parable. Here are the directions. You can't do it wrong.

THE PARABLE

Directions: We write in search of some of the stories we have in our heads. They are stories we've heard told in our families or have told ourselves over and over. We remember them because as each story comes together and turns, it opens out into a meaning.

We write nonstop for five minutes a list of phrases about stories after we've given a couple of samples like these:

- ■ "The story of John and the cat's new kittens."
- ■ "The story of the grown-ups and the ghost stories."
- ■ "The story of the home-made fire crackers."
- ■ "The story about the fight in the ice house."
- ■ "The story of Father and the Christmas roast."

"We call them family parables," Marie Ponsot says, "because they make domestic use of the ancient and noble parable structures in which story turns around and makes a point that identifies character." (CS 23)

We read these lists aloud around the room, listening well and enjoying the hints of ripe stories. Listening to the range, we recognize some of the great narrative types, and their local occasions: weddings, school yards, "firsts," holiday feasts, visitations, eccentric relatives. We take five minutes to jot down more notes for stories other readers have brought to mind. Writers need a good store of parable ideas.

We look over our lists, choose one story, and begin to write it nonstop for 15 minutes. This gives writers a good beginning to take home and complete.

Comment: Sometimes in teachers' workshops I get to hear these beginnings. Experienced writers head so confidently toward the turn that we can foresee the shape of the parable. We realize it's not surprise at the outcome that makes stories good, but our growing confidence and delight in the shape and its new embodiment. I seem to remember scores of such parables and their writers in Kansas City, San Diego, Traverse City, Washington. The anonymity and even discomfort of those conference rooms contrasted with the vivid faces of men and women reading a story in the shape of its meaning.

We don't explain our analysis of the parable or give literary samples. Instead we always present the structures we've devised in an elemental form—a sentence or two sentences—and in concrete language. Let me say this again because it's so important. The structure is always presented embedded in a concrete form which is a version, not a model. Students imagine the structure as they perceive it in the versions they hear, and they embody it in their own concrete versions.

Naturally student writing is uneven, but there are always flashes of writers' discovery. We don't ''cook'' the assignment or critique the results. What's crucial is hearing the variety of student parables. Structure becomes imaginable only as students hear it in variety.

The first apparent strengths and weaknesses of student writing are not significant. Both strong and weak parables affirm the authority of the author. Only the author knows what he or she had in mind and can imagine how an extension of the writing will best embody the original conception. For learning the structure and for succeeding at it, both strong and inexperienced writers must write more than one parable. This is one of the ways we set up a course of work that everyone can do and no one can do wrong. And it's preferable, I believe, to arranging for students to write what the teacher predicts.

Always, the interface between the literary structures we assign and student writing is the imagination of the student writers. It's the form students have imagined that teaches them the possibilities for developing their idea.

But why not give students something richer, a parable of Kafka's, and let them imagine the structure from that? Wordsworth, after all, reading Renaissance sonnets from Shakespeare to Milton, imagined and wrote his own quite different sonnets. Yes, and if this were a late 18th century course in England filled with young Wordsworths we'd get fine sonnets. But for inexperienced writers and readers, to read enough versions to see them *as* samples, get the elemental structure, and then in an act of supreme psychic integrity, go past the energy of the original and re-imagine the structure for themselves—this may be beyond their present powers.

Scholars and critics have for decades been showing us the nuclear forms embedded in long works. In medieval literature we can see how a poet, like Chaucer for example, uses oral literary forms like the fable, fabliau, and exemplum. This relation of developed literary to simple oral form is the relation our students can enjoy with the structure we assign. They may not be Chaucers, but they can have his chance. They develop the structure they imagine just as Chaucer imagined the nucleus of the exemplum, ''The Three Rogues in Search of Death,'' into the suberb irony of the Pardoner's tale. And they can't imagine the structure wrong anymore than Chaucer could, because the point is not to reproduce a sermon or explanation, but to imagine their own experience by conceiving it in a meaningful shape.

We're not after what is often called personal experience in autobiographical narrative. It takes a very experienced writer to turn recent experience fraught with feeling into proper fiction. Inexperienced writers are likely as not to think a "tedious brief epic" of their latest harrowing airport experience will be more entertaining to hear than it was to live through. A family parable may have so much shape through its tellings that it's no longer true at all. I once heard a gifted storyteller from poor, rural southern Indiana tell a tale I was startled to recognize as almost identical to one of Boccaccio's. Whatever its original truth as an account, it had become literature.

It's usually enough to ask students to tell a story often told. Memory selects stories packed with meaning. Many tellings have given them the parable shape: the marked turn, the meaning that emerges in a characteristic act. We can't predict how many illuminating versions of parable we'll get the first time it's assigned. Passive or anxious students may not get to what they know the first time. When they listen to the versions of their more confident colleagues and see what the possibilities are, they come forward in Parable Two.

Observations: The Sentence

Our next step is to make observations on the parable, but here we must backtrack a little, for the writing of observations is a practice we have already put in place by some earlier work on the sentence. At the beginning of the course, after listening to students' fables, I asked listeners to choose aphorisms they remember. The author rereads them, and I copy them on the board. If time permits I say something about what I notice and especially like about the way each sentence is written.

By the third week we're ready for writing observations.

Directions: Here is a sentence of Marie Ponsot's, her translation of an aphorism of La Fontaine (from "Wolf and Lamb," *Fables*, I, 10).

"The strongest reasons are the reasons of the strong." Copy the sentence first. Then write what you notice about how the sentence is written. Begin with the obvious. For example, I notice that the sentence has a balanced ABBA pattern: *strongest, reasons, reasons, strong.* Write for two minutes nonstop a list of such observations. You can't do it wrong. (At the end of this section are other observations on this sentence you might like to read when you've written your own.)

Comment: You will have noticed the phrases "listening attentively," "listening with pleasure," and the assertion that writers get ideas about writing by hearing how variously many writers imagine the same structure. Put this beside the familiar teacherly complaint, "They don't pay attention. They don't know how to listen." Writing observations is the way we teach students to listen attentively, and to contribute to the class in a simple, non-heroic way.

Everyone writes. The most obvious fact is that then no one can say when called upon, "I really didn't notice anything." I say, "Just read whatever you've written. You can't do it wrong."

The central points about observations then are that they are written, are based on listening, and that they describe and define. Once it is pointed out, everyone recognizes an observation. If someone ''disagrees'' with it, it probably does not describe, but evaluates or opinionates.

Observations are the elements of analysis. As analysis they are secondary. The strongest tendency in teaching is the analytical and explanatory. Teachers always begin by explaining everything. To counter this and to say that literature comes first, we give priority to student writing and put the generative writing skills in place before the analytical ones.

I prepare writers for observations in the first two weeks of class by asking them to copy down single sentences they've heard and admired. When I can, I spend the last five minutes of class putting such sentences on the board so we can read and admire them.

I do this also to demonstrate to writers something they don't realize yet, the importance of the sentence. It's the great *generative* structure in thinking and writing. And it's the unit of thought. A single sentence shows the power and idiomatic beauty of a language: ''. . .they see with great exactness but at no great distance'' (Swift); ''*Spes alit agricolam*'' [hope nourishes the farmer.] (Horace); ''*La raison du plus fort est toujours la meilleur*'' [The reason of the strongest is always the best.] (de La Fontaine); ''Es geht auch anders/Aber so geht es auch.'' [You can do it other ways, but you can also do it this way.] (Kurt Weill). It matters little whether students know what's wrong with their writing. Teachers and students usually agree when they are working from the strengths of writing. And we begin to find what's right by listening for good sentences.

Listening has priority over reading because it's less analytical and more imaginative than reading. Reading, students will pick out faults in their colleagues' writing, especially those teachers want them to find. But even inexperienced listeners can hear something imaginative. Essays often sound better than they read. That better ''sound'' is the work's possibilities. They are not fully there yet; they may never be. But at this moment we can catch a sustaining glimpse of them. The writer, like the farmer, lives on hope.

For a week or two, then, I ask students to copy a good sentence and write what they notice about how it's written.

OBSERVATIONS: THE PARABLE

Back now to the day writers bring in their first parable.

Directions: We read all the parables aloud, uninterrupted, on the day they are due and enjoy listening to them. Then I ask someone to reread a parable. We all write nonstop for five minutes what we noticed about how the parable is written, beginning with the obvious. To do this yourself read aloud the family parable part of the essay in part A and write observations nonstop for five minutes. Begin with the obvious. I always give a sample: ''I notice that the story part of the parable is mostly in dialogue.'' I declare that this is description, and that description is free, not evaluative. I ask students, ''What struck you? Say what you noticed about it. Or if nothing struck you, just find the good parts and name them. Writers need to know what they're doing right so they can do it again.''

We read these observations aloud to the author, again without interruption. (At the end of this section are more observations about the parable in section A.)

After this practice writing observations with a sample parable, we write observations on each parable read aloud. This is patient work, but it's the way we say to each writer, ''Your work is important enough to deserve attention.'' We pause to write one minute of nonstop observations after each piece read, but we don't read the observations till all the assigned writing has been heard.

We break up into small groups quickly for reading and observations, and reassemble as a whole class when we practice work that we all do. The point is to read all the papers on the day they are due. I read my own observations along with the others, but I don't interrupt others for comment or correction. I may have to ask more ebullient students to stick to reading their observations instead of using them as a spring board for talk. When everyone writes and reads neither the teacher nor any other loquacious person takes over class time.

If someone says, ''What I noticed someone else has already said,'' I say, ''Please read it anyway. It's important for writers to know how many people noticed the same thing, but in different voices and from different standpoints.''

I don't correct ''observations'' that are really paraphrase or summary. I do interdict negative criticisms and one person's suggestions about what another person could do better. I encourage listeners to express their pleasure. Writers need to know when they do something really well, and listeners need to know when they have identified something literary.

Writers know when they haven't hit the mark from even the most discreet observations. I let them draw their own inferences. The central right thing is to write every day prolifically. So for each small step I keep saying, ''You can't do it wrong,'' Only the repeatable is teachable, and only work that can't be done wrong can be repeated calmly.

More significant for students than praise or blame is definition of what they've done: ''I see you've used dialogue for the most exciting part of the story.'' Definition moves writers to a previously unimaginable standpoint from which they can now see their work anew. What to make of what they see is up to them.

SAMPLE OBSERVATIONS ON THE SENTENCE

Here are two sample sets of observations on the sentence, ''The strongest reasons are the reasons of the strong.'' Set one:

- The sentence builds on repetition and variation of the words *strong* and *reasons*.
- The sentence repeats the word *reasons*, but with different modifiers:
  strongest adds something to *reasons*.
  of the strong restricts *reasons*.

- Forms of the word *strong* come first and last: *reasons* comes second and in the middle.
- *Reasons* keeps suggesting "reason," but it's as far from "reason" as the word *strong* can put it.
- The very simple language and the repetition make the sentence seem artless.
- But the sentence is an iambic hexameter line, so the simplicity must be deliberate. Deliberate simplicity is like understatement; it works like irony.

Set two:

- Two strong words are repeated in this (one is intensified), and convey most of its meaning.
- In the repetition, the sequence of these words is reversed, so that we begin and end, roughly speaking, with *strong*.
- Five syllables before *are* are balanced by six syllables after it.
- *Reasons* appears twice, in the center, flanked by three syllables on each side.
- *strong* is "strongest" doesn't mean quite what it does in *strong* at the end of the sentence: it changes form figurative to literal.
- The definite article appears three times, and seems to increase the statement's definiteness. There are no qualifications.
- The verb is not active but a copula, making the statement an equation, and increasing its apparent tautology.

SAMPLE OBSERVATIONS ON THE PARABLE

Set one:

- The narrative is at least as much design as narrative: everyone in the family is shown in relation to Muffin, through dialogue and characteristic reaction.
- The mother and father are far from being the heroes, though the mother is plenty "responsible."
- The children treat Muffin as seriously in need of help. The mother "drats" her. The father shows little interest.
- Muffin is the one who "acts" both to get herself into trouble and to save herself.
- But John's response to Muffin's trouble encourages a response in Muffin.
- Any age child can play this game, and profit from it. Adults aren't really in it.
- "Response" here is shown entirely within the family, if we include Muffin. Henry the "orkitecter" and the Fire Department are peripheral.

Set two:

- The parable has two parts, a story and an address to Muffin. The first part is dialogue; the second part is images.

- The story-dialogue acts out the conflicts (mother-children) and the harmony (children-Muffin) of "response."
- In the images neither Muffin nor the children are present but are seen in imagination.
- The story is a first-person narrative in the past tense, but it serves mostly to frame a dialogue in the present tense. So the events seem both past and present.
- The voices of the children dominate the dialogue. We get to know them by what they say; the narrator doesn't characterize them. Their voices don't appear in the second part.
- Both mother and father see events shaping into narrative or fiction. The children see events as "real" or unique or history in the making.
- The mother thinks of herself as a charge of the rescue, but the story turns when John and Muffin solve the problem.

Comment: These observations are pretty much in the order in which they occurred to the observers. In confident observers this is seldom the reading order of the text, but the order of their own attention. Listening to writing, as opposed to reading it, helps to free the beginning observer from anxiously following reading order.

I think you'll be surprised by the observations you get from students. Someone always notices something right there that you missed. And it's to students advantage that they don't have standard terms for what they see. They invest more expressive terms for themselves.

CONCRETE TO ABSTRACT

Students write three more Family Parables. Then we take the crucial step toward the essay.

Directions: When writers bring in Parable Four, we're ready for the turning point of the course. Someone reads a parable aloud. We think about the behavior of the main character. We write nonstop a list of four to six adjectives that describe the main character's behavior as it makes a difference to the story.

Taking John as the main character of our sample parable, we might get adjectives like these: trusting, believing, persistent, hopeful, confident, powerful, faithful, devoted, friendly, imaginative, responsive. As students read their adjectives I put them on the board.

We select the most fitting and change it into a noun, like this:

responsive→response

Thinking about the parable, we use that noun as the subject of a sentence, followed by "is." We each write at least two such sentences, like this: "Response is the offer to help." "Response is generous attnetion." We read all these aloud: "Response is faith in good will." "Response is an original answer." "Response is belief in the response of another." "Response is being a ladder between a mother and her kittens." "Response is the power of friendliness." "Response is helping your cat to do the impossible." "Response is persistence in paying attention." "Response is talking to a cat who can only meow back." Notice that some definitions identify the abstraction concretely; they have become metaphor.

We read another parable aloud and do it all again.

For the next meeting students write five adjectives suited to the main character of their Parable Four. They choose the best one, transform it into a noun and use the noun as the subject of three sentences. Then they repeat this with another of their parables.

In the next class we have two people read Parable Four, the adjective and noun derived form it, and their sentences beginning with that noun. We choose one sentence and copy it: "Response is an offer to help." We have the parable it fits read again. Then everyone writes three more sentences which tell more about the noun and move in the direction of the parable. For example:

"Response is an offer to help. It's attention to what someone else needs whether she can ask for it or not. It's using intelligence as an act of friendliness. It's a generous attention that persists till the problem is solved. Response is being a ladder between a mother and her kittens."

We do this again with the second parable.

Writers' next assignment is to develop one of the sentences they wrote for their Parable Four into a paragraph of definition.

Comment: This elemental, four-sentence paragraph has the structure of definition. It opens up one specific meaning of an idea that has been pulled from knowledge of concrete data. It doesn't generalize the data into one lump or summarize it as a take-it-or-leave-it example of a stereotype. A good definition enables us to think about our data in sentences that tell us more about the idea we have in mind. The discreteness of sentences helps us to see and express the parts of this special idea.

Exposition depends on an idea that has parts. The idea is the order of its parts—the parts seen as a simultaneous order. The order remains whole and at the same time is sorted out and expressed by the order of syntax. So definition is the elemental analysis of an idea by the person who originated it.

The discursive writer with a good idea is like a gardener in a windy country who constructs a wall enclosing promising ground. The wall is not mechanical, not arbitrary, though the parts look as if they could be set up somewhere else. This wall rises from the lay of this land. When you look at it you can see the direction of the weather and the ideas of the gardener. The wall begins the garden by defining it as a center. Just so the expository writer must define his or her territory before he or she can develop it.

It's good for students to realize that they don't need a dictionary or other secondary source to tell them what they know. They can originate a definition by studying the data, the experience they have in mind. Some versions of the paragraph may be stilted or choppy, but they teach the structure of defintion.

This paragraph also establishes the idea of paragraph unity, and enables me to comment on something students have done right. I can point to paragraphs well unified by the way all sentences have the same subject, the governing idea, a subject examined from one point of view or governing pronoun, and in one time or governing tense. This beats lessons on transitions, lack of pronoun reference, and shifts of pronoun—lessons which some writers don't need, and others can't learn *in abstracto*.

PARABLE INTO ESSAY

Directions: On the day writers bring their first paragraphs to class they read their parables and the paragraphs derived from them in small groups. As a whole class we ask someone to read first the paragraph and then the parable it came from. Then we all write a new paragraph to show how the story has developed the sense of the first paragraph. We read these aloud. Now I ask the author to read again her first paragraph beginning with a noun; then read her parable; and then read her final paragraph. Marie Ponsot says, ''It's an essay with beginning, middle, and end.'' (Ponsot, CS 150) If this were my sentence, I would accord it an exclamation point: ''It's an essay with beginning, middle, and end!''

I write on the board, and the students copy this sentence, ''An expository essay supports the idea it asserts.''

The next assignment is for writers to choose another family parable and go through these steps to produce Essay one: adjectives, abstract noun, defining sentence, defining paragraph. This is paragraph one. It asserts the idea and defines it. The middle is now the parable from which the idea was derived. It becomes the concrete example or evidence, the support for the idea asserted at the beginning. The ending paragraph, Marie says, returns ''to the idea of paragraph one and expresses the difference the example makes to what you can say about the idea.'' (CS 27)

Comment: I have taken you through about two weeks of Marie Ponsot's course in the elements of the essay. At this point we have seven weeks to go and will write 14 essays, moving in a variety of ways toward writing on a given word, a given quotation, and writing on an unrehearsed subject.

The test of students' work is not that they can write an essay on the ''right answer,'' given them in class discussion. A teacher asks of an essay: ''How much of his data can this writer's idea explain and organize? Or does he have the right data and enough of it for the assertion he's making?'' The test is whether writers can observe and be accurate, derive an idea from what they've studeied, and define their idea by identifying and ordering its parts.

This is the structure of exposition, and there's every reason for teaching it in a concrete form. The work I've described here is not an exercise preparatory to writing a real expository essay, as one would do exercises to get in shape to go skiing. Rather it's the walking a child does in order to learn to walk. It's learning it as you live it—living it in order to do it. It's the real structure of exposition.

Teachers reading tests, essays, research papers judge ideas by what authors have done for them. If an author has honestly done her work, the teacher can say, "Even if I don't agree with you or see it your way, you've defined one center of the material, asserted your idea clearly, and supported it amply."

A writing class works with polar powers: the sentence, which belongs to all writers no matter how naive and inexperienced, and literary structures (such as fable, parable, satire, elegy, expository essay), which, in the beginning, belong to the teacher. Any literary structure may be transformed into expository essay in several ways, one of which is the technique of simple definition developed into the simple essay.

In any course, I believe, teachers begin by making a gift of structure to the students. In the assignments I've described, teachers call into play the great source power of language, the sentence. They show writers how to exercise it imaginatively, steadily, and non-heroically to enable students to realize for themselves that all experience is concrete structure, and that structure is finally what sticks to the mind.

Heather Monkmeyer speaks of "detail." The maxim "show don't tell," has become a truism, but William Zinsser puts skepticism about truisms aside when he says, "What's true about a truism is that they're true" (1989). And no one is going to argue with Zinsser! With a soft touch, Monkmeyer "simply" asks students to add more. But, less softly, she spends time, lots of time, dealing with **quality** *detail. And that's the key. If someone asked you to describe the room you're in, now, you could go on for hours. On the other hand, if someone said, "pick just five details," your choices would narrow. This is what Heather's chapter is all about. Read it along with Will Hobbs's chapter and you'll feel confident about discussing the use of specifics with your students.*

CHAPTER 6
MODELING THE REVISION PROCESS WITH YOUR OWN WRITING

By Heather Monkmeyer

PART A: SQUEEZING INTO THE CIRCLE

It was 7:30. Almost dark. Kelly pulled on her darkest clothes—her papa's pine green sweatshirt, hooded and warm. Her scruffy brown corduroys. Her fast-as-lightning sneakers. Looping the last lace she peeked out her bedroom window to the driveway below. The big kids were already starting to gather for a game of kick the can. Would tonight be the night they finally let her join the game? She glanced in the mirror, brushed her shaggy bangs away from her eyes, scrambled down the stairs and out the back door.

Nathan, Amy, Julie and Beth, Heidi, Alex and Lyndon crowded around a rusty, crushed coffee can. Kelly took a deep breath, looked at the ground and squeezed into the circle.

"All right. Let's get started," ordered Nathan. "I'm the biggest so I'll kick the can. Lyndon, you're still It from last night so you count to 150 with your eyes closed after I kick. Everybody ready?"

"Hold it!" shouted Alex pointing at Kelly. "What's the Pipsqueak doing here?" Seven pairs of eyes flashed to the girl who was so small she hardly reached their shoulders. Her eyes darted from face to face looking for a friend. "Can I play? Please?"

"No way, Shrimp, Beat it," spat Alex.

"We don't need little kids hanging around our game!" said Beth.

''Go in the house and play with your dolls,'' barked Lyndon.

''I don't play with dolls,'' Kelly shouted. I'm fast and I know the best hiding spots.''

''Well I'm not playing with a punky kid,'' said Heidi.

''Me neither,'' agreed Amy. ''She'll slow down the game.''

Kelly jammed her fists deep into her pockets and kicked at the gravel but didn't budge. Determined, she said, ''If you just let me play, you'll see. I'm fast and Lyndon will never find me.''

''Want to make a bet? I could capture you in a minute!'' Lyndon yelled leaning toward Kelly like a tree in a windstorm.

''Let's see you try!'' dared Kelly.

Lyndon glared at the tiny girl all clothed in the colors of the night and then Nathan said, ''Aw, just let her play.'' And with that he kicked the can.

Before he could change his mind, Kelly shot toward the back yard until she was out of Lyndon's sight. She zigged back to the front, around the cars, careful not to crush the gravel, and back on to the silent grassy lawn. Then, making sure no one was watching her, spun around and raced for the big gumdrop-shaped juniper bush that grew tight against the garage. People scattered in all directions scrounging for the best hiding spots.

''fifty-five, fifty-six, fifty-seven . . .,'' Lyndon called.

Scrunched between bush and bricks, Kelly covered her scruffy white shoes with dead needles and earth and imagined herself part of the juniper.

Beth burrowed into a grassy ditch behind the shed. She was invisible except for her white socks that fell around her ankles.

''. . .seventy-one, seventy-two, seventy-three . . .,'' Lyndon chanted.

Heidi hid in the hedge nearby. Only her pink collar could be seen.

''. . .eighty-three, eighty-four, eighty-five . . .'' Lyndon howled.

Alex, in white sneakers, climbed a crooked tree, and Julie and Amy flew into dark corners and secret spots hidden by shadows.

''. . .111, 112, 116 . . .'' Kelly heard Lyndon sing.

''He can't even count,'' she thought.

Nathan rolled under the lilacs and lay like a log near Lyndon and the rusty, dented can.

. . .148, 149, 150! Ready or not, here I come!'' he bellowed.

And there was silence. Don't breathe! Kelly told herself. Don't move a muscle! She listened for Lyndon's footsteps and watched through a tiny peephole in the branches.

Lyndon tiptoed on the gravel and tried not to make a sound. He peeked under the Plymouth. No one was there. He gazed up to the top of the ginkgo tree. No one was there. He craned to see around the corner of the house. No one was there.

Lyndon scratched his head and crept over to the gumdrop bush. He stopped like a statue and searched the yard. He was so close Kelly could hear him breathe.

Her heart pounded like a jackhammer. She was sure the whole world could hear the thump thump. She bit her lip and pressed her hand over her mouth so the sound could not escape.

Just then Lyndon whirled around and raced for the can. "I'm caught," Kelly thought. He stomped his brown boot on top of it and hooted, "One, two, three on Alex crawling in the Weeping Willow tree!"

"Phew!" she sighed as she slumped against the bricks.

Lyndon bolted to the other side of the yard. He listened and watched and listened and then, lightning quick, leapt to the can. He stomped his brown boot on top of it again and shouted, "One, two, three on Amy and Julie peeking over the porch."

In the shadows, Kelly could see Alex, Amy and Julie trudging to the little hill in the front yard, where the prisoners stayed.

Now? she wondered.

A crackle of twigs right next to the gumdrop bush made Kelly jump. Beth, scrunched low to the ground, peered around the bush and watched Lyndon guard the can. Then, as quickly as she appeared, she dashed to the nearest hedge—Heidi's spot.

Soon, a snickering noise came from the bushes. Lyndon heard it too and sprang for the can. He stomped his brown boot on top of it and shouted, "One, two, three on Heidi laughing like a hyena in the hedge!"

While Lyndon watched Heidi head for the hill, Beth bolted toward the can. But Lyndon beat her to it and called, "One, two, three on Beth, right before my eyes!" And he laughed a deep-down belly laugh but not for long because he knew his job was not yet done.

Kelly peered through the prickly branches. She knew if someone kicked the can everyone would be free again. The captured kids huddled on the hill waiting for a hero.

Lyndon paced back and forth near the can. His head twirled with every noise. Dried-up leaves brushing over the gravel made him jump. Creaking branches high-up in the trees made him freeze and listen. Only two more to go. He looked serious. Kelly knew he didn't want to lose his captives.

Now? she wondered.

Just when there was no sound and the nippy night wind was still, a dark figure exploded from the lilacs. It shot toward Lyndon and the rusty can.

As Lyndon sprang to reach the can first, the runner lunged for it. They missed the can but they found each other. Feet and hands were everywhere! Nathan and Lyndon were tangled like a garden hose!

Now! Kelly saw her chance. She darted from the gumdrop bush, flew across the driveway, hurdled over the Nathan and Lyndon pile and KICKED THE CAN!

"Hurrah!" shouted everybody but Lyndon, "We're free! We're free!"

"Where did she come from?" Alex laughed.

"I don't know but Lyndon is still it!" snickered Beth.

While clouds of cheers still billowed around her, Kelly caught Lyndon's eye. He just snarled and clomped toward the can.

''Don't worry about him,'' Nathan said, ''He'll cool off before the snow flies. And, do you know what? You ARE fast.'' Nathan winked at her and gave her shoulder a big brother slug.

Just then Kelly felt something deep inside her smile.

She brushed her shaggy bangs away from her face, stepped back into the shadows, and watched the children scatter in every direction searching for better-than-ever secret spots, while Lyndon's voice called through the moon-dipped night, ''twenty-two, twenty-three, twenty-four, twenty-five. . .''

PART B: MODELING THE REVISION PROCESS WITH YOUR OWN WRITING

INTRODUCTION

As a teacher of writing I am convinced that I must write along with my students. I learn to empathize with them as humans and writers as I too experience the dread of facing a blank page, the excitement of recording a significant moment, the disappointment of a story going nowhere, the satisfaction of tying together the last threads of a piece, the anxiety of "going public" with my own creation and the joy of having it accepted and enjoyed by others. I know what they are going through and they know that I am with them in the process. It gives my teaching validity in their eyes.

As I write alongside my fifth graders, I generate the examples needed to model the work of a practitioner. "Squeezing into the Circle" started as a small scrawled draft of personal narrative and throughout the year it evolved into a short story. Observing the evolution of a piece, as it transforms from an incomplete blur of information to a finished story, is an important experience made more valuable by involving the students in the revision process. It is my hope that while I model the never-ending possibilities of revision in large group lessons and share sessions, in small group and individual conferences, students will make more varied attempts to revise their own work and will become more competent writers.

It takes just a bit of extra work to prepare yourself to share a piece of your own writing in a lesson. I always give my students my work in "as is" condition. I want them to see my scratched-out words, my blotted out or squeezed-in paragraphs, my marginal notes. Therefore, I do not clean up or retype anything in draft form before presenting it to the kids unless it is illegible. If I'd like to focus on one page of a draft, I make a transparency of that page. Sometimes I also make copies of the selection so that students can physically manipulate my draft at their seats. An assorted supply of transparency pens, an overhead projector and screen are the final necessities.

When I have a complete or partial first draft ready, I read it to my students during writing workshop. My students respond to my writing by telling me what they understood, what they liked, what they didn't understand and what they want to know more about. I use this same procedure with students' writing in large and small groups. I take notes as I listen and then spend time later making the revisions that will make my piece say what I want it to say.

There are many ways to shape a revision lesson. I start by looking over my drafts and examining the changes I have made. These changes may be at the word level, sentence level, or on a larger scale. The revisions may be superficial or they may deal with the very meaning of the piece. Analyzing the motivation for change allows me to pull together information I can share with the students. Perhaps I substituted many words. Some may have been changed for the sake of accuracy. Others may have been altered to make my prose sound more poetic. The children need to hear these ideas. I group similar revisions and use them as the thrust of the lesson. Before and after transparencies illuminate the revisions. Underlining with different colored markers make them easy to see.

DETAILS THAT MAKE A DIFFERENCE

As I considered two drafts of "Squeezing into the Circle," I saw that I had attempted in the later draft to paint a clearer picture of the opening scene, dropping in detail that would play into the story, extracting that which was insignificant. I highlighted this for my students:

Draft A:
It was 7:30 and almost dark. I slipped into my darkest clothes: my dad's baggy navy blue sweatshirt, my ugliest brown corduroys, dark blue knee socks and sneakers.

Draft B:
It was 7:30. Almost dark. Kelly pulled on her darkest clothes—her papa's pine green sweatshirt, hooded and warm. Her scruffy brown corduroys. Her fast-as-lightning sneakers.

In her book *Writing Down the Bones*, Natalie Goldberg (1986) encourages writers to be specific, to take the blur out of the reader's mind. Not just any detail will do, of course. If we simply ask students to add more detail children will often answer with gluttonous portions of indiscriminate verbiage. So I spend time dealing with the quality of the detail. As I see it, selecting details to include is like choosing buttons for a piece of clothing. The selected buttons must be the right size and shape to function properly. So too, we must choose the details that will serve our purpose—those that will set the scene and help us tell our story. The number of buttons must be considered—too many and the garment becomes heavy and cumbersome; too few and gaping holes will leave it an ineffective piece of cloth. Likewise, excessive detail will leave a story cluttered and without focus; insufficient detail will leave the reader without understanding and empathy. Finally, the chosen buttons must match the determined look and feel of the frock. Our words also must complement the mood and the style of the writing. I ask the students to look at the changes and discuss them with that goal in mind. The observations may include:

■ The sweatshirt transforms into a pine green, bulky hooded type that will emphasize the character's small size and will allow her to be warm and well-hidden in the shrubs on a cool, autumn night.

- Her sneakers become "fast-as-lightning" to further develop the attitude of the character.
- Eliminated were details like "dark blue knee socks" and "ugliest" brown corduroys because I could make my point with less detail.

Observant students might look at the draft and find other legitimate changes like the switch from first person to third person. Wonderful. Follow up on those insights in individual conferences. The focus of the large group lesson is getting more specific. The objectives will be different from day to day.

From there we look for other places in my draft that seem blurry or vague. Students offer suggestions for changes that might make the section more effective. I listen carefully to my students and take their response seriously by marking their ideas on the transparency. Throughout the lesson we discuss the changes and applaud those that really make a difference.

Finally it is time to bring it all home. I ask my students to dive into their own pieces and look for blurry places they can make more specific. They write. I circulate silently peeking over their hunched shoulders, quietly conferring with individuals. Later we informally share our revisions with each other and consider the effects of the alterations.

Scott worked on making a short passage more visible to the reader by simply focusing on the vague word "everything."

Draft A:
> That night he could not sleep. The reindeer that was shot in the woods boggled his mind.
>
> He got up at six o'clock. He rushed down the stairs trampling over everything, swung on his parka and was out of the house in seconds.

Draft B:
> That night he could not sleep. The reindeer that was shot in the woods boggled his mind.
>
> He got up at six o'clock. He rushed down the stairs trampling shirts and towels. He picked up the towel, swung on his parka and was out of the house in seconds.

As the author, Scott visualized the things his character was trampling. Trampling shirts and towels showed his single-minded desire to get out to the woods. He had his character pick up one towel that would later play an essential part in the story.

Scott did not write in a lot of detail, but only the information that would serve his purpose. In that he was successful.

REVISING CONTENT

Research has determined that writers of various ages and abilities make predominantly superficial revisions [See J. Fitzgerald (1987) for a review of revision research]. My goal is to nudge my students toward more substantive changes that deal with the content of the piece. As I studied my drafts I found several examples to which I could bring the children's attention.

At one point I discovered by listening to the questions the students asked that I had misjudged the prior knowledge of my audience. They did not know how to play kick-the-can, and I had not given them enough information to help them make sense of the text. I had to find a way to insert the rules without interrupting the flow of the story. I asked students to suggest places where I could add the missing information. I marked my draft and went back to work.

Considering the missing information, I added the following lines throughout the piece, reshaping the text to welcome the additions:

- She knew if someone kicked the can everyone would be free again.
- Only two more to go. Kelly knew he didn't want to lose his captives.
- In the shadows Kelly could see Alex, Amy and Julie trudging to the hill in the front yard. That was where the prisoners stayed.

A few days later I brought back my piece and tried it out on the students to see if I had answered their questions. I had.

Similarly, Scott knew his audience probably didn't know much about the real reindeer of Manitoba. He inserted the information necessary to move kids from the miniature cartoon cliche to the bulky beast that really exists:

> How cruel, he thought, to shoot an animal and let it suffer. Eric got a patch out of his pocket and laid it on the wound. He then got the towel and wrapped the reindeer and tried to help it up (for reindeer are four to five feet at the shoulder and lifting it would be impossible)...

Scott's additions gave his piece authority and made it more interesting to his readers. This attempt at improvement and others like it are highlighted for students during share time and in mini-lessons.

CONCLUSIONS

Instruction should not take over and crowd out the exploratory process writers need to experience daily, but as teachers, there is much we **can** do to nudge our charges toward good writing.

Endless lesson possibilities will surface as you pursue your own writing. Simply allow the discoveries that are made to become the teaching points. If you turned personal narrative into fiction, show the children how you did it. If you rearranged the episodes in your story, show them why.

You don't need to churn out a new piece of writing every week. As you take a piece through multiple drafts and finally to a finished piece, use the different stages to show your students how writers revise. You will learn along with your students and have a story in the end.

REFERENCES

Fitzgerald, J. (1987). Research on revision in writing. *Review of Educational Research. 4,* 57. 481–506.

Goldberg, N. (1986). *Writing down the bones: Freeing the writer within.* Boston: Shambhala.

SUGGESTED READING

Atwell, N. (1987). *In the middle: Writing, reading and learning with adolescents.* Portsmouth, NH: Heinemann.

Atwell offers rationale and methods for setting up a writing workshop. Discussion of revision is woven throughout the book.

Goldberg, N. (1986). *Writing down the bones: Freeing the writer within.* Boston, MA: Shambhala.

Goldberg's book is packed with ideas that will help get you writing. Many of the suggestions will work in the classroom. Her discussions of the qualities of good writing are most useful.

Murray, D.M. (1985). *A writer teaches writing* (2nd ed.). Boston, MA: Houghton Mifflin.

This book has been most helpful in its discussions of the qualities of good writing and revision.

Ponsot, M. & Deen, R., (1982). *Beat not the poor desk.* Upper Montclair, NJ: Boynton/Cook.

See chapter 10, ''Rewriting,'' for a helpful discussion about revision.

*For the people who live in Michigan, **Terry Blackhawk**'s lessons on voice embedded within a short story framework will come as a surprise. Terry is a well-known poet in the Midwest. But she chose to share a short story and accompanying lessons on finding one's narrative voice because of the spirit in which **Writers in the Classroom** was conceived. A major premise of the book is that to teach writing one must remain, on some level, as vulnerable as one's students. As Terry grapples with finding the voice she would use in "The Truth About the Easter Bunny," we grapple with her. That she'll bring this process to her students is a given. The issue of time needed to write rings true as well, "It was six weeks before I got Bonnie off that porch and worked toward the focus of the piece: the death of the chicken." Terry Blackhawk teaches with the same generous spirit you've found, or will find, in Leonora Smith and Rosemary Deen: They all know students are worth listening to carefully, and that their job has much to do with helping students recognize their own voices and strengths.*

CHAPTER 7
FINDING A NARRATIVE VOICE

By Terry Blackhawk

PART A: THE TRUTH ABOUT THE EASTER BUNNY

It was the last day of Easter vacation and I was next door in my turquoise dress, the one my parents liked to argue over. Blue, Mommy said, but Daddy said it was green. They would laugh and go back and forth, blue green blue green, like it was some kind of game. "It's blue *and* green," I would tell them. "It's both!" But they wouldn't back down.

"Well, I don't believe you. That's not what *my* daddy says," Sandra started up again. But I could tell that whe wasn't entirely sure. "Besides, if you don't believe me you're just a boo-boo."

"What's that supposed to mean?"

"Na-nanny-foo-foo. You're just a boo-boo."

"So," I tried. "At least I don't believe in a stupid Easter Bunny."

I wished to be anywhere but here. We were supposed to go out for dinner. We'd go and sit down at Miss Hankie's table and she'd serve okra and other strange stuff I didn't like. I couldn't go back inside because I'd been jumping off the bunk bed in my new shoes and it was hard for Mommy to keep us quiet in our half of Miss Bessie's house. Miss Bessie owned our house and she owned the gas station and she owned the store next door and the apartment behind the store where the little girls lived, all in one big room with their parents.

"You might get stuff your momma buys, but our stuff comes straight from the Easter Bunny," Sandra bragged. "It's magic."

I was waiting at the little girls' house, but now I didn't like it. I didn't like Sandra telling me about magic. I didn't like being up here on their porch in my blue-green dress that I wasn't supposed to get dirty. I didn't like having to be so careful in our house just because Miss Bessie would complain if we ran up and down and made her cakes fall. I asked Mommy how could a cake fall if it was already in the pan. And how could I make it fall in a kitchen I'd never even been in, on the other side of a wall?

The porch stuck out from behind the little girls' apartment high up over the back yard. I wanted to be down in the cool long grass in the corner of the yard by the fence. I didn't care if the outhouse was back there too. I remembered the first outhouses we saw last summer when we moved south from Massachusetts. I liked the tiny buildings and how they were usually back in the corner of a yard or field. Daddy called them "backdoor trots," and we all laughed. Trotting was something you did when you were in a hurry. We had a bathroom in our house at Miss Bessie's but the little girls had to use the backdoor trot.

I used it once, too, when I spent the night and we all four of us, me and the three little girls, crowded into the hide-away bed in the middle of their apartment. The little girls' daddy walked around in his t-shirt and hung blankets on wire strung across the room and divided up the apartment for sleeping. Then the little girls' mother asked if we were ready to go out to the outhouse. It was dark so Sandra, the oldest, got to hold the flashlight and lead us through the dewy yard, and she and Betsie and Lissie and I stood around in our nightgowns waiting for each other and listening to the soft sound of our pee falling to the ground. I held my breath when it was my turn to go in, but I liked being back in the corner of the yard where the grass grew so shiny and tall. The little girls giggled and shivered and Sandra hurried us up so the boogie man wouldn't get us, but I didn't believe in the boogie man, and I liked being out in the night.

"Na, na . . ." Sandra started again.

"Stop," I said. "That's dumb."

"I won't stop. Who's gonna make me? Your mom-mee?" Sandra always called her mother "momma." "Muske-dine, muske-dine. Your momma hasn't got a dime."

I looked out across the yard. If we were down in the grass playing fairies and making houses and thrones and chains of dandelions, I could make up the games and we could take turns being Wendy or Tinker Bell. I knew all about fairies and kingdoms. Sandra usually liked to play my games.

"This is MY porch," she said. "If you don't like it, you can just leave."

When Mommy called I was glad to run down the steps and across the gravel to the car. I didn't think of Sandra as I pressed my face to the window and watched the pastures flash by. That spring was the first time I played in a pasture. I went down the highway, climbed through the barbed wire fence with the little girls and we wandered through the pasture, watching out for cow-pies. The pasture land was bumpy and uneven and a cow-pie could be hiding behind any clump of grass. We laughed at the silly idea of cow-pies, and we chewed on grass stems and wild green onions. I learned how those can spoil the taste of milk and I tried to imagine the multiple stomachs of cows.

The weeks after Easter passed slowly and somewhere in those days Biddie died. I hadn't liked Biddie very much, especially as he got older, though I felt jealous of Sandra for having a pet of her own. Secretly I thought Biddie was a dumb-sounding name, but I liked seeing all the little chicks in their Easter basket. I got to hold the fluffy bodies, and though I didn't much like their scratchy feet, I liked the peeping sounds they made and the way they looked, all packed into the basket when the little girls' daddy put them out on the back porch for the night.

Sometimes I felt afraid of the little girls' daddy. He took care of cars that came to the pumps in front of Miss Bessie's store. Their mommy stayed in the back. Sometimes she fixed other ladies' hair and sometimes she ironed and washed clothes. She listened a lot to the radio. ''You're too old to cut the mustard any more,'' the radio would blare and the little girls' mother would sing out loud, real loud. Even after my mommy explained that mustard was a plant I couldn't understand why someone would want to cut it or why they would be too old to cut it if that's what they wanted to do. Still, I liked it and I'd sing it to myself and think of piles of cut up leaves.

Sandra had wanted Biddie to stay in the house with her, but her daddy didn't want animals ''on the inside,'' though he changed his mind when the other chicks, the blue one and the pink one that belonged to Lissie and Betsie, died out in the cold. Biddie had been dyed green and at first they thought he was a she. Then she got bigger and was not cute and fluffy any more. After she attacked my legs, I started to make wide circles around her and I would run fast to get to the steps leading to the little girls' porch before attracting her attention.

One day Sandra's mommy explained to us that Biddie was probably a he. The soft feathers were almost gone, though if I looked hard I could still see traces of green dye. He had a little red comb on the top of his head and had started to grow something Sandra's mommy called spurs. We were supposed to stay out of his way until Sandra's daddy could make a pen for him.

''I don't care,'' Sandra said. ''He's still mine.'' And she bragged about how she was going to make a leash for him and walk him like a dog.

The next day Lissie greeted me at the top of the steps before I could knock on the door. I could hear crying from inside, but then Sandra pushed her way past us and slid down the bannister like she wasn't supposed to do. She stood at the foot of the steps and looked out into the yard.

"Biddie's dead," Lissie said in my ear. She pretended to whisper, but I could tell she wanted Sandra to hear.

"He is not!" Sandra shrieked. "You say that one more time and I'll beat your brains out."

Lissie stepped behind me. "I'll tell," she rang out. "Who cares about a dumb old chicken? And anyway, you didn't even cry when Squeaky died."

It was true. I remembered how Sandra held on tight to Biddie as her sisters cried over their dead chickens and how for a while she took charge of the Easter basket they had in common, carrying Biddie in it everywhere until he was too big to fit inside.

Lissie went on, almost happily. "Poppa just *told* you he took him to a farm, but it's not so. He took him and drownded him. I heard him. I heard him tell Momma . . ."

"You shut up, bratface. My poppa wouldn't do no such thing." Sandra was coming up the stairs, two at a time. Sandra was a year older than me and two years older than Betsie, the next oldest, and she was bigger than any of us. But she didn't grab for Lissie like I thought she would. She went inside and came out holding Betsie's arm in one hand and Biddie's basket in the other and then she marched downstairs and got a shovel from under the steps.

"We're gonna have us a funeral," she announced and she led us back to the soft earth by the outhouse where we dug a hole, all of us taking turns, three digs each, and buried the basket and the few feathers still sticking to it. We piled some rocks on top when we were finished and Sandra made us all swear that we wouldn't go in or out of the outhouse without bowing to Biddie. "If you don't," she warned, "that boogieman will get you just as sure as you're born."

I knew there was no boogieman, but I felt a coldness on the back of my neck and a tingling feeling in my stomach, as if Biddie were still around ready to run at my legs. Sandra gave me a hard look and said, "Here. You can carry the shovel." I didn't like carrying the shovel and I thought if we were going to do it right we should have more than just a pile of rocks to mark the grave. But we all practiced bowing in front of the stones, and Sandra checked us to see that we bowed correctly with our right foot stuck out behind us. I shouldered the shovel and walked up the slope to the house without talking.

We were halfway there when Betsie let out a loud wail and we all stopped and looked at her.

"What's wrong?" Sandra wanted to know.

"The b-b-basket . . ." she began and gulped a little. "The Ea-. .the Ea-. . the Eather Bunny."

"What about him?"

My stomach started to feel kind of fluttery. I didn't want to start talking about the Easter Bunny again.

"Where's he gonna put our stuff when we ain't got no basket?" Betsie went on. "You just went and buried it. And Poppa said there wouldn't be no buying of stuff we lose."

"I don't care," Sandra said, "but why don't you ask Miss Bonnie-know-it-all? She can tell you all about the Easter Bunny." She gave me another hard look. "Well, go on, Miss Easter BON-nie."

Betsie and Lissie looked up at me and Betsie rubbed her face with the back of her hand and left a dark reddish streak on each cheek. "I saw him, that's all. I peeked out my window and there he was," I said and twirled around the shovel like I was dancing with it.

"You did not. Liar, liar. . ." This was Sandra, but Lissie and Betsie were still looking at me.

"That's for me to know and you to find out." I gave the shovel another twirl.

"But she doesn't even believe. . ." Sandra started just as the door from the little girls' apartment opened and a broad beam of light came down into the yard below.

Lissie was still looking at me. She hadn't moved. "What'd he look like?" she wanted to know.

"Kinda big," I said. "Just a big old rabbit. With glasses. He had on little glasses." And I could almost see him, hopping busily along the hedge between our houses, where Mommy and I saw the cedar waxwings in the fall with their black masks and creamy feathers and the bright waxy touches of red and yellow upon them.

"What're you all doing down there in the dark?" It was the little girls' mommy calling. I could hear music. "The shrimp boats are a-comin' " floated out across the yard. "Come on in and wash up," she told them.

As the little girls headed up the stairs to their porch, I heard Lissie and Betsie tell their mother about how they had a funeral and about how Bonnie saw the Easter Bunny. And I watched as Sandra put away the shovel and walked heavily up the steps behind them. I turned toward Miss Bessie's, thinking about shrimp boats and why there'd be dancing the night the shrimp boats came in and who would be dancing and where. I guessed they would dance on the boats and lots of people would come to the boats and dance around. I sang as I ran, "Why don't you hurry, hurry, hurry home? Why don't you hurry, hurry, hurry home? The shrimp boats are a-comin'; they'll be dancin' tonight."

PART B: FINDING A NARRATIVE VOICE

A STORY AND ITS MESSAGES

Writing this story showed me how the barest hint of a childhood memory could blossom into narrative. The crucial element in this process was finding a voice for my character. It was also a matter of trusting and going with first thoughts, of turning barely remembered neighbors into characters and then of watching, in some surprise, as the characters established themselves. Since "The Truth about the Easter Bunny" grew from a class assignment, I write this chapter as both student and teacher. From my experience as a student, I will describe how the story unfolded for me and how the guidance of my teacher, Mimi Schwartz, (in a class on autobiographical writing at the 1989 Martha's Vineyard Institute of Writing and Teaching) helped my story along. From my point of view as a teacher, I will explain how I apply what I learned to help my creative writing students at a public high school in Detroit develop their voices as writers.

Trust the Images. "Ha, Ha, Ha, I'm glad Biddie died." The words stared at me from the top of my page. Mimi had asked us for a list of memories, and suddenly I saw myself, six years old again, on our neighbors' back porch. It was a memory which I rubbed against with some discomfort: an embarrassment, a sense of shame, the type of topic suggested by Stillman (1984, p. 40) "not only because it continues to stir a guilt in you, but because somehow it was also a part of growing up." This is what I remembered: Two groups of children arguing and myself whispering to a younger child, "Say 'Ha, ha, ha . . . and so forth." I wasn't willing to say it myself but was perfectly happy to let her hurl out what seemed to be the perfect taunt. And I got caught and embarrassed, as an older child accused me with: "You know you told her to say that!" It was my first encounter with the terrible power of words.

According to Natalie Goldberg (1986, p. 38), "Writers end up writing about their obsessions. Things that haunt them; things they can't forget; stories they carry in their bodies waiting to be released." When Mimi told us to write down the first thing that came to mind, there were those words, facing me on the page. I think of those thoughts or scenes that suddenly pop into my mind as generative images, images that are spontaneous, unconscious links with our own unique fabric of memory and emotion. I often follow such imagery in writing poetry trusting it to lead me forward. So I tell my students that first thoughts, even the most seemingly incongruous, occur for a reason and should not be censored but rather greeted with Stafford's attitude of "welcome, welcome, welcome" (1978, p. 125).

LISTENING: TRUST THE VOICE TO EMERGE

At first I wasn't sure what I was writing—story, poem, or essay. My exploratory drafts were monologic ramblings about our first house in Georgia where we lived for about nine months when I was six. Memory provided me with place, but not with personalities. I had a vague notion of situation—the chicken, children arguing, three "little girls." But who were they? What were they saying?

I went through several drafts and began to get a hint of a child's voice emerging through a rather adult-sounding memoir. As that voice became clearer, I excised analytical statements such as "a gullible younger child" or "silenced by their verbal audacity." At this point I had no real plot or characters and even tried making my narrator a teenager as I groped for realistic sounding dialogue. Mimi's responses were crucial. She highlighted places where the narrative seemed strong, gave me a sense of confidence in the piece's possibilities, and kept encouraging me to find the voice in which to tell the story.

Perhaps it was returning to my original impulse, i.e., trusting that first image, that helped open my character up for me; but it was shortly after I knew she would *not* be a teenager that I started to "hear" Bonnie talking. Her voice began to control diction (words like "audacity" no longer belonged) and syntax. The text had free-associative childlike speeches, but no action. I didn't know it was Easter, wasn't sure what the girls were arguing over. But the voice was there. At the end of the class, Mimi's final comment was that I should "let it go into fiction."

Let it go.   Once I found the focus of the piece, the death of the chicken, the writing took on an energy of its own and events began to unfold. I heard the characters talking and watched them do unexpected things: Sandra slid down the banister, Lissie tattled on the father. So when the girls marched off to bury the basket, where else to send them but the outhouse? Plot began developing from setting and character. I described the burial of the basket before I knew that Bonnie and Sandra had a disagreement about the Easter Bunny. Then I revised the beginning, clear at last that the initial conflict between the two was an argument over belief.

As the writing evolved certain things surprised me. I often tell my students to surprise themselves, but am still surprised at my own surprises. One surprise was Sandra's father. In retrospect I see how he was necessary as an agent of Sandra's grief, anger and her need for control. But that interaction emerged through the writing. It was nothing I planned. In a recent article, Mimi Schwartz (1989) cites a precept from her teacher, Russell Banks, on letting go. "You have to be able to 'give up your initial ideas once the story takes on its own momentum.'" I learned that both intent and the giving up of intent are crucial. My intended goal was the original scene of two groups of children arguing. But once it was under way, the story took several unexpected turns, and I followed along.

STRATEGIES: PRACTICING VOICE

What exactly is meant by voice? Must it remain, in Cramer's (1989) words, "a mysterious, other-worldly concept . . . as unanswerable and omnipresent (in writers' vocabularies) as God?" The student writings that follow will, I hope, give some examples of this notion of voice, which is easier to illustrate than to define, although one definition might be the felt presence of a personality behind the words.

Unfortunately much traditional writing instruction would have young writers assume a voiceless, neutral stance. How many times are students told not to use the personal pronoun I, as if their authority and experience are suspect or insufficient? It's no wonder that when students are confronted with such depersonalized tasks, they either freeze up or turn off. My goal as a writing teacher is to get students to listen to themselves and to trust their ideas and their imaginations. When I knock on the doors of their stories and essays, I want to find somebody at home.

The longer I teach the more convinced I become that there is no direct, programmatic way to help students discover their voices as writers. My general approach is open-ended. I offer a smorgasbord of ideas, stories, visual prompts, sets of words. Students freewrite or cluster, work from an object or a memory or a role-playing situation in class. These efforts are triggers, ways to help them arrive at their own topics for writing. Once they have a way in to their imaginary worlds—once their ideas or one of the suggestions I offer clicks for them—we work together in a dialogic fashion. I respond as a reader, questioning, trying to see possibilities and to hold a mirror to the minds I see at work underneath the surfaces of their drafts.

Using Monologue to Find Character.   According to Gardner, fiction is first a matter of character. We understand characters by the way they act, talk and think as well as by the way they interact with others. To hear a character's voice or to tune into a character's consciousness is not a step-by-step sequential process but a matter of listening and imagining. I got a sense of Bonnie's emerging character from a monologic rambling in her voice as she mused over the details of her new environment. To imagine a character, therefore, I ask my students to start from the inside and work outward, to start, that is, with inner monologues or imaginary scenes—anything that can generate an inner world.

Monologue: States of Mind.   Monologues put students into imaginative states in which they can begin to hear and/or visualize a character. Emotions give one entree into character. Emotional states can yield varieties of tone and diction, different rhythms; each can also conjure up a host of specifics: persons, places and situations. To begin this activity I might put a word such as anger or boredom on the board and ask for a quick freewrite in response. Other states of mind that could be used include pride, jealousy, comfort, nervousness, elation, loneliness, fear, triumph, giddiness, and so on. In *Inside Out* (1988), a fine and useful text on working with teenage writers, Kirby and Liner offer good examples of how different emotions produce different "tones of voice." The following example in response to "anger" is fairly typical. The student's use of dialect is intentional.

> She makes me sick. I can't stand her dumb class, giving out stupid assignments all day long. Set up in a dumb class for hours, and it's so dumb and unorganized you can't learn nothing. Then she just jump up and give out a fat assignment for homework and don't explain nothing. I go home with some stupid assignment I don't understand. I wish I had some dynamite. I'd blow that ##@# up. I am so sick of that class I don't know what to do. When the tests come around I don't be knowing nothing.

Although this is hardly grand literature, it is worthwhile to consider it seriously and to make the point that any student writing can be dignified as indicative of hidden drama, tension and interest. One might ask the student at the very least to "see" the classroom. Where is the narrator in this "world"? What's happening around him/her? We could also "show" and not "tell" the teacher's disorganization and lack of concern. What would she be doing or saying? Or we could "show" and not "tell" what it feels like to say "I don't be knowing nothing." To capture the full extent of the speaker's feeling of futility and stupidity might make for a powerful indictment of rote, meaningless teaching. On the other hand, we might question this narrator's sense of self. Is this character truly responsible and/or believable? What makes him/her sit and seethe and think of dynamite? Through open-ended follow-up questions like these, students can come to see how, like Japanese paper flowers dropped into water, their ideas and writing can unfold.

Assumed Name Monologue.   The following monologue explores how a character feels about his/her name. The activity developed after students wrote about their own names, the stories of their names' origins and how they felt about their names. I followed this activity (which I first encountered in Mimi's class on the Vineyard) with Marge Piercy's poem (1988) "If I had been called Sabrina or Ann, she said" and a paragraph from Margaret Atwood's "Kat" (1990) in which a character ruminates about her name. Next we brainstormed a list of odd or whimsical names to write about. What would it be like to be an Egbert? a Poindexter? John assumed one of the names and suddenly donned the voice of a new character.

> Every brand new day I wake up and ask myself one question. And I quote: "What is a fine guy like myself doing with a name like Felix? What am I, some kind of cat?" So before I go to school, I drink a brew in order to make it through the day. You should hear the girls as they say, "Hey, Felix baby, you're looking fine." And then I say, "I'll look a whole lot better if you call me John."

Moving Ahead with Monologue.   I heard a strong voice in this fragment—a mixture of pride, bitterness and humor—and I responded with enthusiasm to Felix. Once a student seems to be on the trail of a character, I sometimes suggest hypothetical situations that require the writer to show inner feelings, or reactions to people or places. Some samples follow.

- Your character is suddenly thrown into a completely new environment. What is that environment? How does she respond?
- He wants to keep peace between two friends. What is the conflict and how does he feel about each of his friends?
- He's trying to persuade a parent of something he wants very much. What might that be? How might that parent respond?
- She has a confession to make. To whom does she confess? Where? and why? Describe the scene.
- Your character is self-conscious about his appearance. What makes him so self-aware? Where is he? What thoughts is he having?

Putting his character into a new situation was an idea which seemed to click with John. Felix became a kid from a northern city who facing a new life in Alabama. The sketch involves characterization (Felix, his pious aunt, a less than manly teacher) as well as plot (Felix goes to his new school, gets the best of his teacher, renames himself and wins the approval of the girls in his class) and setting (his aunt's house, rural setting, bedroom, classroom). This excerpt will show how John keeps Felix's voice consistent as he establishes the setting of the story.

> from "Down South" by John Pitts
> Ten o'clock. Sunday morning. The sheets were off my bed and I coasted toward the front door to smell the great city smog when all of a sudden, I heard the disturbing crow of a rooster. Then I remembered. I was in a place where people chew on nasty old tobacco and the nearest party store is a thousand miles away. To my left was a stable of horses older than Columbus and a barn loaded with hay and hens; to my right, a field of what looked like a lot of work for a guy like myself who hates to lift a finger; and beneath me, stuff the animals just had to let out so I could place my foot in a pile of it.
> I don't mind being surprised, but this time my parents had gone too far. They knew how much I hated Alabama or any part of the South for that matter, yet they took a chance on losing their very lives and sent me here for a full year. You know, like twelve months, fifty-two weeks, three-hundred-sixty-five days, and a whole lot of hours. I didn't think I could take it. Then I heard Aunt Cathy as she walked down to the kitchen singing out my name in her innocent church-toned voice, "Felix—Felix," and I wished deep down in my heart that I could have left that take-my-parents-to-court name back in Pontiac.

A Few Points about Monologue.   Monologues help students explore dimensions of character. They can serve as the focus of class discussion and can be developed with further detail. Here are a few points to remember about monologues.

- They start with emotion or an emotion-laden situation.
- They are deliberately open-ended and general.
- Without being directed to do so, students will imagine settings and events as spin-offs of the monologue exercises. They will be further into plot than they realize, closer to story—through and because of voice.

■ A reminder: monologues are practice activities, ways of getting started. But once a student gets into a role, the details of the monologue may prove restrictive (as with my original intent in ". . . Easter Bunny"). She may need you to give her permission to let the specifics go.

■ A postscript: One way to follow up a monologue is through a character questionnaire. With their characters' voices in mind, I ask students to explore the characters' personalities with questions such as the following: Where is she most at home? What is he most afraid of? What does the character want? How does she act when she gets/doesn't get what she wants? How does he react to crowds? babies? loud music? the color purple? spiders? being alone? A mix of frivolous and serious questions requiring on-the-spot answers keeps the exercise loose and may yield surprising insights.

WITHIN THE MASK: STORIES AND ROLES

Surprise, which keeps writing lively, cannot be legislated in the classroom. I never know exactly what will work and find I must maintain a certain wariness, a kind of sixth sense, about my students and the possibilities for their writing. As I get to know them through their writing, I sometimes suggest writing roles that seem tailored to their personalities.

David's Story.   In a freewrite one day David wrote about a boy who confused his name with a brand of peanut butter. It was an amusing idea and I suggested that David might expand the story to lead up to what felt like a final scene. The result was "The Peanut Butter Kid"—a witty story which received a Scholastic writing award. David blends third person narration and his character's internal monologues into a text that he laces with puns about food: 13-year-old Jeffrey Skippy Smuckers the 3rd is in love with Cookie Manor, who of course ignores him. In the opening, Jeffrey is in a rhapsodic reverie as he compares women to peanut butter and jelly ("kinda crunchy and sweet at the same time"). When we see him in the final scene he's sitting on a park bench, eating a sandwich, licking a trail of grape jelly off his arm, as Cookie approaches.

from "The Peanut Butter Kid" by David Ramsey

He crossed his legs and took a vigorous bite of his sandwich once more. "Oh no!" His heart sank as peanut butter and jelly flew everywhere. "She's looking at me. God, she's really looking at me. Here she comes! Fast, Jeffrey, what do I do? Talk to her, man! No! I can't do it! Why? Okay, okay, I'll do it. I'll talk, I'll talk! Dammit! Peanut butter, I have peanut butter breath! God, I can't go through with it. Terrific, she's right over me. I swear, I'll never hate peanut butter more. I hate it! Did I hear—? Yes!! She's saying Hi. THE Cookie Manor wants to talk to ME? I have to. I can't take that voice. Lift your head man, she's waiting. Go ahead, Skippy. Peanut butter never killed anyone."

Jeffrey slowly lifted his head as he beheld the center of his life for the moment. His mind was oblivious to everyone and everything else.

"Hi," she repeated. "My name's Cookie. Don't I know you?"
"H-hi," he stammered. "My name is Jiffy. I mean, Jeffrey."

David is a skilled actor who participated in many student productions and is pursuing a career in theater. I can't help but think that his acting abilities enhanced and enriched his writing in countless ways. So much of creating a character is involved in writing from within a role, and David clearly lives in Jeffrey.

Ways into Roles.   I'm intrigued by the possible connections between acting exercises and writing, and I've found that role-playing exercises in the classroom can create possibilities for voice. Here are some suggestions that have been useful.

- Small groups of students create an impromptu scene to depict a conflict involving a teenager, a parent, and a grandparent. Classmates watch, then write a monologue in the voice of one or more of the characters.
- Use photographs or portraits as prompts. Tell students to imagine the portrait as a mask that they are wearing. They write from behind/within the mask.
- Bring in stage props—hats, toys, tools, odd clothing, objects. Students create a monologue using one or more of the objects. It's amazing what the imagination can do with a simple rolling pin.

The following piece shows how voice can move a student into poetry as well as prose. I am taken with this poem because of the way Catrina enters Van Gogh's world and uses his voice to capture a sense of anguish and loneliness as well as the necessity for the saving grace of art.

Vincent Van Gogh: Self-Portrait

by Catrina King

Can you see the uncertainty I feel
or are you fooled like countless others?
Through my eyes my afflicted heart begs
for release, but no one comes to call
or quench my fires of frustration.
So I paint.

Can you not see that the sky is
burdened with birds of ill omen,
darkened with fluttering anger,
a hell-bent fury, the storming winds,
they loom larger, fly faster and higher
on their damning flight to rage,
and still I paint.

As I look out into the streets
even the town trollops no longer
approach me, but with a sudden quickness
their feet walk diligently out of reach.
Yet still only can I paint.

Surely someone has the key to let me
out of my dungeon of everlasting torment.
Trouble won't last always
but for the constantly haunted, morally
wounded, and rapidly aging
always sounds longer than all ways,
so yet, and still, I paint.

Dezmon's Story.   A story that developed directly from an acting experience
was Dezmon's "My Only Home Boy." The year before he wrote this story, Dezmon acted the part of Leroy in a student-written and produced play that dealt
with the problems of urban youth. Leroy was the slow character—stolid, angry,
full of inarticulated feelings. When I suggested that Dezmon might want to try
on the voice of Leroy, I needed to say nothing more. Dez was off and running.
In this excerpt, Leroy, who has recently been released from an institution, goes
to the L.Q. (Latin Quarter—a Detroit nightclub) in search of B.C.—his best friend
from the "home."

from "My Only Home Boy" by Dezmon Faulkner
    I approached the L.Q. with a determined look on my face thinking B.C. gotta
be here. A middle-aged man wearing a raggedy Raiders hat opened the door and
began to search me up and down with a metal detector. Obviously the man didn't
know I was on a mission, looking for my boy of course. So before he tried to make
any more contact or rush me in with these ugly babes in line behind me, I asked him.
    "Yo! You know my boy, B.C.?"
    "Listen, kid. People come through here all day. I don't know nobody named
B.D."
    "B.C., Mr., not B.D."
    "Well, son, I still don't know what or who you're talking about," he said as he
tapped my shoulder.
    Maybe I didn't tell you. The reason I was in a home was because I didn't like
nobody touching me. Last guy who touch me and call me crazy, I beat 'im half
to death and threw him through a library window. Put him in a coma for a few days.
B.C. always said when I get out I should chill with my temper.
    "Yeah, all right sir, you touch me again and I'll break your neck," I said under
my breath.
    I thought maybe I should go in and check and see if my boy B.C. was in there.
Naw, that's awright, somebody might make the mistake of their life and bump me.
I decided to head on back to the crib.
    Back home, at the door of my grandmother's two-family flat, I began to knock
hard, since my Grand said she wasn't givin' me a key till I learn how to come in
at the right time. Guess I won't be getting a key.
    "Who is that bamming on the door?" she yell.
    "It's Leroy, Grand. Leroy," I said.
    She peeked out and as she unlocked the screen she fussed at me, you know, the
regular, don't-be-calling-me-Grand-you-ain't-grown, all that kinda stuff.
    I went in, threw my coat in a far corner, fell backwards on my bed like a diver,
and began to think. I still ain't found my homeboy. I know he somewhere. I'm really

getting frustrated. People been touching me, bumping me. I'm trying to hold off, but if the next person who touch me ain't Grand, I feel for 'im. I still ain't gon' stop looking for my boy, though.

At the story's end somebody does, in fact, touch Leroy: it's B.C. who gets clobbered before Leroy recognizes his friend. Beyond the ironic twist to the plot, notice how many careful details emerge in this excerpt—the momentary yet typical confusion between B.C. and B.D., the man in the Raiders hat who is just doing his job, oblivious to the seriousness of our hero's mission, and the loving, chiding but largely oblivious grandmother. Indeed, much of the world is oblivious to Leroy. Besides B.C., the only other character who takes notice of him is the proprietor of an Arab-owned party store who falsely accuses him of stealing some potato chips. Through its diction, its understated tone and the odd mixture of innocence and aggression of its narrator, this story gives voice not only to Dezmon, but also to the existential situation of disenfranchised youth in our cities today.

CONCLUSION

I began Part B of this chapter by talking about trust—how we need to trust first thoughts and not censor ourselves in order to let writing happen. I try to apply the same principles in my teaching and encourage students to trust themselves. Over the years I have come to see cook-book, proscriptive how-to's of writing pedagogy almost as a form of censorship, and certainly as control. The antithesis of these approaches—and another lesson I learned from my story—is letting go, which also requires trust. I trust my students to follow their imaginations and their language in the belief that, as Bell (1985, p. 15) states, "one learns to write interestingly, if not well, by abandoning oneself to the materials, the actual materials of language. One discovers content." One of my goals as a teacher, then, is to help students trust their own authority and to wean them away from relying on me as the arbiter of their writing. I try to do this by sharing my struggles as a writer with them, by encouraging a sense of community in the classroom and by being as open-ended as possible. I am as likely to respond to a question with another question as with an answer.

This is not to say that anything goes. Life is not art, and in a creative writing class we are interested in art, or, as one student put it recently, "how you spice the chicken." A straight rendering of experience, "as we all know from our students, is likely to emerge as bathos, inertia, formlessness" (Vendler, 1980, p. 153). It seems to me that assuming a voice or role helps students avoid flat, cliched writing by giving room for the imagination to play. Writing in other voices can also promote self-discovery. When we put on the voice of others, we end up finding out new things about ourselves. My writing ". . . Easter Bunny" certainly revealed some of the dynamics of growing up in a kind of perpetual culture clash. According to Summerfield and Summerfield (1986, p. 210–211), "the framework of the role. . . (its) vicariousness. . . is perhaps its greatest virtue. No personal confession is involved. But the very detachment of the fiction promotes, paradoxically, a greater intensity and concentration of 'existential presence,' of personal truth." To help students express these personal truths is what makes a writing class an exciting and surprising place to be. Putting on roles and assuming fictional voices enable student writers to approach the underlying dynamics of their lives with a measure of both safety and control.

REFERENCES

Atwood, M. (1990, March 5). "Kat." *The New Yorker.* pp. 38–44.

Bell, M. (1980). In N.L. Bunge (Ed.), *Finding the words: Conversations with writers who teach.* Athens, OH: Swallow Press. 1985.

Gardner, J. (1982). Interview. University of South Carolina writers' workshops, SC Educational Television.

Goldberg, N. *Writing down the bones.* Boston: Shambhala.

Kirby, D. and Liner, T. (1988). *Inside out: Developmental strategies for teaching writing* (2nd ed.). Portsmouth, NH: Heinemann.

Piercy, M. (1988). *My mother's body.* New York: Alfred A. Knopf.

Schwartz, M. (1989). Wearing the shoe on the other foot. *College Composition and Communication, 40,* (2) 203–210.

Stafford, W. (1978). *Writing the Australian crawl.* Ann Arbor: University of Michigan Press.

Stillman, P. (1984). *Writing your way.* Montclair, NJ: Boynton, Cook Publishers.

Summerfield, J. & Summerfield, G. (1986). *Texts and contexts.* New York: Random House.

Vendler, H. (1980). *Part of nature, part of us: Modern American poets.* Cambridge, MA: Harvard University Press.

*Rewriting is such a mammoth task that **Juliana Janosz's** attention to just **leads** feels like a break. In this short but effective chapter, she shares her knowledge of lead writing by having her students try many. But hers is not a directive without support. Through modeling her own attempt to get her piece off to a good start, she shares four approaches her students might try. While most children begin their stories with background information (e.g., "I was in my babysitter's house last year"), Julie prods them into trying dialogue, description, or action. The results are impressive. Impressive, also, is the way in which this writing lesson spills into reading time. Many of this text's authors use models by published authors during prewriting. Julie does, too. But like researchers who do **post hoc** statistical analyses, her students keep mucking around long after the experiment is over.*

CHAPTER 8
INVESTIGATING LEADS: A LESSON IN ALTERNATIVES

By Juliana Janosz

PART A: SHIFTING GEARS

The last new bike I remember owning arrived as a Christmas gift in second grade. I can still remember visiting my grandmother's house to find my Christmas present hiding in her basement. There stood a black bike with fat tires and no handbrakes. A basic model, it added chrome handlebars, a black leather seat, and shiny black fenders, front and rear as options. Fully assembled and leaning on its kickstand, it waited for me to hop on and go for a ride. Grandma's large basement allowed for an eight-year-old to take a few spins around the center support poles. Wow! I became the envy of all the cousins, who each begged a ride. All that winter I rode in Grandma's basement, anxiously waiting for warm weather and the chance to ride through the neighborhood.

I remembered the fun as we rode the streets of the old neighborhood. I could bicycle to Vicky's or Cecilia's for an after school visit. Sometimes we rode back to the school yard just to ride the swings. Sometimes my mom even sent me to the little store on the corner to buy bread for her. Somehow, back then, the thoughts of exercising never once crossed my mind.

Years later however, getting more exercise became more important. If only I owned a new bike. One that worked. One that would allow me to visit my friends in the neighborhood and get exercise at the same time. A new bike I would be proud to take on our summer trek to Lake Michigan. I envisioned leisurely rides along the bay. I saw myself riding to the village for flowers and muffins.

Both of may kids rode new bikes, and my husband's new red Schwinn stood proudly in the garage. Next to mine. The old one. The second-hand bike with the broken brakes, rusty chain, and handlebars that never seemed to stay in one place. No trek into the quaint little village on this antique. So much for my visions.

My birthday approached, along with Christmas and Valentine's Day. A new bike seemed the perfect choice for a husband always on the lookout for unique gifts. Special events flew by like dead leaves in a fall windstorm. I didn't mind though. I was a little old to be riding my bike in the basement anyway. I could wait until spring. Soon Mother's Day passed without a hint of a new three-speed. Summer filled the air. The Lake Michigan trip had been planned. Still, no new bike appeared in the garage next to the other three new ones. By July, I left for a week-long seminar convinced the summer would pass without a new bike for Mom.

When the week ended, my family arrived to rescue me and take me to the beach. My daughter greeted me first with strange giggles and a cheshire cat smile. With my mind still engaged from an exciting week of study, only those all too familiar Mom thoughts came to mind, "Oh, no. Now what?" When my husband wheeled a shiny red Schwinn from behind the van, I knew the secret. Finally, three speeds and hand brakes, I thought! I could be part of the New Bike Family, and my handlebars would stay in one place. They gave away my old bike, my daughter bubbled, and bought the new one. And, she continued as I climbed on the seat, since it was just the right height, she could ride it, too. She had spent the last few days test riding the new bike for me. She couldn't wait until I tried out all *ten* speeds.

I sat atop this new Schwinn with sudden trepidation. Getting on was the easy part; and, of course, I could ride. But, did she say ten speeds? My stomach did a flip. My old bike had three speeds, two of which didn't work. I slid slowly off the seat and oohed and aahed and thanked them all profusely. I would ride as soon as we arrived at the lake, but right then we really had to hurry.

Before long we were unloaded and everyone was ready for a ride. I had completed every possible unpacking job: Clothes hung in order from short to long, plastic bags lined every wastebasket, fresh tissues popped through each tissue box, beach towels lay folded at the foot of each bed, fresh soap lay neatly unwrapped next to each sink. No more stalling! As I began alphabetizing the food packages in the cupboard, wails of, "Come on, Mother!" brought me outside to face the mechanical marvel. All I wanted was little exercise. All I wanted was to be able to ride a few miles to enjoy the scenery. All I wanted was to buy a few muffins without burning any foreign oil. I had no intention of entering the Tour de France. What would I possible do with ten speeds? I had complained about my old bike, whined that everyone else in the family had a new bike, and nagged that summer was on its way and I still didn't have a new bike; so how could I complain now that there was no way this unmechanical, non-athletic, mother of two was going to ride this complicated machine? I climbed on.

As we pulled away, my husband offered instructions in the finer points of handling of a ten speed. The gears were set so I would have no need of shifting, he said. Until we reached the hill. I might want to shift to a lower gear, he offered. I heard the rattling of gears as I tried shifting to make pedaling easier, and it worked. My feet spun wildly around on the pedals. No control. No speed. Just wild spinning. My hands white-knuckled the handlebar grips as I frantically shifted again. "Remember to keep the pedals moving when you shift," he called after me. Right! I might as well spin plates at the same time I wanted to yell.

I heard scraping and rattling as the gears shifted into place and tightened. The wild spinning stopped. The pedals gripped and felt slightly more in control. "See," he said, "just keep practicing. Get the feel for each gear position and keep your feet pedaling." I glared back at him ready with an unkind comment, when the chain suddenly dropped off the sprocket. Now what? I never owned a bike that lost its chain. Convinced the bike needed to be returned to Schwinn, I yelled at my husband. It was all his fault. He insisted I needed ten speeds. He came over to help.

With the chain returned to its sprocket, we continued. Back on level ground, I shifted once or twice to feel the gears, like he told me. As I approached each hill, I concentrated. I slid the lever into the lower gear and heard a clank as the chain dropped, as it should, to the smaller sprocket. Only two gears on this lever made shifting easier and smoother. Only one slide of the lever shifted from high to low. The clank had a less ominous sound to it; less like the sound of losing one's muffler and more like the sound of a miniature train rolling on its metal tracks.

Shifting through the five speeds on the other lever however, sounded like a bouncing bucket filled with nuts and bolts. In the first few shifts, I even lost a gear or two. I was sure Mr. Schwinn had forgotten one of the five I was supposed to have. The clicks and clanks continued for a few more days. Sometimes loudly, but slowly they became fewer. I begin to feel the difference in the gears. Gradually, all I heard as I shifted was the smooth touch of metal against metal. I began to feel a rhythm in the gears as the miles clicked by. By the time the leaves began to change, I felt comfortable with this new bike. We had gotten to know each other.

Before long, snow covered the pathways my bike followed. Time to put my wheels to sleep for winter. My new bike hung quietly from the garage rafters waiting patiently. Come spring, would I remember to keep my feet moving as I shifted?

PART B: INVESTIGATING LEADS

My new bike piece began as a short draft written in my fifth grade classroom. I often write with the students and had shared this piece many times as it began to take shape. It soon became a tool to help teach a lesson on writing story leads. The lesson evolved from a desire to help ten-year-olds focus on this one aspect of revision. When writers begin drafts, they often start without giving much thought to a beginning. Children are no different. The following are first draft beginnings from fifth graders.

> Two years ago I started collecting baseball cards. I have about 5050 cards. My best cards are Eric Davis, rookie. . .
>
> *by Ryan*

> I was at my babysitter's house last year. They were giving away free rabbits. When my mom got back to the sitter's house, I begged and begged if I could get a rabbit.
>
> *by Jared*

> Everytime I come home from Latchkey and we're going to have company, I have to clean my room. After that I feel like I can't do anything until the company gets here.
>
> *by Justin*

> I like to hike in the woods. I especially like to hike at Obrien Lake in Huron National Forest.
>
> *by Eric*

Although not bad, when rewriting starts, I want my students to think of other possibilities. After everyone has written four or five drafts, I set aside one writing period to discuss the importance of good leads and to investigate how authors we enjoy start their books. Although tempted to begin with my bicycle piece, I prefer to discover with the children good leads that already exist in published literature.

I introduce the lesson with a discussion about ways readers select books. While the jacket and title may attract my attention, I explain, I usually open to the first page and read. If I find myself sitting down, trapped in the prose, I know I'm into something. The beginning captures my attention, enticing me to read on. The lead is important to a good story. Then we begin investigating various author's beginnings.

Authors lead readers into their work via many paths and for a variety of reasons. I have to start somewhere, though, so I begin by telling my students we are going to look at four beginnings commonly used by authors. (See Orange County Public Schools, 1986 for full discussion.)

First, I read the opening to *Charlotte's Web* (1952) by E.B. White. We see Fern and her mother at the breakfast table talking about Mr. Arable going to the barn with an ax. Through this dialogue, White establishes the problem in the story; the runt of a litter of pigs is to be killed. I explain that White began his story with *conversation or dialogue.* I ask them what else they want to know after hearing this short conversation. We discover that White has captured our curiosity. We want to read on. Will Mr. Arable really kill the pig? Why doesn't Fern want this pig killed? What will Fern do to stop Mr. Arable?

Next, I read *The Indian in the Cupboard* (1980) by Lynne Reid Banks. Banks describes the birthday present Omri receives from Patrick, and we wonder what's going to happen to this unwanted plastic Indian. My students learn that Banks began her book with a *description.* I might follow this discussion by reading the beginning of *Sounder* (1969) by William H. Armstrong. The first page describes the tall man on the porch and introduces the boy and the dog, Sounder. I ask, "Has this beginning description hooked you?" They want to know about the tall man and wonder if he is a stranger. They ask why the characters are standing on the porch in the cold.

Encyclopedia Brown Takes the Cake (1983) by Donald J. Sobol is the next beginning I read. Sobol begins with information about Idaville, its chief of police, Mr. Brown, and his son Leroy. We need to know the setting and characters before we read the mystery. This beginning gives us *background* information necessary to the rest of the story. The students soon discover that each book in the Encyclopedia Brown series begins with background information. The lead generates interest in solving the mystery. The students ask why Encylopedia is a secret weapon. "What did he do to save the town?" someone asks.

Finally, I read *Alexander and the Terrible, Horrible, No Good, Very Bad Day* (1974) by Judith Viorst. Most of my fifth graders remember hearing and reading this book when they were younger. The boys and girls discover Viorst has used Alexander's *actions* as a beginning. Since everyone wants to know what other misadventures befall Alexander, I am pressured into reading the whole story.

By this time many students sneak novels out of their desks to examine the first page. Look at the beginning. Can we classify some of them? Hands go up quickly. Conversations are often first to be discovered; perhaps special punctuation makes them easy to spot. We also discover that many children's authors begin this way. As students share their discoveries, I post a chart with four separate headings: conversation, background, action, and description. The class will fill in the chart. As they come across an identified beginning, they add the title and author to our chart. If students find leads with a combination of action and conversation, for example, they are also added. These examples can be placed under both headings, under one of the two headings, or under a separate heading called other. Gradually, our chart fills. My students unintentionally prepare a bibliography to share with each other, subsequent classes, and other teachers interested in using this lesson. Many teachers collect their own bibliographies after I introduce this lesson in their classrooms.

After this discovery period, I ask my students to examine their current drafts. If someone finds an example in his own work, that title is added to the chart with published authors. At this point, however, few papers are found. We discuss the possibility of writing new beginnings for work that is in progress. Since the class is familiar with my new bike draft, I use it as a model for this lesson. I show them how I could possibly begin in four different ways.

One at a time, I project the following four paragraphs on the overhead for discussion.

1. I've decided that getting a new bike is as exciting when you are "somewhere in your thirties" as it is when you are ten-years-old. Something about a shiny, candy apple red bike makes you want to ride around the block to show it to the world. With its upright handlebars, fat tires and hand brakes, I am sure I can ride for miles. It has a soft lambswool seat to cushion the ride and ten speeds to make the hills flatten out before me! It even sparkles as the sunlight dances off the chrome handlebars and wire spokes.

2. The last new bike I remember owning arrived as a Christmas gift in second grade. I still remember visiting my grandmother's house to find my Christmas present hiding in her basement. In the middle of the basement stood a black bike with fat tires and no handbrakes. A basic model, it sported chrome handlebars, a black leather seat, and shiny black fenders, front and rear. Fully assembled and leaning on its kickstand, it waited for me to hop on and go for a ride. Grandma's large basement allowed for an eight year old to take a few spins around the center support poles. Wow! I became the envy of all the cousins, who begged to take a ride.

3. "I haven't had a new bike since I was in the second grade," I whined, staring at my husband's brand new, shiny red Schwinn.

"OK!OK!" he said. "Of course you need a new bike. Maybe in November for your birthday. How about Christmas? Can you wait until December?"

"What good is a bike in the winter? Besides that's the last time I got a bike, but I was in the second grade and could ride it in my Grandma's basement. I need to get out in the spring. So I can exercise. I need to lose weight, tone my muscles, increase my heart rate."

"Uh-huh," he muttered under his breath.

4. I could hear the clicking of the gears as I shifted to make pedaling the hill easier. I heard scraping and rattling as I tried to make the change from one gear to the next. There had to be something wrong with this thing, I thought. I listened closely to the gears; more rattles and then a loud clank. Keep practicing my husband told me; still more rattles and scraping.

The kids quickly identify each of my beginnings as one of our examples. Number one, description, is so, because I describe my bike. Number two, background, tells about the last new bike I owned, so I can convince the reader I need a new one. Number three is barely on the screen before all hands are up. Although this contrived bit of conversation is not my favorite, the children seem to enjoy it. Perhaps they like it because they are familiar with the many children's authors who begin their books with conversation, or they like the whiny voice I have written. Number four easily identifies as action because of all the sounds and movement. We discuss how authors try many different beginnings, liking some more than others, but it is the author who makes the final choice. The children also notice parts of my discarded leads appear elsewhere in my final draft. By now, it is the students' turn to write.

I ask the class to search for and re-read a draft in their folder. They decide what kind of beginning it has and attempt to recast it into a form they have not tried. They begin silent writing time with this new task in mind. Some students even raise hands during silent writing (usually a no-no) asking if they can try a different beginning after they do the first one! I assure tham that this exercise plays with words; we are in the thick of it, doing what writers do. There is no intention to direct them one way or another. The author decides. The following is my fifth graders work, after my beginnings lesson.

Ryan decided to expand his beginnings by giving more background:

> Two years ago, I started collecting baseball cards. My friend, Mike, had been collecting baseball cards for three years. He told me he had a Willy Mays. It was worth $35. That card had gotten me interested in baseball cards. I learned you can make money off the cards you buy. Now I have about five thousand fifty cards.

Conversation begins Jared's rewrite:

> "Mom, Mom! My mom got home from work, and I was at my babysitter's house. "Can I get a rabbit from Ryan? They're giving away free rabbits. Can I get one? At first she said no, but I wouldn't give up. I begged and begged. Finally she gave up. She said, "All right you can have a rabbit."

Justin thought a description at the beginning of his draft might attract other fifth graders to read his work:

> My room is always a mess. I have clothes on the floor, my instrument up (stand and everything), and sometimes my closet door can't shut because I have clothes on the floor, some games, and two boxes full of old toys under my clothes hangers.

Eric also chose to begin with conversation:

> "Hey mom! Can I walk in the woods?" I asked.
> "Well," she said, "you better be careful and watch out for hunters. We're camping in a national forest you know."
> That's my mom. She's always worried about me. You see I love to have long walks in the woods. I drift from trail to trail on soft, noiseless feet, searching for animals, almost stalking them, hunting them but with my eyes not with a bow or gun.

As I compare these rewrites with the originals, I am impressed by the wonderful changes many students make. Their smiles and eagerness to continue these drafts to publication tell me they are as impressed with their work as I am. I also discover a number of unexpected benefits never planned for when I first prepared the lesson. The lesson objective is to show students different leads and attempt to create new ones for their own work. However, as they attempt to rewrite, many of them choose richer language. Eric's new conversation does more to hook me than his original. I want to know what animals he will find or if his mother's concern becomes warranted. Ryan's rewrite explains why he now has over 5000 cards. The students also appreciate this richer language and the added interest given to their stories.

Another unplanned benefit is an increased awareness of revision. Remembering the lesson, many students give more attention to the beginning of their next piece. They might ask a peer to help them rewrite a lead, or they might bring the question to a conference with me. I often refer a weaker writer to this lesson to encourage revision. Students also begin to understand the concept of multiple drafts when they try writing different beginnings to the same draft.

This writing lesson spills into reading time as well. I hear discussions about how an author begins a story. Some students stop to tell me about the beginnings of their latest novel. My students sound more like writers as they talk about books. Sometimes I ask them to share a book by describing the lead and its impact on the reader's attention. The best part of this lesson is that after three years, I am still excited and encouraged by the results it produces.

REFERENCES:

Armstrong, W.H. (1969). *Sounder.* New York: Harper & Row.
Banks, L.R. (1980). *Indian in the cupboard.* New York: Avon Books.
Orange County Public Schools. (1986). *Weaving literature into writing.* Orlando, FL: Orange County Public Schools.
Sobol, D.J. with G. Andrews. (1983). *Encyclopedia brown takes the cake.* New York: Four Winds Press.
Viorst, J. (1974). *Alexander and the terrible, horrible, no good, very bad day.* New York: Atheneum.
White, E.B. (1952). *Charlotte's Web.* New York: Harper & Row.

SELECTED BIBLIOGRAPHY:

Asher, S. (1989). *Wild words! How to train them to tell stories.* New York: Walker & Co.

Sandy Asher's delightful new book helps young writers with their stories. She offers good ideas from which a writing teacher can develop revision lessons.

Atwell, N. (1987). *In the middle.* Portsmouth, NH: Boynton/Cook Publishers.

Cited by many writing teachers as a useful resource, Nancie Atwell gives concrete direction in establishing and managing a process classroom. She also offers help for developing writing lessons.

Orange County Public Schools. (1986). *Weaving literature into writing.* Orlando: Orange County Public Schools.

This manual offers a handy bibliography of children's literature that can be used to teach a number of writing skills. The titles are organized under various skills including good leads, good endings, writing descriptions, and so forth.

Olson, C. (Ed.). (1987). *Practical ideas for teaching writing as a process.* Sacramento: California State Department of Education.

Practical Ideas is an inexpensive handbook written by classroom teachers. It offers a variety of lessons from prewriting to publication.

*No one but **Will Hobbs** could open a chapter on fiction writing with, ": . . it is the most effective weapon in my bag of tricks." Not, and get away with it. But get away, he does; he's that fine a magician. While Hobbs's advice for getting started in this chapter will undoubtedly prove helpful, it's his methodical approach to rewriting, all the cutting and pasting, that will help teachers the most. "Cultivate humility," he says, "look for ways to improve. . ." Attention to audience, point of view, effective use of detail, the nitty-gritty of style. strong verbs, nouns, modifiers, tone and diction— it's all here, and delightfully readable. Suggestions and advice from Hobbs, combined with Hilla and Blackhawk's insights, should leave readers with enough on short story writing to last a lifetime. Of course, the qualities of good writing cross the genre, so readers, truly, have tools for all writing occasions.*

CHAPTER 9
TURN YOUR READERS INTO WRITERS

By Will Hobbs

PART A: EXCERPT FROM *CHANGES IN LATITUDES*

"*TU MADRE.*" That's a Spanish expression, one of the worst insults there is. It translates as "your mother."

It came to mind as I brooded over a Tecate in the cafe—*palapa* at the Playa Tortugas. I'd never properly appreciated that expression. Now I could. If someone had walked up to me right then at the beach and said that to me, I would have ripped his lungs out and then agreed with him.

I really wanted to rip somebody's lungs out.

Teddy kept looking over to the next table at a big, muscular, blond-haired gringo hunched over a Spanish-looking newspaper. He was munching *empanadas* and drinking a *cerveza* as he read. Finally he looked up, and when he saw Teddy his face broke out in a smile as golden as Robert Redford's.

"Say, how's it going?" he said. "Teddy—right?"

Teddy nodded, and told me enthusiastically, "Casey's the marine biologist I told you about."

He didn't look like a marine biologist to me. In his muscle shirt, swimming suit, and thongs he looked more like a surfer. Or considering the tattoo on his arm and his three-day beard, like a biker.

"This is my big brother Travis," Teddy announced proudly.

"Glad to meet you, Travis," he said with that smile.

As savage as I felt, the smile disarmed me. There wasn't anything phony about it, maybe because of his eyes. There was a lot of mileage around his eyes.

"Your brother really knows a few things," he told me. "How 'bout you—are you interested in marine biology too?"

Though it had never occurred to me before, I told him I was. "I don't know much," I said, "but Teddy's been getting me into it."

Teddy was surprised and pleased, I could see that. I was surprised myself. I'd never heard myself say anything like that before.

Casey smiled. "How'd you guys like to go offshore and see if we can locate some turtles?"

A few minutes later and we were in Casey's motorboat, picking up speed and heading out to sea. Teddy and I sat on the front thwart and helped weight the bobbing bow as Casey opened it up full throttle and really gave us a ride. Teddy was grinning like a mule eating briars. I glanced back to Casey. He nodded to me and broke into that smile, as if to say, "This ain't bad, eh?" It seemed as if the three of us had been together for years.

When we were a good mile offshore, three other small boats appeared at a distance. Casey eased up some and steered in a big arc away from them.

"What are they doing?" Teddy asked.

"They're . . . fishing," Casey said. "We should do okay over this way."

Casey cut his speed, shaded his eyes, and started searching the water for turtles. We did the same, though I couldn't keep it up after a few minutes. Finally, Teddy saw one and cried out. It was paddling around just below the surface. We had no idea what Casey had in store for us. He fished two sets of snorkeling gear—masks, snorkels, and flippers—out of the rear thwart, coached us, and sent us after the turtles. "They mass offshore, the males and females both, well before the arrivals. Maybe we'll get lucky and you'll see some more."

We got the hang of swimming at the surface and breathing through our snorkels while we kept our faces down and scanned for turtles. Then we practiced diving until we could stay down a minute or two. After a number of dives I'd convinced myself we wouldn't see any, but then like an image in a dream they appeared in front of us, six of Teddy's olive-green ridleys swimming silently and effortlessly along, and we were right among them.

With the flippers we had no problem keeping up. Strangely enough, they showed no fear of us. I'm sure they could have sped up, or dived deep where we couldn't follow, but they held their own course. I felt like we were of the moment, and they were of the ages.

When we couldn't stay down any longer, we surfaced with a shout and let Casey know we'd found them. He called his encouragement and we dived again. We hadn't lost them. This time we took hold of two of them, and let them lead us around. If we kept kicking we didn't hold them back. Then we let go and swam alongside them again. It didn't seem right to hinder their graceful movements—just to be there with them in their own element was enough.

For the first time in my life I was filled with awe. I was overwhelmed with the kind of appreciation for them that Teddy must have felt. As beautiful and perfect as wild geese, they swam like birds of the sea. Just as birds had mastered flight, these turtles were reptiles who'd taken to the open sea. If anything, they were more graceful than birds because the water slowed their movement to the speed of a hypnotic dance. It seemed a pity that they ever needed to return to the land to lay their eggs. Creatures of freedom and flight in the sea, they became awkward and hapless once they climbed out onto the beach.

Without realizing it, I'd started daydreaming the daydreams of a marine biologist.

For me that swim was a waking dream wrapped around and around with beauty. I was sharing it with my brother, and I was happier than I'd ever been. We'd left the land and the weight of our troubles behind, and for a short while in another dimension we experience together the weightlessness of pure joy.

There's a place where that swim keeps on happening forever. That place is in my memory. I go there often. Teddy and I are swimming along with the turtles and looking to each other to share the wonder. We're the brothers we always wanted to be.

PART B: FICTION WRITING IN THE CLASSROOM

"When he said to make a 1200-word story I about fell over. But I started to write and it was easy, because we learned all the tools to a good story. It gave me confidence in myself. I can do anything I want to. I still have to practice a lot before I could do anything that was perfect or even close. But just knowing with a little work I can."

When my students review what they have learned in the course of their English class, they invariably value their accomplishments as writers most highly. I am thrilled. I can remember the attitudes they'd brought with them to class at the beginning of the semester. "I'm just not a good writer. I just don't like to write."

Fiction is only one of the genres in which my students write, but it is the most effective weapon in my bag of tricks, and has everything to do with building their confidence as writers. Especially in secondary school, story writing is considered an extra-credit option for the talented few, or as fare in a creative writing elective, but I've found it to be the key to writing success for all the students in my English class, regardless of aptitude. When students write fiction they care deeply about their work, and writing becomes rewarding, as it did for the student I quoted above. Their ears are open when the teacher makes suggestions about mechanics, grammar, usage, stylistic choices of any kind. Here's the friendly and motivational arena in which teacher and student can work on punctuation, capitalization, spelling, fragments, comma faults, run-on sentences, misplaced modifiers, parallel structure, word choice, sentence variety, unity, coherence. . .and it all transfers to any other form of writing. (What can't you teach through fiction? It's a shorter list, but topic sentences and formal argumentation would be on it.)

It only makes sense that students would enjoy writing stories, if they thought they could. People love stories; it's human nature. The novels we read, the movies we see, most TV shows, songs: These are all stories. If you have ever been moved by a good story, you have the motivation to write a story. It's up to the teacher to demythologize the process, to show that anyone can write a story. Authors are not members of a select priesthood; they're readers who've picked up the pen.

I would like to suggest that we're largely neglecting the most effective genre through which to teach writing because we do not recognize it as such. We know that students generally prefer to read fiction rather than non-fiction, but when it comes to *writing* fiction, we assume that the task is too difficult. Students who have learned that writing a story, like reading a story, is not that hard once you get started, will develop writing fluency on their way to their immediate goal: producing stories and enjoying the self-esteem that comes with authorship.

I wouldn't suggest that students at any level write exclusively fiction, only that it should become an integral part of the writing they do, because it is the most reinforcing. Through story writing, a teacher can foster a positive attitude about the process of writing in general. More personal forms of expository writing—letters, journals, profiles of other students, personal narratives—contribute to the same effect. Students are never so proud of themselves, however, as when they've written an original story.

When it comes to their fiction, students *listen* to suggestions for improving the writing. It's a special feeling to be creating a story. They want it to be good, especially if it's going to be published in any form. Oftentimes our trash bins are full of crumpled papers dropped by students on their way out of class; not so when students are writing original stories.

SETTING THE TABLE

Because the motivation for writing springs from reading, any class in which you're going to teach writing should have a strong reading component beyond the reading the class is doing in common. If you can put the right novels in the hands of your students, and if you devise a system that rewards them for a great deal of independent reading, they'll become emotionally involved with fiction and therefore predisposed to try writing a story, not to mention all the other benefits they'll derive. In my English classes, I would require one book report per quarter and reward students with extra credit for reading up to five more (each 250 pages counted for one extra). All book reports were oral, pass-fail, in a one-to-one conference with me. The conferences kept the students honest, and they could quickly start their next book without having to do a written book report, which they loathe. Having the opportunity to meet with my students individually was wonderful for rapport as well. Students welcome the opportunity for their own dialogue with the teacher; it's a refreshing change from being lectured to as one of the pack.

It's vital, I think, to allow students latitude in their independent reading. They'll snap up the titles you recommend to them personally, if you're usually right that the student and the book are a good match. A short required list is deadly. In high school, students chose from my list of one hundred titles for their required report; extra book reports were wide open. Often they continued to choose from the list for their extra book reports. (Each title was accompanied by a blurb clipped from a catalog, so they could see what the book was about.) By emphasizing reading in the English class, I saw students rediscovering reading in a big way. Some of them told me they hadn't really read a book since their last required reading class years earlier. They'd fudged a number of written book reports, but they'd pretty much quit reading.

Oral reading as well, at any level, creates excitement about language that carries over to writing. When you read dramatically to the class from their anthology, for example, students have the phrasing and the inflection modeled for them which will enable them afterwards, in their silent reading, to hear vividly through the printed word. The words on the page won't be there two-dimensionally; they'll come to life. As I'll go on to demonstrate, it's good stories fully brought to life through oral reading that provide the springboard—both the motivation and the seminal ideas—for fiction writing in the classroom.

How Do You Get Students to Write Stories?

If you ask a classroom of 30 students to dream up a story out of the air, how many will you get back? Maybe one or two. That's why we don't assign fiction writing outside of the creative writing class: We assume we'd be setting our students up for failure. An original story seems so intimidating, because students' own experience, that they can draw on so comfortably in a personal narrative, seems to be ruled out.

Stories start as a "what if"—a premise. A story is a "what if" tested in the laboratory of the imagination. Students will readily write stories, but at first, only when the teacher supplies the "what if." It's hard enough for professional writers to come up with their next idea. Most students need a catalyst to help them turn their experience into fiction; they need the "what if" supplied. Teachers at any level who've never written fiction themselves can become good at producing "what if's" to supply their students, if they get used to thinking in that mode.

The tall tale is an example of a comfortable, introductory genre for fiction writing, and it's not just for younger students. I used the tall tale to elicit a short writing sample the first day of school from my sophomores and juniors. First I read them a humorous story from an anthology, "Snapshot of a Dog," in which James Thurber told, as if they were totally plausible, the implausible exploits of a bull terrier. Then I asked the students to tell their own story, starting perhaps with a dog they knew and whose traits they could amplify, and make up some fantastic exploits for the dog, only tell them dryly and straightfaced, as Thurber had done. "Does it have to be a dog?" a student asked right away.

"No," I replied. "How about a pet duck? I just read in the paper, that there was a really mean hog in a small town in Texas, that wasn't being fenced and was more or less terrorizing the town. Maybe your narrator's pet duck could take on that hog and defeat him."

"How long does it have to be?" came the inevitable next question.

"No certain length."

Most of them wrote two or three pages. It was a non-threatening assignment, non-graded, and they got into it. I got a good look at their writing, and they started out the class associating writing with pleasure. I had also signalled them, without even mentioning it, that we were going to be writing some fiction in this class, and it was something they could succeed at.

My students were writing fiction without being intimidated by the task, and they were learning that fiction isn't something made out of nothing. They hadn't suddenly become Leonardos. They were applying their own experiences, their own sense of the people they'd known and situations and outcomes, and filtering them through their imaginations in light of the "what if" I had given them. Students' experiences are by no means ruled out in fiction writing; after all, don't writers always say, "Write about what you know"? Rather, students' experiences are transformed in the process of writing fiction into a new, imaginative form. And they'll be delighted to find themselves practicing this creative alchemy.

Fiction writing is a process that most of us practice little, if at all. It's no wonder we think of it as near-magical. Fiction writers, on the other hand, know that the magic happens only with plenty of practice and time.

When you read the daily paper and watch the evening news, you can be watching for a premise, a "what if," that might catch the fancy of your students. What about the story of an abducted child, from the child's point of view? Would it be a boy or a girl? How old? Where were they and what were they doing when they were abducted? Their imaginations will kick in.

The news can inspire ideas for fantasy as well as realistic fiction. Suppose you're reading about the discoveries in Montana of fossil dinosaur eggs. You think, what about a living dinosaur egg? What if a child plucked a large egg from a stream, and then heard something rapping inside? What if a small dinosaur hatched out of that egg? What if the little dinosaur could talk?

But my best and inexhaustible source of fiction-writing ideas is closest at hand: It's the reading that we're enjoying together in class. As with the Thurber story, almost any form of reading can be turned into an idea for a fiction writing assignment. Reading myths can lead to writing myths, whether it's how the bear lost its tail, or a new adventure for Odysseus. Reading fables can lead to writing fables. Reading fairy tales can lead to writing them, and will probably result in fractured fairy tales, but that's fine, too.

Most often my ideas come right from the stories in the literature anthology. Think about the premise, and you've got the key. Even the moldy standards of early American literature can generate exciting story ideas. I'll give three examples. If they'll work, anything could.

The premise of Hawthorne's "Dr. Heidegger's Experiment," for example, is the finding of a new fountain of youth. As the class finishes the story, take the premise and give it a twist. Ask, for example, if a fountain of youth of some kind were discovered near your own home, or in your town or city, what form would it take? Who would discover it? Who would be in on the secret? What would happen to them?

Perhaps you're studying the Salem witch trials. Now give the witch hunt idea a spin: A fictional writing assignment might be to write "A Short History of a Modern Witch Hunt" with characters, a plot, a contemporary setting. You might add the restriction that it can't be a literal witch hunt; their story should demonstrate an understanding of the derivative and broader meaning of the term.

Afterwards, you might follow up with more reading to see what sort of spin other authors have put on the same idea. *Visit to a Small Planet* (1955), the short play by Gore Vidal, would be perfect, and students could take turns bringing it to life by reading the parts. They'll be learning that writing and reading are inextricably connected, always fueling each other.

I have a particular attachment to Herman Melville's "Bartleby the Scrivener," and so I wanted to see if I could interest my students in the story. As they were put off by with the difficulty of the diction and the syntax, and of course by the length of the story, I started them out by reading to them, and they soon became, like me, intrigued with the title character. They wanted to strangle him for living in the law office and refusing to work, but at the same time, like Bartleby's employer, they cared about him. My students read on, on their own, and then we finished the story together.

As we and the narrator wrestled with our consciences upon concluding the tale, I asked my students if Bartleby wasn't essentially a homeless man, and the narrator his only connection to humanity. They agreed. We proceeded to talk about the homeless people of our own era, in our own small town. Everyone knew a few of the most visible by sight, but no one in the class had ever met one of them, knew their real names or anything about their personal histories. A "what if" came to me on the spot. With "Bartleby" so fresh, it wasn't a blinding piece of inspiration, it was merely an association: What if you were to write a story in which a homeless person came into your or your narrator's life? How and where would the first meeting occur? How would a relationship develop? What if your narrator discovered, like the narrator in the story did, that he or she was the homeless person's only connection with humanity? What would happen? What would be revealed in the course of the story about their personal history? How would they change, how would your narrator change?

I sensed I had a winner. I proposed, for our major second quarter writing assignment, that students choose either a personal narrative, something we had worked on earlier, or an original short story based on "Bartleby." Most of them had never written a short story before, but ninety percent of them chose to write one, after initially saying they couldn't make up a story. It was a challenge, and they felt they had the tools. It came toward the end of the semester, after we'd written in a variety of fictional and non-fictional forms while studying the elements of style (a brief discussion follows in this chapter). Their imaginations were primed as well by all the reading they had done, especially "Bartleby," the occasion of the assignment.

We used the same prewriting techniques as we had for personal narratives and essays. Only this time the students were brainstorming characters, setting, plot. They were soon scribbling away in class on their rough drafts. Once they had the first draft of their own original story to work with, they were much more interested in revising and in proofing each other's work than ever before. As the final drafts were coming in, I was looking them over and was able to say, "Wow, these are *really* good," which they were. I'd been pointing out in our reading and in their writing all semester what makes for good, strong writing, and here they were doing it! For example, they were writing with the five senses—tactile, specific writing, nothing vague, images the reader could see, smell, touch. If we could publish these, I started thinking, it would cement their confidence.

"Now," I said, "let's get serious. These are good, but they still need work. If you'll spend two more class periods trading them around and doing some serious proofing, and if you'll type them or have them typed over Christmas vacation, we can go to print. Let's put out a book of your stories and personal narratives. Extra credit, of course."

Over the next two days those juniors demonstrated more curiosity and learned more about language mechanics than I could have force-fed them in two years. It was no longer a matter of a grade; this was for publication, and they wanted it to be right. They cared about style as well. They wanted their sentences to flow, to sound right. Each of them received their own spiral-bound book. They funded them at $3 apiece, and students in art classes created covers and inside art for us. (Students in the school print shop photocopied, collated, and bound them; the cost would have been $5 if we'd had them printed professionally off-campus.)

My student writers were more than pleased. So was I. Their writing had taken a quantum leap, and they had each written an original short story that was also a response to "Bartleby the Scrivener." A number of students said they were going to hang onto the books for a long time, and I believe they will. (I know I will. I still have the books of poetry that my classes published in my first year of teaching 18 years earlier.)

The books were a gold mine: homemade literature, a different book from each class. My students could read their own stories to the class, and I had the opportunity to reinforce strong writing, quoting a passage and emphasizing a string of strong verbs perhaps, or a particularly well-turned phrase. They loved to hear their own sentences quoted back to them. Because of their ownership, they were imprinting on *why* the writing was good.

As they read each other's stories, as well as those from the books produced by the other classes, they were amazed at how dissimilar the stories were, in narrative voice, in characters, settings, and plots. The variety was a testimonial to the power of their own imaginations and the unique quality of their own life experience. They'd all started with the same premise and created stories solely their own.

My three junior classes that wrote the short story based on "Bartleby the Scrivener" were not honors classes. It was so satisfying for me to award the grades and write the individual comments. A couple received *B's*, and all the rest *A's*. (The *B's* were for stories that read like summaries, covering much ground indirectly, typically failing to zero in with specific detail and dialogue.) When they said, "Thanks," I was able to shrug and say, "You earned it." And they knew they had. The stories had been proofed so well, there was no need to mark on them. I wrote my comments on separate sheets of paper. The author of "The James Early Story," which ran to 5,000 words and was better written, in fact, than my first effort as a junior in college, came after class and asked me to sign the comments. "I'm going to take this home," he said. "My parents aren't going to believe this. It's going to blow their minds."

"It should," I said. "You wrote an awesome story."

He looked at me, this junior in high school who was bigger than I am, and said, "Would you mind adding that?"

HOW TO WRITE FICTION: GUIDELINES FOR STUDENTS

Find a Subject You Know and Care About, That is Interesting to You.   Once students are excited about writing fiction, some will want to try out their own "what if" instead of working on the group's "what if." I would encourage them to. Advise students, when they're dreaming up totally original stories, to build from what they know. Otherwise they won't be able to invest their writing with specificity. If they know even a little, and care about the subject a great deal, they can do the research and gain enough new knowledge to be able to write about the subject. That's how I came to write about sea turtles in my novel, *Changes in Latitudes*. I cared about them first, then learned more about them as I wrote the story.

Along with extra credit for extra book reports, you can offer extra credit for original short stories. I remember one that should be added to the Christmas literature. It was from the point of view of an ornament.

Keep to the Point.   Detail is good, but too much of it is boring. If it doesn't advance the plot or reveal character, leave it out. If a character lifts up the hood of his car and the narrator goes on for two pages about the motor before getting back to the action, this is bound to be boring. After publishing two novels, I still hadn't incorporated this point sufficiently myself. I wanted to set a novel in the Grand Canyon, and pour my love for the canyon into the novel, and so I did: my first draft was natural history and geology thinly disguised as fiction. I didn't recognize that when I sent it in, of course; it took my editor to point out that my story was "bloated." Her comments couldn't have been more accurate or helpful. *Downriver*, my third novel, is now a hundred pages leaner and bears only a superficial resemblance to my first version, which leads to my third point.

Be Ready to Cut and Rewrite.   Don't get too attached to your first draft, I tell students. Very few of those words, as it turns out, should be engraved in stone. Cultivate humility, look for ways to improve, to change things around. Add characters, drop characters, change who's telling the story, cut out the stuff where you were just enjoying listening to the sound of your own voice. Listen to advice. Try out suggestions instead of being defensive. Look at everything you put down as moldable. Compare every line to your original or new vision of the piece. Does it contribute to the effect you're trying to create, or is it a side-track?

The great thing about a first draft, I encourage students, is that now you have something to work with. Don't be disappointed if your writing is technically weak at first. It will lack specific details, sentence variety, and the connecting elements essential for coherence. And of course, the majority of verbs in a first draft will be weak ones.

It's in the revision that a writing student who knows he has the tools experiences the satisfaction of seeing the writing assume a pleasing, fluent form. Students don't mind the work when it's obvious to themselves they're getting results. What they can't stand is working over and over, and not improving. It's only natural and face-saving to give up, and declare, "I'm just not a good writer."

It's so much easier to sell revision when what the students are working on is fiction. They'll care about their stories, and want to make them better. They'll think of you as the person who can help them get where they want to go, instead of the taskmaster who's making them do something they could care less about.

The language you'll see will be more natural and unforced than what you're used to seeing. Encourage them to think of their writing as talking on paper, and you'll see a more fluent style. They won't have worked themselves into the self-perpetuating syntax tangles, the uncomfortable, artificial language they've concocted for trying to think analytically on paper.

When you go back to teaching the essay, you'll be able to say,

Remember how well and how smoothly you wrote in your short stories? When you read them out loud to the class they sounded perfectly natural, didn't they? Now write your next essay that way. Don't overreach. Don't try to sound fancy. Just talk. Get a flow going, the way you did with your stories. Avoid those writing errors that kept turning up in your short story: Refer to your personal list of "goofers." But don't expect your essay to be "ready for prime time" with the first draft. Once you have your first draft, say the sentences out loud to yourself. Yes, really out loud. Do it in your room, so nobody will think you're weird. Do the sentences sound pleasing? Is there a rhythm; do they fit well together? Are you saying what you mean, or are you just blowing smoke? If it sounds confusing or awkward to you, you can bet it will sound at least that bad to someone else. Try it another way. Make it flow. You can do it!

Think about your Audience   It always helps to keep a distinct picture of your audience in your mind as you write. When I started writing young adult fiction, it was comfortable and natural for me, because I'd been a teacher of adolescents for so long, my sense of audience was already ingrained.

Some writers write with one person in mind. That might be helpful for students. When students ask if the teacher is the audience, I say no, you're writing for each other. That way they care much more about their writing; there's more internal motivation. It's not for a grade, really, or to please the teacher. Audience makes more sense when they actually read what they've written to the class. The audience is right there. Writing was for a real purpose, not to satisfy an assignment.

Choose a Comfortable Voice. Change Point of View only for a Specific Purpose.
More than anything else, it's the voice of the narrator (whether first or third person) that grabs or disenchants a reader within the first few pages of a story. In choosing a voice, students should foremost choose one that's comfortable. They'll have

the most success sounding like themselves. Writing fiction does marvelous things to your own voice. The narrator isn't you but the voice is familiar.

Writing in the first person is automatically comfortable for most students. It's a good way to start. First person is inherently more immediate than third person, and exerts a powerful attraction for young adults across all ability levels, both as readers and writers. In the first person, the entire text has that immediacy that's gained from everything being seen from that one character's perspective. As an example, turn back a few pages and consider the voice of my first-person narrator in the excerpt from *Changes in Latitudes*, which introduces this discussion. Does Travis, my 16-year-old narrator, have that "immediate" quality to his voice? Note as well, as Travis relates his transcendental swim with the turtles, that a first person narrator who's worth his salt needn't be limited to the colloquial. Travis' voice is capable of lyrical flights because that's part of his nature, albeit a side he's neglected. I use some slang (e.g. "rip somebody's lungs out"), but largely I avoid it. Slang, especially name-calling, is simply passed over by a reader's eyes, because those words and expressions are so overused they convey almost nothing. When I had Travis call his little brother a name, it was "cheeseball."

A third-person narrator, on the other hand, alternately zooms in on a character's thoughts, then steps back to view the action from a more removed perspective. Consider the narrative technique in this excerpt from *Bearstone*:

> . . .With a jump, the roan gained the rock ledge and they were standing right where Cloyd wanted to be, in between those sheer walls like towers. He watched the swallows put on a show. He could even see the rainbow in their wing patches. To the north, across the Rio Grande country, a whole new world had opened up. It seemed like the wilderness had no end.
>
> If only the old man could see us standing here, he thought—me and Blueboy in the Window. I wish my sister could, my grandmother, and Susan James. But especially the old man.

In the opening of the first paragraph, note the omniscient narrator's distance from the point of view of the character: "With a jump, the roan gained the rock ledge. . ." Then the narrator approaches the point of view of the character by stating his intent ("right where Cloyd wanted to be"). Thereafter, we're in the character's point of view; note that the narration is not coming from inside the character's head.

In the second paragraph, the narration speaks directly from the character, but must use "he thought" in the first sentence to signal that we are now inside the thoughts of the character. In the following sentences, the signal ("he thought") can be dropped because the reader now knows we're inside. From this point, the narration can either stay in the character's head, transition back out while remaining in the point of view of the character, or return to an omniscient point of view.

When writing in third person, there are constantly these kinds of narrative decisions to be made. Third person narration for me is more like driving a stick shift than an automatic. And it took awhile for me before the shifting became smooth and unconscious.

In my first attempts at writing a novel—my early drafts of *Bearstone*—my third-person narrator had little authority, and it took me years to figure out why. I hope my diagnosis, looking back, will help you and your students short-cut the process. In an early scene in the book, for example, I had three characters involved as the Ute boy arrived at the ranch for the summer: Cloyd, his housemother (who was delivering him), and the old rancher. I wrote the scene with frequent shifts in point of view among the three characters. I was thinking of myself as a sort of movie director, and I was using the camera to show each of the characters from the other's point of view. What I came to realize was that I was preventing the reader from forming a strong identification with the main character—the boy—by switching points of view for no good reason. It wasn't important at that point in the story to know the inner thoughts of the old man and the housemother.

What I learned, and what I'd suggest you pass on to students writing in the third person, is to stay in the point of view of the main character except when there's a strong reason to see that character from the point of view of another character. Never do it randomly: You'll lose control of your horses and the reader will intuit your lack of authority. In *Bearstone*, I ended up going to the old man's point of view occasionally, but only when it was plainly useful. In one of my favorite parts, the boy and the rancher have a major falling-out, and the old man drives Cloyd back home to Utah, in the middle of the night. Confused and heartbroken, the boy waves good-bye, and Walter drives back to Colorado. The chapter ends as Cloyd resolves to hitch-hike back to the ranch. He knows and the reader knows that he's on his way back, but the old man doesn't. The next chapter, from the rancher's point of view, has him sitting on the ditch bank back home, full of regret, thinking about the years and the boy. The point of view shift for this scene made the dramatic moment possible, at the end of the chapter, when the boy comes trudging back to him across the field.

The handiest advice, to my thinking, for a student trying a short story in the third person for the first time, would be to channel everything in the story through the point of view of one character. This narrative technique is technically third-person narration, but actually in its effect it's more like first person, and it's so much easier to control. *Sounder* is an example of a short novel written in this sort of modified third person.

Voice is one of the wonderful and mysterious features of fiction. Whether you're telling a first- or third-person story, every time you begin a new project you happen upon a different voice with which to tell the story. Finding the voice that seems to match your vision of the story can be easy at times, difficult at others. Experiment. If it doesn't seem to work in first-person, try third, or vice-versa. If you want to stay with first, and your narrator isn't cutting it, try another character as the narrator. With my novel *Downriver*, three different characters tried their hand at telling the story. (It's about what happens when seven teenagers who have run away from an outdoor-education program sneak onto the Colorado River

in the Grand Canyon.) Two of the narrators were rather flat, and their versions
remain in the desk drawer. Eventually I found the right person to tell the story,
a 15-year-old girl named Jessie from Boulder, Colorado.

Show, Don't Tell.   This maxim has to be the most-repeated caveat for aspiring fiction writers, but it remains the most important. I heard it early, but I didn't
really understand it for a long time. I've found a way to teach it, and it's a concept that students get genuinely excited about, because when they understand
it, they feel they have a powerful tool in their possession that they definitely know
they never had before. Now they can work wonders!

Consider the following excerpts from *Bearstone*. The scene has to do with the
falling-out I alluded to earlier. Cloyd is terribly angry with the old man for reasons
he and the reader understand, but which the old man does not. Cloyd is taking
a chain saw to Walter's beloved peach trees, which his wife brought as seedlings
from Missouri to Colorado many, many years before. Compare the version in
my first draft, the first quote below, with the published version which follows:

   I. He made a cut in the dozen or so peach trees, about a third of the way through.
       He didn't want them to die. He just wanted the leaves to wither and yellow,
       and the peaches to shrivel.
   II. He cut through the skin of the nearest tree and winced as he withdrew the saw.
       Beads of moisture were forming along the edges of the fresh wound. From one
       to the next he ran with the saw roaring at full throttle, and he cut each of the
       twenty-two peach trees most of the way through. Each time, as the saw's teeth
       bit into the thin bark, he hollered with hurt as if he felt the saw himself. He
       didn't want to cut them down, he wanted them to die slowly. Before they died,
       their leaves would yellow and the peaches shrivel, and they would look just like
       his grandmother's peaches.

What made the difference? Writing with the five senses. In the first version,
the narrator *told* that Cloyd cut the trees. In the second, the narrator *showed* it.
Showing means using the five senses as you write. It means writing with imagery,
but if you tell that to students, they draw a blank, unless you always say
"imagery—the five senses." In the second version, we *see* a very specific picture,
the little beads of sap forming. We *see* him running from one tree to the next. We
hear the saw roaring at full throttle. We *see* the teeth of the chain saw biting into
the thin bark. We *see* and *feel* the cut as a wound in a living thing. Implicitly, we
feel the saw in our own hands. We *hear* Cloyd hollering with hurt. We *picture* the
leaves withering and yellowing; we *picture* his grandmother's sickly peach trees
back home in Utah.

When the reader is told, the reader remains uninvolved. When the reader is
shown, that's when writing comes alive, and the reader becomes emotionally involved. The scene becomes so real, it's as if you were there.

Vivid imagery can work hand-in-hand with motivation, as well as advancement of the plot. Good fiction is characterized by a number of things happening
at once. Compare the two paragraphs again, this time for motivation. In the second, we understand what the boy is feeling. He's in torment, because he loves

the trees and he loves the old man, while at the same time he hates him and seeks revenge. Motivation, I learned, had to be fully integrated rather than written occasionally into a plot.

If every class period that you're reading from a poem or a short story or a novel to your clsss, you stop and rave over remarkable imagery, and talk about how and why it's so incredible, your students will quickly learn what makes for good writing and lively reading. Announce triumphantly to the class, ''That's what good writing is!'' They'll take notice, since it seems to make such a great impression on the teacher, even if it is a little odd to be carrying on about it.

When you turn them loose on a story assignment, your last words to leave hanging in the air should be, ''Write with the five senses!'' Because you've pointed out countless examples all quarter, especially from their own writing wherever you find their own vivid imagery, they'll write that way. ''All right! I get it! Now give me some space and let me write!''

When they're reading each other's first drafts, ask them to look for places where the writer *told* instead of *showed*, to find examples of where specific imagery would make the writing come to life. They'll realize, in come cases, they've only summarized the story, without using specific details rooted in present action and dialogue. (Note that present action doesn't mean present tense; if you're writing in the past tense, stay in it. The effect of a lively scene written in the past tense seems very much of the present moment to the reader.)

Oftentimes, as I've read the first drafts of my own stories, I see scenes that I've thrown away by simply alluding to them, that could and should come to life in present action: I've *told*, not *shown*. If the scene brought to life would detour the story or bog it down, it's fine to allude to it, or to briefly summarize, but if the scene is an important one, it should come into focus through dialogue or description or both. Telling has its place when we want to speed things up; it serves often as a bridge, for example, to the next important scene.

TEACHING THE NITTY-GRITTY OF STYLE

Use Strong Verbs   Early in the year, a sophomore in one of my honors classes was shocked to get a piece of expository writing back that I'd graded as a C. It was his first year in high school, and he was worried. It wasn't the kind of result he was used to. My written comments were lost on him. He was hurt and confused. ''There are no mistakes on this paper,'' he pointed out, as calmly as he could. I admired his restraint, because I could tell he felt he was talking to an arbitrary sort of teacher. Was I punishing him for being gone two days a week for golf tournaments?

We had a writing conference. ''You avoid mistakes very well,'' I said, ''but you don't write well—yet. Good writing amounts to much more than avoiding mistakes. This year we're going to take it up to a much higher level—writing with style.''

"Style?" he objected, investing the word with the ring of subjectivity. He looked at me like, "So I have to write in a certain style to succeed in this class?"

"In writing, style is everything. Let's look at your paper, let's look at the verbs."

"You underlined about every one."

"I've been hammering on verbs on the overhead . . ."

"I was on a school trip."

"Let's catch you up. Verbs power sentences. Weak verbs leave sentences just lying there. Strong verbs provide drive. They embezzle, dream, jump, investigate, carry, crash, dissect, laugh, cry, win, or lose. Almost every verb you used, in three pages of writing, is a verb of being or a linking verb. All they do is serve as equal signs—they hook parts of sentences together. Almost always, you begin with the subject, you followed with a verb of being, then had no choice but to conclude with a predicate noun or adjective. That's why this writing is so flat."

"You just used two weak verbs."

"Good—you can spot them. Now try to limit yourself, the next time you write, to one weak verb per paragraph. Including the forms of 'to have'—it's usually vague and weak. You'll force yourself to learn how to use strong verbs. Nothing wrong with weak verbs if they're only one of the clubs in your bag."

"But you can't substitute strong verbs into these sentences."

"That's right. You rebuild the sentences, searching for good, basic, strong verbs—don't get too fancy or you'll sound phony. That's one of the things you do when you're revising a rough draft. The first draft is full of weak verbs—everybody's is. But when you revise, that's when you make it shine. As you come up with the strong verbs, concentrate as well on sentence variety and a pleasing, natural rhythm. Say the sentences aloud to yourself and listen for a smooth flow."

He went back to work, because he felt like he had the tools. He knew what he was supposed to do and why. It didnt' come automatically. He had to wrestle with old habits, force himself out of an old and deeply worn groove. But he did, because he cared about quality. (In fact, he was a state championship golfer.) By the end of the semester he was writing vigorous prose, and he knew it. Maybe he came to think of me as his writing coach.

Even with verbs that are not inherently weak verbs, there are stronger and weaker ones. The weak ones are vague, e.g. "to have," "to go." When possible, use a *particular* verb to give the reader an image, something the reader can see or touch or hear or smell or taste. "She inched through the tunnel" is more particular than "She went through the tunnel." Paint a precise picture with your verbs. Did she inch, or creep, or crawl, or slide, or grope, or elbow her way through the tunnel?

"Elbow" above is a good example of a strong verb, precise, a little unusual. The process for coming up with such verbs can be taught to students. Originally, I thought, "She went on her elbows." When I realized that "went" was weak, I looked elsewhere *in the same sentence* for something I could make into a verb. Students can get the hang of this skill, and it should be on their short list of what to look for when they're reviewing first draft material and considering how to revise it. If they see "We had a disagreement," they could consider, "We disagreed. . ." If they were to spot it in a first draft, "There was a protest from the team," they might revise by transforming the predicate noun into a strong verb: "The team protested. . ." Oftentimes, first draft sentences get out very little—all those words for one bit of meaning. By changing the predicate noun, predicate adjective, or object into a verb, we're natually going to try to combine sentences with something close by in order to complete the thought. That's how you build coherence in revision: tying things together, showing relationships, instead of leaving concepts isolated form each other, as if they were afraid of getting acquainted.

As you do with imagery, every time that you're reading a poem or a story to the class, stop when you find an especially good string of strong verbs and rave about them. Whenever you find a good run of them in a student's own writing, read those sentences aloud to the class and lean into the verbs. Act like you're about to have a stroke out of pure joy. They can hear with their own ears how good the sentences sound, and they'll be writing many more to please themselves and their apoplectic teacher.

Verb Tenses and Voice Counsel students, when they're writing fiction, to stay in the simple past unless there is a specific reason to deviate from it. ("He *cut* through the skin of the nearest tree and *winced* as he *withdrew* the saw.") The simple past is clean and pleasing to the reader. Sometimes, when you're referring to previous action, you need to use the past perfect (e.g. "had exploded"), but even when an entire paragraph is going to be set in that previous time, it suffices to start the paragraph off with only one or two uses of the past perfect, then slip into the simple past.

The -ing endings, if used throughout a paragraph or piece, tend to clutter it up. The present or past participle should be used for a specific purpose: continuing action. For example, "Beads of moisture were forming along the edges of the fresh wound."

Once in awhile a writer successfully writes a short story or a novel in the present tense. But it's to be avoided. Extended narration in the present tends to sound artificial and affected. Sometimes you go to it for a specific purpose. When you do, use the simple present, (e.g. "he drives") unless the meaning involves continuing action (e.g. "he is driving").

Some students tend to load their first drafts with verb constructions in the passive voice, for no particular reason. A writing teacher should demonstrate to them, with dozens of examples, the difference between a useful passive and a gratuitous one that weakens the writing by leaving out responsibility—namely, who did the action. If the house was robbed, and we don't know who did it, that's a good passive. It's like being run over; it's definitely something that happens *to* you. If a student wrote, "a man wearing a yellow windbreaker was observed running out of the house," there was no good reason to leave out the person doing the observing. The revision might read: "Mary Dermotty, a neighbor, saw a man wearing a yellow windbreaker run out of the house."

Nouns   As with verbs, the more particular nouns are generally stronger. "Trees grew by the river" doesn't paint a precise picture; "Cottonwoods grew by the river" does. It comes back to writing with the five senses. Abstract nouns (e.g. love, hatred, courage) are difficult to use well, especially in fiction. Students should be encouraged to dig in and provide the sense images that involve the reader and make the reader feel those things. To make the point, I like to hand out slips of paper to students, with different abstract emotions written on them, such as the three listed above. I ask them to write a short piece involving them or family members or made-up characters, which demonstrates that emotion without ever mentioning it by name. When they read it to the class, everybody will be listening closely to see how soon they can figure out which one it is.

Modifiers   Sometimes modifiers only weaken the nouns or verbs they're supposedly strengthening. My first drafts are peppered with "just" and "really." Usually they should be scrubbed. To say they "really weaken" is not as strong as simply saying, "they weaken" my writing. Moments ago, I revised a sentence by dropping an adverb: "Extended narration in the present tends to sound *awfully* artificial or affected."

Sometimes adverbs in your rough draft can signal a weak verb for you. If you wrote, "the skater moved *fluidly*," you were subconsciously trying to do something about the lack of specificity in "moved," so you tacked on the modifier. What improves the phrase? Yes, a strong verb. The skater glided, or danced, would do nicely.

It's easy to overuse modifiers. Laid on thick, unless they're in the hands of an Updike or a Faulkner, they lead a writer into false emotion, fanciness, or any number of forms of overwriting. Please turn back to my revised version of Cloyd chainsawing the old man's peach trees. Note the modifiers. They shouldn't stick out. The sentences should be carried by the nouns and the verbs. while you're studying that paragraph, note the noun and verb choices. Are they strong, are they particular? Why did I use "yellow" as a verb, when I could have used "turn yellow"? Why did I depart from the simple past, in choosing "were forming" instead of "formed"?

Once you talk about the principles of good writing, point them out when you spot them embodied in a short passage of whatever the class is reading together. Whenever you're reading together, you can also be teaching writing. As the principles add up, it's fun for the class to take one paragraph, like the one above, and talk about everything that's going on: voice, tone, imagery, verbs, nouns, modifiers, sentence variety, rhythm, connecting elements that contribute to coherence.

Tone and Diction   When you talk with students about choice of nouns or verbs, adjectives or adverbs, it's worthwhile talking about how the tone of the piece, which flows from the writer's choice of audience and voice, provides a natural guide for the writer when it comes to diction. If students believe they should be writing in a comfortable voice, they won't think they need to write from a thesaurus, and they won't create syntactical mare's nests.

Dialogue   Too many stage directions (e.g. "she exclaimed, looking astonished" or "he replied coldly") make a piece of dialogue look amateurish. It's another case of telling rather than showing. The reader's mental ear mostly fills in the motion from the contact of the actual conversation. When in doubt, use "said" instead of something overwritten like "jeered" or "fumed" or "snapped." "Said" can be repeated often without drawing attention to itself. Note in published dialogue how cleanly a conversation runs, how much restraint the narrator uses.

CONCLUSION

I've been looking at writing instruction from a writer's point of view as well as a teacher's. From my own experience, I know why writers write and why they want to be published: they want to have readers. They aren't laboring for the pure satisfaction of increasing their proficiency. We should recognize that the same is true of students in our classrooms. They largely view writing as an unrewarding exercise. By inviting them to write stories, we're inviting them to partake in the most fulfilling aspect of the reading-writing connection. When we invite them to write their own story for a real audience—each other—and then make the reward happen for them, by publishing some of their work and reading it as literature to that audience, we'll have made writing worthwhile for them. When they have readers, they'll think of themselves as writers.

REFERENCES

Guthrie, A.B. (1965). *The Blue Hen's Chick*. New York: McGraw Hill

In Chapter 18 of his autobiography, A.B. Guthrie provides invaluable maxims and specific examples that illustrate the do's and don'ts of fiction writing. Concise, ideal aid for teaching fiction writing in the classroom.

Hall, D. (1988). *Writing well*, (6th ed.) Scott-Foresman.

Donald Hall is a prose stylist as well as a poet, and he shares his ear for language in this practical text.

Hall, D. (1985, April 15). Bring back the out-loud culture, a "My Turn" essay, *Newsweek*.

Hall knows what's missing, and what will help to revitalize language arts education.

Hobbs, W. (1988). *Changes in Latitudes*. New York: Atheneum.

Hobbs, W. (1989). *Bearstone*. New York: Atheneum.

Hobbs, W. (1991). *Downriver*. New York: Atheneum.

Vonnegut, K. "How to write with style."

A two-page gem with advice to students or any aspiring writers, printed widely as a public service ad. For reprints, write: "Power of the Printed Word," International Paper Co., Dept. 5-H, P.O. Box 900, Elmsford, New York 10523.

*I've been writing short stories and childhood vignettes for about eight years now, and it wasn't until I read Paul Darcy Boles's book, **Storycrafting** (1984), that I understood how to revise my dialogue. I knew dialogue should move a plot forward. I knew it should reveal character traits. But once I understood Boles's concepts of surrounding description and explanatory action, I knew I could get better, and that my dialogue could, and would, do more than what mine was doing. From experience, I can tell you this lesson works. Children who write all dialogue have a strategy for breaking their talk apart, like planting cactus on a sandy hill to stop erosion. Children who use no dialogue in their stories, ever, learn that they've a head start on all of us, but that there's more to learn. Combine your own rewriting strategies with my chapter and with the rest of the chapters in Part II, and you'll be well-served, thanks to Boles, the other authors, and your own, sound intuitions.*

CHAPTER 10
WRITING DIALOGUE: TALK WITH INNER TONE

By Ruth Nathan

PART A: OATHS FROM *ALLEY PICKING: AN AMERICAN CHILDHOOD*

I promise never to forget you, best buddy, even upon my death bed you will be on my lips. I'll speak your name with my last breath. This I promise you, my faithful ally, copartner in prank, trusty champion—pal.

I know the words slipped between my lips as I fell asleep that night. And in my mind's eye I saw Marilyn listening, felt her breath on my cheek. We had promised never to forget, so I was setting the oath deep into my subconscious.

It had been a Saturday, grateful day of the week when all cares were buried deep because I knew she would call and we'd be off soon.

The season was summer of '55. I finally had my bike back, free to roam the neighborhood once again, my punishment for running away finally over. Marilyn called saying she wanted me to come to her house—no alley picking. A summer Saturday without alley picking. "Okay," I said wondering.

When I walked in, Mrs. Henry said Marilyn was up in her room. "She's acting weird," Mrs Henry said. "She ate breakfast with a turban wrapped around her head. An old dishtowel!"

Hmmm, I thought as I raced up the steps. This is getting good.

Marilyn's room was locked. Well, not locked, there was a chair pressing the door shut. "Let me in," I whispered, "it's Ruthie." I could hear music in the background, strange sounds. Marilyn's voice materialized from beneath her closed bedroom door. I stooped down and asked her what on earth was going on.

"Shhh," she said. "I'm going to open the door. When I do, come in fast so Bobby doesn't see." Bobby was her older brother.

"Okay."

The door opened just enough for me to squeeze through. I couldn't believe what I saw. Marilyn was dressed like a gypsy in a long flowing skirt, a tight blouse tied at the waist so her belly showed a bit, the dish towel around her head, long spindly earrings, and two black circles, one drawn on her forehead and the other on her nose. "Weird!" I said, "really weird."

"Shhh. Come here," she said as she took my hand. She'd made a dwarfish den out of four chairs and a dark green army blanket. We crawled under and into her inner-sanctum. "It's time we took our first oath."

"First oath for what?" I whispered.

"First oath for everlasting friendship. First oath for everlasting belief in the power of the Forces. First oath to be veterinarians."

"I don't want to be a veterinarian," I protested.

"Well, first oath to BE somebody, not just anybody."

I thought a minute. "Okay," I said.

With that Marilyn took out a pin. "We have to poke our fingers—and swear with blood."

All of a sudden I felt like the day Marilyn opened her mouth when it was full of bananas. And I thought of the demonic nurse at the doctor's office that thrived on pricking hard. "No, I don't want to."

"Ruthie, trust me! And trust the Forces."

"The Forces?"

"The Forces," she said in a slow, bewitching way.

"The Forces."

"Yes. The Forces."

"Okay," I said. "But how far will you put the pin in?"

"Not far. Swear to the Forces," she said.

I thought if I didn't do this now, with her, my best friend in the whole world, I might never get the chance to say a real oath again. So, I closed my eyes, remembered how I'd always fasted on Yom Kippur, held out my finger and said go.

And she did. It wasn't too bad, either. Then she pricked herself. I was awe-struck. How could she prick herself? Oh, how I wanted to be that tough, that self-assured, that daring. Then I had a thought. "I'll make up the oath." I said. "Close your eyes." Looking straight at Marilyn, who was squinting in disbelief, I demanded once again, "Close your eyes!" She did. "Good," I said. "Now say 'I'."

"I"

"Marilyn Henny"

"Marilyn Henny"
"promise"
"promise"
"never to forget my best buddy, Ruthie."
"never to forget my best buddy, Ruthie."
"Even upon my death bed,"
"Even upon my death bed,"
I was making this up as I went along—Even upon my death bed."
"I already said that," she said.
"her name will be on my lips," I continued,
"her name will be on my lips."
"This I promise you,"
"This I promise you,"
"my faithful ally,"
"my faithful ally,"
"copartner in prank,"
"copartner in prank,"
"trusty champion,"
"trusty champion,"
"pal,"
"pal,"
"until death do us part."
"until death do us part."
"Amen," I said.
"Amen," she said.
And with this done, I closed my eyes and knew beyond a shadow that surely I would be somebody someday. I felt, then, as powerful as I ever would.

PART B: WRITING DIALOGUE

The blue jay we had was like another friend added to the family. He was a great pet, too. It all began like this . . .

I was at school, but my brother, who was five, was at home with a babysitter and his friend, Jamie. My brother was riding his bike when he saw something on the driveway. He rode over to it and called Jamie. She ran over to my brother, Jon. They took a short look at the baby bird and ran into the house and got their sitter.

Michelle came outside with Jon and Jamie. She saw the bird and said, "Jon, find a shoe box. Jamie, find some rags." They soon came back with a shoe box and rags.

This is Jessica Faigle's opening to *Our Blue Jay*, a book she wrote while a fifth grader at Midvale School in Birmingham, Michigan. The excerpt exemplifies a lesson I learned about writing dialogue years ago from a master American storyteller and the author *Storycrafting* (1984, p. 82), Paul Darcy Boles. "Real dialogue," says Boles, "is shaped, balanced, and trimmed to fit the exact contours of the story it graces. One word too much of it and the story will slip out of motion like a gyroscope top jumping the string. One word too little and the story will have a vacancy in it, a space that needs filling . . ."

Notice how Jessica has fit "Jon, find a shoe box. Jamie, find some rags" into the contour of her piece: She's shared her view of the rescue scene first, somehow knowing that we'd need it in order to understand the call for the box and rags. It comes at just the right time, too, and trimmed to perfection. And, why do we sense the dialogue is a call, rather than a whisper, even though Jessica has used, "said?" Maybe all the action before—with the children riding bikes and running—has something to do with it.

Boles helps us understand Jessica's success when he tells us that prose encircling dialogue has the "inner tone of surrounding description and explanatory action." To understand the "inner tone" Boles refers to, try doing what I did: First get a pen or pencil. Now, underline the lines/phrases around her dialogue that you think *describe* Jessica's scene with two lines (lines which detail background information and/or visual aspects of the scene), and the lines/phrases that *show action* with a single line. (Sentences like, "I was at school but my brother, who was five, was at home . . ." describe, while ones like "he rode over to it and called . . ." show action.) The description and action surrounding Michelle's call give her words meaning, making them not only believable, but needed. (Below, see one child's attempt where a double line represents description, a single, action.)

The blue jay we had was like another friend added to the family. He was a great pet, too. It all began like this . . .

<u>I was at school, but my brother, who was five, was at home with a babysitter</u> <u>and his friend, Jamie. My brother was riding his bike whe he saw something on</u> <u>the driveway. He rode over to it and called Jamie. She ran over to my brother Jon.</u> <u>They took a short look at the baby bird and ran into the house and got their sitter.</u> <u>Michelle came outside with Jon and Jamie.</u> She saw the bird and said, "Jon, find a shoe box. Jamie, find some rags." <u>They soon came back with a shoe box and rags.</u>

We see action working its magic again with Jessica's indirect dialogue later on in her story, where we get a detailed view of Michelle's actions before she tells her charges that the bird might die. I've put the indirect dialogue in italics:

Michelle padded the box with the rags.
She put a rag on her hand and carefully
picked the baby bird up and put it in the
shoe box. Then she put the bird in the
kitchen and left it alone. *She told Jon*
and Jamie that the bird might die.

It's interesting that Michelle's actions help us see what the shoe box might look like. With the use of the word "padded" we get the idea that there's not just one piece of cloth, but many, and that all together the box might be a comfortable nest for the wayward jay.

Now let me share some more conversation, but this time from my introductory piece, "Oaths." First, let's look at my dialogue striped down to its bare bones:

"Let me in," I whispered; "it's Ruthie."

"Shhh," she said. "I'm going to open the door. When I do, come in fast so Bobby doesn't see."

"Okay."

Take a look at it now, as I place it back into its full context, with the inner tone of the story supporting the interaction between Ruthie and Marilyn.

Marilyn's room was locked. Well, not locked, there was a chair pressing the door shut. "Let me in," I whispered, "it's Ruthie." *I could hear music in the background, strange sounds.* *Marilyn's voice materialized from beneath her closed bedroom door. I stooped down and asked her* *what on earth was going on.*

"Shhh," she said. "I'm going to open the door. When I do, come in fast so Bobby doesn't see." *Bobby was her older brother.*

"Okay."

The door opened just enough for me to squeeze through.

I find children are very excited to learn what Boles and Jessica know, and what I have learned. I often ask children who are writing dialogue frequently to do what I did when I read Boles's work (and what I asked you to do when you read Jessica's): Copy some dialogue and then underline the surrounding description and explanatory action—be it from Jessica's piece, from one of mine, from a book by a published author they admire, from a classmate's book that has dialogue they like, or from a piece of their own. (Most books by Chris Van Allsburg work beautifully.)

Sometimes I ask a small group of children who are writing stories, whether they're writing dialogue just then or not, or whether they've asked me to help them with their dialogue or not, to embellish a few lines that talk with description and action. Then we take turns underlining what's what. I do this for two reasons. First, many young children's stories have no dialogue, but lots of description and action. The reader nearly begs for dialogue. When stories are long, readers often get bored and want to hear what the characters would say. This exercise gives children who don't generally write dialogue a chance to begin rewriting from their strength. (That is, they've got the dialogue and are good at adding background, visuals, and movement.) Second, some stories come to us as all dialogue, and we—the children and I—get lost. We want to cry out, Who's saying what? What's happening? Individually, or in a small group, this is a fun exercise to try.

Mindful of my reasons, here's an example you might try underlining. It is the opening of second grader, Jonathan Dalin's book, *One Mystery is Tough Enough*.

Chapter One: Can You Help Me

I was coming home from school one day when I saw something weird.
I looked and saw a warehouse.
It had a little door. I ran off to the side of the street.
I sneaked around the corner. I ran on top of a crate.
I looked and saw a man. I was very still. I called my agent friend from a nearby phone. "Can you help me?"
End of "Can You Help Me."

Chapter Two: Silence

I waited to hear his answer. He said, "No, I can't. I have a piano recital."
I hung up.
   End of "Silence."

The children and I have discovered many things through underlining, the first of which is that Boles doesn't mention everything that supports dialogue: Characters' inner thoughts and feelings also surround conversation. For example, here's an excerpt from the middle of fifth grader, Adam Palmer's book, *My Stuffed Animals*, a class favorite. (The book begins with a listing of all the stuffed animals Adam has, where we learn that the animals talk back.)

Once I ran away with my animals. I was 4 years old. I was on my bigwheel and all of my animals were in a sack. I was running away because I didn't like the babysitter I had. I packed crackers, bread, cheese, and a cold hamburger. I was all prepared.
   "Let's go," said Chubs. We left.
   I kept going around the block, and never noticed! I got very tired and stopped right in front of my house, and still didn't notice! Then my babysitter came out and told me to come in. I was scared when I saw her for I *thought* she was far away. Then Ace popped his head out and said, "We've been going around the block, silly."
   Then Guineas said, "Aw shoot! I don't like that babysitter. Do we have to go back in?"
   "We better," I said.

After enjoying the story for its own sake on many occasions, the children and I copied the passage I've shared above into our journals and began underlining. We had already tried this with one of my paragraphs, where we discovered sometimes it was hard to tell what was description and what was action.

When we go to Adam's line, ''I was scared when I saw her for I thought she was far away,'' we talked about how thoughts and feelings often embellish good dialogue too, something we hadn't discussed before.

Another thing we learned was that not all good dialogue needs embellishing! Sometimes dialogue works with absolutely nothing surrounding it. Here's first grader, Eric Rothfeder's, piece called *Big Bear*. We agreed that background knowledge on everyone's part would be so high that nothing more needed to be said:

> ''Good morning Big Bear. Time for breakfast.''
> ''Okay.''
> ''What did you do to the playroom?''
> ''I did nothing.''
>
> ''No, you made a mess. Now you clean it up.''
> ''Okay.''
> ''But I still love you.''

Of course, it's not important that Eric, or any first grader, know what an older child, or an adult, might benefit from knowing. (Personally, I'd never ask a first grader to do what I've mentioned here.) But I do stand by the notion that by sharing writing strategies professional writers, such as Boles, tell us about what is *worth* doing with an appropriate audience. Critics might argue that this type of direct teaching isn't worth doing because it interferes with natural development. But I find that children who understand the possibilities provided in this lesson make use of them if the time's right, and don't if it's not. Of course, I always *try* to make the match.

You might consider taking another look at my piece. Check my dialogue against Boles's insights, as well as Adam's class's insights. Of course, test you own dialogue, too, in order to discover more about *your* writing. I've argued over and over again (Temple, Nathan, Burris, and Temple, 1988; Nathan, Temple, Juntunen, and Temple, 1989; Nathan and Temple, 1990) that writing teachers must write if they're going to teach the subject. This lesson, as well as all the other lessons in *Writers in the Classroom*, is predicated on the assumption that you do, in fact, write with your students often.

FROM WRITING DIALOGUE TO WRITING PLAYS: EXTENSION ACTIVITY

Once children understand the choices authors have when writing dialogue, changing their stories into plays is easier. Description and action become parenthetical notes in script, or accentuated speech; while inner thoughts and feelings need to be said out loud, or shown through action notes in parenthetical remarks. Here's an example your class might begin working with. It's the opening page from fourth grader, Terry Strother's book, *Clones*, followed by the opening page of his play, *Clones*. Notice how Terry begins by giving the narrator lines that s/he will use to set the stage: "it's the year 2010. . ." I'll leave the rest to you and your class. Discover how Terry moves from one to the other. I think you'll have an easy time of it now that you know more about how dialogue is frequently written.

The Book

One day in the year 2010, I was sitting at the shuttle station. While sitting I noticed something I had never noticed before. It was a very old house with lights blinking on and off inside. I decided to investigate. As I got closer and closer, I felt chills running up and down my spine. I found a small dirty window and peered in. I saw an old man working on somebody or something, on a table with a device in what looked like a mouth. Then somebody grabbed my shoulder and said, "What are you doing here, son!"

"Nothing," I said timidly as I turned slowly around. Then I said, "Is that a person? What are you doing to him?"

"Nothing he said sharply."

The Play

Setting: Curtain closed, narrator at one side of the stage.

Narrator: It's the year 2010. Our story opens with a boy named Terry waiting for a shuttle ride home. While sitting at the station, he saw something that he never noticed before. There was an old house nearby with the lights blinking on and off. He decided to investigate.

Curtain opens outside of house.

Terry: (Walks across the stage and looks in a window.) Wow, what a neat old house! (Rubs his hand across a dirty window to see inside.) Oh, my gosh! It looks like an old man working on something. . . .or somebody. . . .with some kind of device in what looks like a mouth!!
Guard: (Walks quietly across stage and grabs Terry's shoulder. Terry jumps, frightened.) What are you doing here, son!
Terry: (Turning around) Nothing. Is that a person? What are you doing to him?
Guard: Nothing, kid. Now scram! Shouldn't you be in bed?

CONCLUSION

Conclusions usually recapitulate, give the reader a chance to be told, yet again, what's been learned. I think my point's been made; but rather than leaving you just yet, I would like to do the unheard of: introduce a new idea, here, in my conclusion. Don't worry about your dialogue until your draft is pretty well done. What I've tried to show you in this chapter is how to help children, and yourself, look at your dialogue upon rewriting. Actually, I do most of my serious crafting after I've got a good part of my rough draft out—sometimes I'm talking about the whole first draft—not just pages, or chapters. That's the way it goes with me. Please ask yourself what you do. And, ask your students what works best for them.

REFERENCES

Boles, P.D. (1984). *Storycrafting*. Cincinnati, OH: Writer's Digest Books.

Nathan, R. Temple, F., Juntenen, K., and Temple, C. (1989). *Classroom strategies that work: An elementary teacher's guide to process writing.* Portsmouth, NH: Heinemann Educational Books.

Nathan, R., and Temple, C. (1990). Creating reading and writing environments. In Shanahan (Ed.), *Reading and writing together: New perspectives for the classroom.* Norwood, MA: Christopher-Gordon Publishers, Inc.

Temple, C. Nathan, R., & Temple, F. (1988). *The beginnings of writing.* Boston: Allyn and Bacon.

SELECTED BIBLIOGRAPHY

Asher, S. (1989). *Wild words! How to train them to tell stories.* New York: Walker and Company.

Several chapters in this priceless little book show how dialogue works to set the stage, develop characters, and move a plot forward, all traditional uses of dialogue.

Kohl, H. (1988). *Making theater: Developing plays with young people.* New York: Teachers and Writers Collaborative.

One of the best ways to understand how dialogue works is to have children write their own plays from the literature they are reading. This marvelous book will help you and your students do that.

Roy Peter Clark is daring the way Will Hobbs is daring. Says Clark, "I admit that I learned something in my grammar and syntax classes: I learned to hate grammar and syntax." With openers like these (see my preface to Hobbs), readers know they're in for a ride. But, as with Hobbs, Clark doesn't let down. He's funny. And he weaves grammar (what's a verb, anyway?) and correct syntax into issues more related to style, a much easier pill for students to swallow. Combined with Hobbs's work, these two chapters might easily provide points of entree into a writer's handbook.

CHAPTER 11
BORN TO BE WILD: USE HUMOR TO TEACH GRAMMAR, STYLE AND USAGE

By Roy Peter Clark

PART A: BORN TO BE WILD:

I always favored busing, but, then again, I had no choice. I lived about three miles from the Catholic high school for boys, so, lacking a private chauffeur, and not wanting to ride my bike through the snow, I learned to accept as part of my life that ubiquitous American symbol: the bulbous-nosed yellow sardine can on wheels.

Through most years, the experience of riding the bus was little more than tolerable, but for one year it became exquisite, thanks, in part, to the antics of our bus driver, a criminally irresponsible adult who became known to us, then and forever more, as Bussy.

I never knew his real name, and it didn't matter, because every boy would greet him each morning and bid him farewell each afternoon using his honorary title. "Hey, Bussy," or "Take it easy, Bussy," or, eventually, "Kiss your wife for me, Bussy." Bussy was probably twice our age, a short man with a round, open face, his thin lips set in a crazy smirk. I remember a tan cap he wore, taxi driver style.

It's fair to say that for the 1964–65 high school year Bussy brought joy to our lives. He made our bleary-eyed mornings delightful and helped us celebrate our afternoon escapes. He never missed a day of work, which was probably his only exercise of professional responsiblitiy.

Bussy was a maniac, pure and simple.

Let's start with the gears.

His bus probably had five gears, but Bussy was basically a two-gear driver: slow and fast. He would intentionally adjust the clutch and engine speeds so that each shift of gears brought a grinding noise so profound that it seemed to come from the bowels of some dying animal, a brontosaurus, perhaps. "Hey, Bussy, gind me another pound!" was the standard joke, yelled at least once a day from the back of the bus. Bussy did more for grinding than Gypsy Rose Lee.

Then came the bumps. In short, Bussy never met a curb he didn't like. On every right turn, he would try to run the right rear tire over the curb. The effect was to shake up the boys in the back, and we loved it. In anticipation, we'd sometimes sit on the backs of our seats to see if we could ride through the bump without hitting our heads on the ceiling.

The largest curb was right in front of the school, and he'd shoot for it every day, sometimes taking so much of it that our books spun through the air like rabid Frisbees.

One day he missed the curb, and we booed ferociously. But Bussy aimed to please, so, to the shock of the traffic behind him, he backed up and took the curb at ramming speed, a 6.5 on the Richter scale.

About midway through the year, Bussy took the art of curb jumping to new depths. One morning we were running early, so Bussy decided to take a detour through one of the little suburban towns near the high school. He drove down a quiet street lined with tall trees and neat two-story houses. On the corner was a single, empty lot. None of us guessed what Bussy had in mind.

He made a hard left turn over the curb and took the bus through the lot, tearing up turf all the way, and leaned on the horn. When we realized what was happening, we broke into a cheer, yanked down the windows, stuck out our heads and screamed. Bussy roared the bus out of sight before the startled neighbors could get our number.

Bussy could speed through his route with the cunning of a moonshiner, but he was also famous for his unscheduled stops. On a whim, he might drop you off three blocks from the appointed stop, or, in bad weather, might drive well out of his way to deposit you at your front door.

One day Bussy was driving us home when we caught sight of a commotion outside a local junior high school. A fight was going on, and a crowd gathered as a greasy punk dressed in leather pounded on a kid half his size. The crowd, of course, was rooting for the punk.

"Bussy, stop!" yelled Billy, the tallest kid on the bus, and one of Bussy's favorites. We screeched to a halt, and Billy busted out the emergency exit in the back and landed on the tarmac like something out of Marvel Comics. Justice was swift and unmerciful. The crowd of kids gawked in awe as Bussy reclaimed Billy, shifted into some unspeakable gear, and set Old Yeller lurching into the afternoon sun.

It was as if Bussy were our squadron commander, by God, and we were his black sheep.

The apotheosis of Bussy's evil genius took place near the end of the year on one brutally hot afternoon. As we staggered on board, fatigued from our studies, Bussy greeted us with a mad smile, and there, in fill view of the principal's office, as if he were handing out diplomas, offered each one of us a can of beer.

We knew it was insane, but there we were, inmates driving in circles around the prison, right past the priests' residence and through Our Lady's Courtyard, knocking down cold ones. This rebellious act became the ultimate revenge on our oppressors in the school, and, I suppose, on our parents who sent us there.

Let me set the record straight. If my kids ever rode a bus to school and I discovered the driver was passing out beer, I'd perform a citizen's arrest followed by a summary execution.

But every kid on our bus would have appeared before the Supreme Court to testify in Bussy's defense. We loved him because he was the only adult we knew who didn't tell us what to do. In a year when Lyndon Johnson was elected president, it was Bussy who became our hero, the champion of our unwritten Constitution, which protected, most of all, our right to be wild.

PART B: USE HUMOR TO TEACH GRAMMAR, STYLE, AND USAGE

Teaching grammar can be funny. See, it worked. I made you laugh.

You are laughing, no doubt because *fun* is not the f-word you associate with grammar. You prefer *frustration*. I understand. Learning the rules of language was certainly no fun for me. I was one of those kids who memorized parts of speech, circled subordinate clauses, and diagrammed sentences while our teacher, a grim nun, smacked her desk with a yardstick for emphasis.

"But you learned the stuff, didn't you?" you ask, "and see, now you're a writer."

I admit that I learned something in my grammar and syntax classes: I learned to hate grammar and syntax. As I remember the experience, and think of the experiences of my three daughters, who hate grammer and syntax in their own way, I see two key problems:

1. Technical aspects of language were never taught in the context of writing. Learning this grammar stuff through drills, homework, and worksheets was one thing. Writing, if assigned at all, was another.
2. Grammar was taught as a set of rules rather than a bag of tools.

I was probably in the fifth grade, for example, when I learned the distinction between the active voice and the passive voice. Being a diligent student, I mastered this distinction by the age of 11. If pressed, I could even recite something like this: "If the subject is the doer of the action, the verb is in the active voice; if the subject receives the action, the verb is in the passive voice."

How come you aren't laughing any more? Not much fun, is it? Not only is it funless, but it seems, in that old formula, irrelevant to the needs of students. So I learned the distinction between active and passive? If I hadn't feared Sister Grammatica's yardstick, I might have shouted: "So what?!"

How much better if Sister had confided: "Hey kids, I'm going to teach you a little trick to make your writing better." She could have taken her cue from Strunk & White's *The Elements of Style* (1979), which explains how active verbs help make your writing more direct, more concise, and more vigorous. "There were a great number of dead leaves lying on the ground" magically becomes "Dead leaves covered the ground," if you can only find the active verb.

As I describe in my book *Free to Write* (1987), students use active verbs all the time, from their first stories in the earliest grades. They lack only the name *active* verb to turn a grammatical concept into a tool they can use to improve thousands of sentences.

Which brings me to those 51 sentences that compose the story of Bussy. They came to life because a friend of mine laughed at a dinner party. At such feasts, we often regale each other with humorous tales of our childhood. He spins yarns out of Indiana. I respond with legends of New York. Suddenly, I remembered Bussy and spat out the string of anecdotes that became my story. Tom French convulsed with laughter. ''You've got to write that one,'' he said. Even my wife, who is annoyingly nonchalant during the liturgical recital of my boyhood adventures, offered encouragement.

Two days later I blasted out a draft of the story, not my usual mode of writing, but I attributed my speed that day to my rehearsal at the dinner party. During revision, I tinkered with almost every sentence, paying attention to dozens of tiny details of language and information. During one stage of revision, I employed three favorite writing strategies:

1. Not every verb has to be active, but I want to make sure that, generally speaking, I'm writing in the active voice, especially when I describe action.
2. I try to keep subjects and verbs close together at or near the beginning of sentences. This placement informs the reader quickly and makes even long sentences comprehensible.
3. I look for opportunities to put special words or phrases at the end of sentences and pararaphs.

I learned these tricks over time from teachers willing to reveal them to me. In return, I feel a responsiblity to pass them on to another generation of students in a way that empowers them to improve their own sentences.

So one hot summer day in St. Petersburg, Florida, I offered copies of my Bussy story to a class of 24 high school students. The students, aged 13–18, were participating in a program at The Poynter Institute called ''Writers Camp.'' My job that day was to share some ideas about the technical aspects of grammar and language. When I entered the room, they were on their guard, definitely not laughing.

The climate changed when I read Bussy. After every few paragraphs, I would stop to get their reactions to the story. ''Is there anything in the story that you find interesting or noteworthy?'' I asked. ''Or anything that you want to ask me questions about?''

''I liked the bulbous-nosed sardine can.''

''Why?''

''Because it's odd to think of a bus with a nose. It kind of gives it a personality.''

Another student: ''I like when you say the books spun through the air like rabid Frisbees.''

''Thanks. It took me a while to come up with the word 'rabid.' 'Frisbees' was easy. But books don't travel through the air the same way, so I needed a word that meant crazed and dangerous. I think I made a list and then came up with 'rabid.' By the way, what do you call it when you compare one thing like that to something else?''

One student answered: "Is that a metaphor or a simile? I always get them confused."

"It's a simile, because I use the word 'like.'"

Throughout this process, I asked them to read the story with me carefully to see how the language works. "Writers read their own stories more closely than anyone else," I suggested. "That's how I decide to make changes in the story."

"What kind of things do you look for?" asked one young man.

"Well, when it comes to the language of the story, I look for lots of things. But I have three favorite things to look for."

The trap was baited. They were about to learn something about language, grammar, and syntax, and they may not have been laughing, but they were certainly not frowning. The humor in the story had relaxed them.

I made sure that all the students had a draft of a work in progress on their desks as I taught these next lessons. I divided them into groups of four so they could help each other.

"OK, I'd like you to take any paragraph in your story and underline the subjects and circle the verbs. If you are not sure how to do this, go ahead and consult a neighbor; if you're still unsure, raise your hand."

This process took about five minutes. I heard chatter and consultation, exactly what I'd hoped for, as the more confident students offered advice to the confused or uncertain. I walked around the room and spot-checked the exercise.

"Now let's talk about the relationship between the subject and verb. Has anyone here heard the expression 'active voice' before?" About half the class recognized the phrase, but only two or three understood the concept. Several students confused voice with tense.

Using the most basic examples, I moved through a mini-lesson on the board. THE BOY HIT THE BALL.

"What is the relationship between subject and verb in this sentence? Does the subject perform the action, or receive it? Right, it performs the action. Therefore, the verb is active."

Then I write: THE BALL HIT THE BOY.

I turned the sentence around, so some students assumed I'd changed it from active to passive. I explained why the verb is still active.

"Now, let's turn these active verbs into passive ones. Spend a minute doing that."

Several students got it: THE BALL WAS HIT BY THE BOY. THE BOY WAS HIT BY THE BALL.

"What makes the sentences with active verbs better?"

"Well, the active ones are shorter and more interesting."

I asked them to count the words in each sentence. Five for active. Seven for passive. And the extra words, *was* and *by*, added nothing to the reader's understanding.

We look at a paragraph in my story:

He *made* a hard left over the curb and *took* the bus through the lot, tearing up turf all the way, and *leaned* on the horn. When we *realized* what *was happening*, we broke into a cheer, *yanked* down the windows, *stuck* out our heads and *screamed*. Bussy *roared* the bus out of sight before the startled neighbors *could get* our number.

They see that all 11 verbs in the paragraph are active. Some, they understand, are more vigorous than others, but the cumulative builds action.

"Now look at your paragraph. See if you can find a sentence with a passive verb or a form of the verb 'to be.' What happens to your sentence, and to the paragraph, if you revise it to the active?"

Back to the small groups. More chatter, pointing to pages, crossing out, and scribbling. I cruise around the room again, keeping my eyes and ears open.

Phong Luu had written this paragraph.

"One reggae artist *has left* his legendary imprint on the world with lyrics and music that *overcame* racial, political, religious, and language barriers. 'Bob Marley's songs *carried* a message of freedom. They *taught* morals. You *listen* and *become* one with his music. You *understand* what he *was saying*,' says Thompson."

She discovers all her verbs are in the active voice.

Jacob Moon wondered about this sentence in his story: "Ingalls is very knowledgeable in her own culture, as well as many others." What would happen if he turned it into: "Ingalls knows her own culture, as well as many others?"

The sentence was more simple and direct, but did he lose something by revising "knowledgeable" to "knows?"

"That's exactly the kind of question you should ask yourself," I responded.

I used the same teaching strategies described above to teach them the value of keeping subjects and verbs close together near the beginning of sentences, and the power of emphatic word order. First I taught a mini-lesson, using examples from my own story. Then I'd have them turn to their own stories to look for examples where they used the same technique. Finally, I'd ask them to attempt to revise one or more of their sentences using their new tools.

They enjoyed the lesson on emphatic word order most of all. They recognized how the technique contributed to the humor of my story, pointing to sentences such as: "Bussy did more for grinding than Gypsy Rose Lee." (I was surprised that a number of students understood the joke.)

". . .that our books spun through the air like rabid Frisbees."

". . .as if he were handing out diplomas, offered each one of us a can of beer."

They also took pleasure in the story's final phrase: "our right to be wild."

"How can you think about all those tools while you're writing?" asked one young woman.

"I usually don't think about them at all during the first draft. I try to let the language take over. Some of those things happen automatically. Later on, though, while I'm revising, I can do anything I want with the sentences. Go ahead and check your stories. I bet you use the same tools. You just haven't had names for them."

Sure enough, Frank Witsil had concluded his story this way:

"Rick LaMore, English teacher at the school said every year the English department decorated a bulletin board. This year, they hung in the halls a tribute to Martin
Luther King, Jr., as a black leader and for his contributions to the advancement
of civil rights. But shortly after it was put up, it was set on fire, and burned.

"No one knew who burned the board. Perhaps it was a joke, or it might have
been a statement. But the next day a simple note was found pinned to the charred
board.

"It said: 'You can't burn a dream.'"

I pointed to the word "dream." I said, "Look what happens when you end
with a powerful word."

No one was laughing, but I couldn't help smiling.

REFERENCES

Clark, R.P. (1987). *Free to write: A journalist teaches young writers*. Portsmouth, NH: Heinemann
    Educational Books.
Strunk, W. Jr. and White, E.B., *The elements of style*. (3rd ed.). New York: Macmillan.

*Few published teacher-poets would expose their evolving work in class and admit the day that they did so was a turning point in their **writing** careers. Perhaps their teaching careers, but not their writing careers. I've been inside many writing classrooms taught by some of the best and the brightest, and more times then I'd like to admit, feelings of inadequacy lingered. **Gloria Nixon-John** turns all that horror (ubiquitous, I've learned) upside down and inside out. She dares to **ask** about an author's intent. She dares to suggest. If you prefer Nixon-John's delicate approach to revision, read the Steinberg, Blackhawk, and Monkmeyer chapters right away. They make a fine quartet.*

CHAPTER 12
REVISION
AND BALANCE
IN POETRY
By Gloria Nixon-John

PART A: MY POETRY

*It is difficult to get the news from poems
but men die miserable every day for
lack of what is found there*

William Carlos Williams

Drought

My father's angry words hang
zig zag, hidden in grey clouds
passing, silenced by molten blue.
And if it would rain a soft
summer shower, I would dance
in his anger, anoint his
pouting child, and if the rain
would stay for a day or more
to move the river of denial,
we would mold cool forgiveness
out of the amiable mud, and
the little white flowers of his
embrace would grow again, and
I could gather them at his grave.

Nests
for Renee

There's risk in building high or low.
Between the boughs, I've seen them, chalices
of twig and twine and daily news,
of swooping, fastening tree to sky,
and life that teeters on the edge
and tumbles into flight . . .

As a child I climbed to them.
Warned not to touch the wedgewood
shell, I balanced brave for days
but always missed the birth of beak
and wing and novice song. How I
mourned the fallen egg, unsure of what
to do with life held neatly, still
inside.

Once on the North Shore,
my head craned toward the waves in search
of sanderlings, you buried yourself
in sand. "Take my picture," you said,
only toes and hat exposed. Today
you walk up the steps of Wesley Hall,
an overwrought magnet, Gallagher
would say, hair flushed into November's
wind.

As you notice me, birds scatter.
Their shadows slice the earth.

The Guilford's Dog

Weeks after my visit I imagine her
curled beneath the ficus tree.
I recall her resolute breath lifting
fur whimsical as down, the creak and
curve of spine, the carved hope of miracle.

Her snore makes the Guilfords laugh,
lean toward the hearth, touch one another
and speculate about dog dreams.
It's a T-bone dream, one says,
or chasing the colt beyond the barren
apple grove, up over the hill that August
afternoon, to swim in Little Lake.

Remember how that baby dove right in
beside that silly dog?

The Guilford's dog is dying
and it is a visitor she dreams about.
In the dream she becomes wet clay
that the visitor shapes and strokes deliberately.
She chooses the visitor's coat to make her bed,
looks to him, slants an ear,
feigns against all withering,
so that he might fetch up the finest dry bone
to toss beyond their reach
into the barking shadows.

Salmon Cakes

She made him salmon cakes
every Thursday for years,
fresh sometimes or Sockeyed
from a can. When he was always
late for dinner, she would place
sprigs of parsley on them and
robe them in Saran Wrap.
It was no surprise to her
the day he decided never
to come home. Still she made
salmon cakes for a dozen Thursdays.

Eventually she phoned old beaus
and met them one by one.
Some held wine glasses like
religious offerings to a
chandelier god. Others sported
Detroit Tiger caps and caressed
her with cliches. One little
sullen man put his cheek to her breast
and promised a forever of forevers.

Careful not to make the same
mistake again, she cooked more
exotic things for the men
that followed. And it was only
occasionally that she thought
about the salmon, their agate spines
twisting against the tumbling thunder
of some far off current.

PART B: REVISION AND BALANCE

Writing poetry is one of the ways I celebrate life. It is, for me, a sustained meditation, an evaluative look at nearly everything that mind and time will allow. While this weighty description may make poetry writing seem like a painful deliberate process—it comes, in fact, quite naturally. I don't mean to say that I write great poetry or that my poems are born without need for refinement. I mean that lines—visions and images—just seem to happen and I best write them down when they do. I mean to say that an inner voice speaks to me about my ordinary experiences that lead to extraordinary feelings and thoughts. Later I take care to nurture some of these ideas and dismiss other ideas and the result is the promise of a poem. I have come to realize that this is a slow, sometimes painful, sometimes exhilarating, process and that I do all of this in order to create a work that satisfies some artistic need.

Poet Robert Pinsky, in his remarkable work *Poetry and The World* (1988, p.3) articulates his feeling regarding poetry, and in so doing, helps me comprehend the need for poetry in my life and justifies my desire to encourage my students to write poetry as well. Pinsky says:

> It has occurred to me that many of my favorite works, recent and historical, involve a bridge or space between the worldly and the spiritual. Poetry itself suggests such a dualism, related in ways I can't unravel. That is, the medium of words is social, yet it can also be the fabric of the most rarified—introspective ideas, and the sensuousness of poetry is to give elegance and significance to the sounds that breath makes vibrating in the mouth and throat, animating by art those bodily noises of communication.

I know that many teachers steer clear of teaching poetry writing; some avoid dealing with poetry altogether. And I must admit, I once approached poetry teaching reluctantly myself. In fact, it was difficult to convince my students of the merits of poetry, and that their own poetry writing might be worthwhile, until I started writing poetry myself. In so tooling with the art (alone as well as under the direction of many fine poets), I discovered much. The two most significant and immediate discoveries that had an impact on my teaching came first from what I learned about how personal poetry writing is, and secondly, what I learned about revision.

Let me explain how I came to this point.

In the summer of 1986, I had the fortunate experience of working with poet Stephen Dunn, and seven other poetry students at The Aspen Writers' Conference. The loss of my mother in 1985 had catapulted me back into my poetry as a source of expression and therapy, so I went off to Aspen, as one might guess, with a collection of rather maudlin stuff. And while my poems served my most immediate need—personal expression and healing—I knew, because of my unsatiable appetite for reading poetry, that my poems could be better.

Up to this point, my own idea regarding revision dealt with sharpening: putting a better word here or there, using poetic devices, expanding or cutting the poem in certain areas. I didn't really have the bigger theoretical picture that a good poet needs. Stephen Dunn helped me see the poem as a whole. Specifically, Dunn pointed out through many fine examples the need for poems to contain a balance of opposites—of good with evil, of sorrow with joy—the dark with the light. He pointed out the need for the poet to meander a bit, to avoid linear or predictable poems.

I left Aspen, needless to say, with my ego a bit dented; but with the bigger picture about poetry writing looming, slightly out of reach, but there.

STARTING WITH THE BIG PICTURE

I wanted to share what I learned with my students without hurting their feelings or slicing into their egos. I decided to present certain elements of this bigger picture before we did anything else in the area of poetry or poetry writing. That is, instead of working on creating metaphors or using other poetic devices, we talked about theme. We looked at many contemporary poems and discussed what we thought was the author's intent—or focus. We even discussed when we felt intent broke down or was lost and why. We also looked at the careful balancing act that many fine poets have mastered.

Next in a brave move, I brought one of my poems to class. I put all four drafts of my poem up on an overhead. I explained what I had hoped to do with the poem, and explained the changes I made in an attempt to reach my hopes for the piece. I also admitted that my poem still needed more work. Then I turned and asked them for suggestions.

Thinking back on this day, I know it was a turning point. It was the day my students started to view me as a writer—as someone open to criticism, as their catalyst as well as their cohort and confidant. You might say I balanced the scales that day, and we all seemed to be working on an equal basis—equally vulnerable and equally accepting.

Eventually I do suggest that my students work on such things as imagery, rhythm, metaphor, and so forth, but I have learned to start with the bigger picture and, in so doing, teach appreciation and theory as well as craft. That is, I don't suggest work on a line or a word. I ask questions with regard to intent, theme or focus, and I let the artist tamper with specific choices in order to create the needed delicate balance.

DESIGN ASSIGNMENTS THAT PRE-EMPT REVISION

Eventually, I learned to design assignments that suggested theme. I have even learned how to design assignments that pre-empt one or two suggestions for revision: assignments that might prompt the dynamics necessary for an interesting poem. Let me illustrate.

The following pre-emptive assignment was given to several of my students:

> Select any one of the topics below and write in any form you choose. If you are inclined to write poetry, do so! Know also that if you start out with an essay, story, or letter, I may suggest later that you try poetry as an alternate form. Write about:
>
> 1. Something that you would like to change but cannot.
> 2. Something bad that turned out good.
> 3. Something good that turned out bad.
> 4. Something you love, but cannot have.

Built into the above assignment, or predisposed here, is the suggestion that the poet create a work that includes himself/herself in some way, as well as opposites, a poem that does not go neatly from one point to another in a predictable way.

Looking back at my own poems in Part A my meandering is hopefully obvious. To illustrate, in one of the poems we see the Guilford's dog at a younger and healthier stage in life, even though we discover that the dog is dying. In "Salmon Cakes," notice that not all the men are "bad." "Drought" deals with various good and bad elements of the father-daughter relationship, and "Nests" has the reader reaching high and low physically as well as emotionally.

The balance of good and bad is especially important for a longer poem like "Salmon Cakes," in that a change in direction or tone serves the same function that comic relief might serve in a serious drama. I also feel that this balance lends a sense of reality to the piece—shows the gray of life as well as the black and white.

Notice how in all the poems I have avoided predictability, being linear. So I bathe my students in a sea of unpredictability in order to help them avoid too many hours of treading. I like to use: "University Hospital Boston," by Mary Oliver; "Accidents of Birth" by William Meredith; and "Rain" by William Carpenter.

After putting the idea of balance along with meandering together and after sharing the poems above, I ask my students to fold a piece of paper down the center, label one side "Good" and one side "Bad." Then I have them list words, ideas or actions that occur in a poem as either "Good" or "Bad."

Here is one such list that a student produced after examining my poem "Nests":

Good	**Bad**
Chalices	there's risk
Tumbles into flight	life teeters on the edge
balanced brave	warned not to touch
life held neatly still	missed the birth
you walk the steps	mourned the fallen . . .
	unsure of what . . .
	an overwrought magnet

(The student wanted to place some ideas in the center which led to a good discussion about the subtlety of good poetry or the grey areas.)

Here are poems I received from students—their first go around with the assignment. Even their first drafts will impress you, I'm sure!

Untitled

his face is a small hopeful triangle
pocketed deep in the life preserver
we are waiting for summer, for the first violent
sparkle of silver to flash by Daddy's immense
rubber boots

waiting
as his hands made timid loops through the
air
casting shadows against the dim basement wall

Michelle Ritter
Age 17

Something

something
an angry man with a unlit cigarette in his mouth
driving by
it's fall
a rusty car racing a readheaded girl on a bicycle
with a banana seat and her hair is fiery behind her
her bike is faded blue
something
a boy about 13 running through the woods
with a plastic machine gun tucked tightly under each arm
something
alone here
with my spine on a tree
staring at woodchips
something
in a meadow somewhere?
I imagine something
something about how the wind feels
when it pushes at my face
about how the earth feels
when the bones of my butt are perched upon her
something
in the way the trees
fold the wind towards me
while their leaves sing and dance above me

Renee Helen Nixon
Age 18

Walt Whitman's Biographer

Walt has always loved to walk but it is harder now, still she struggles to her feet. We confine our walks these days to the park behind my house. Her world is constantly getting smaller. Soon it will fix to a point as small as her pupil and she will close her eye.

As with everything, there is wisdom in Walt's approach to death. She lifts a leg above the yellow flowers of Spain. She is curious about the bees that settle in the Chinese gardens. She follows a crazy scent over the ragged tar and asphalt of the Americas. Some are embarrassed by her confusion but she is not. "One day you will never be confused," she says, "what a happy person you'll be then."

There is a pond in the park that is calm and graceful with the gliding of mallards. Some poets would gaze at the water for hours. Today Walt tries their approach but cannot stand it. She must be wet and foolish and blatant. The mud must coat her under-belly and the ducks must scream and flurry and the poets must throw their pencils to the earth and their paper must be set and worthless. "The world was founded in chaos," she says—water barking from her lips. She is circling in the middle of the pond mystified by her own blurry visions. For a moment she is frightened. It is up to me to call her attention and dry her off—this is all part of being a biographer and I am good at my job.

Can you hear Walt Whitman's voice from where you are? I cannot imagine the distance rising to dissuade or disperse it. I like to think that somewhere the tyrannies of governement pause—distracted. That for a second they forget what they were doing—whiping or wailing—and they fumble awkwardly with their car keys. I like to think that in the heart of some frightening city a malnutritioned child bursts out of a sweaty sleep and says, "Oh, that's just Walt Whitman—nothing to be afraid of."

David Turkel
Age 19

"His Face" needed not so much revision as it needed expansion or development.

"Something" needed tailoring and perhaps expansion.

In the case of the Whitman poem, I wanted to edit it slightly and rush it off to *The New Yorker*. And I feel comfortable in saying that the student, in this case, may outshine the teacher.

All of the poets, I felt, would gain something if they would venture to experiment with cadence and typography; but, in general, one would have to agree that the assignment had a built-in success mechanism and that all three poems contained some balance. The first drafts do show promise.

REACTING/CONFERENCING—SUGGESTIONS BASED ON THE AUTHORS' INTENT

If there were first attempts, imagine what could be accomplished with a few more suggestions! "Suggestion" is a key word here, as some of the authors' choices may have been stylistic. Keeping in mind that writing (in any form) is an idio-syncratic subjective act (Macrorie, 1974, p. 14), we will want to suggest ideas for revision based on the authors' intent and the degree to which they succeeded based on this intent. In other words, it is important that we keep in mind now and always that the authors—not the teacher—has ownership of the piece.

What I did next was give each student a copy of their poem along with a note that was primarily an emotional reaction to the poem on my part, which in general stressed the positive. I then asked each student to write out what they intended to communicate with their poem, as well as an assessment regarding how close they came to their own intentions. I know that in so doing the student would have to consider the poem as a whole, not as just a series of images or metaphors.

Here are the students' answers to the question I asked about intent.

You will find these answers to be nothing less than impressive literary criticism, plus much, much more.

Response From Michelle Ritter:

Dear Ms. GN-J,

I want to communicate—a sense of maternal pride, almost, of fear, a slight ap-prehension for him (my brother). A sense of loss over the Daddy figure, true to life—foreboding is a poor word.

I wish to describe the hero-worship I see in the boy's eyes for his Daddy, an im-mense man who fills the room, who is silent, who spends hours in the basement with his little boy—in the corner playing with a truck, glancing up to watch, wide-eyed, as the man explains something grown up about fly-fishing.

I am always a distant, motherly figure when it comes to Jeff—always protected him when he was little. Does it work to put myself in the poem?

Love,
Michelle

Response From Renee Nixon:

Mo:

My poem—how grand the somethings are deals with how inadequate I am to understand any of them, how impossible it is to piece it all together.

Renee

Response From David Turkel:

Dear Ms. GN-J,

I wanted "Walt Whitman's Biographer" to operate on three distinct levels. The first two are obvious—a boy coping with the eventual death of his dog, and a homage to Walt Whitman. The third unifies these two and contains what I feel to be the bulk of the theme and movement of the piece. That is, it is a piece about writing and the examination of life.

Love,
David

EDITORIAL CONFERENCING

My next correspondence with each student was more specific and based primarily on what each student suggested as intent.

I call this level of interaction editorial conferencing, and I approach it face to face, in letter form, or I tape my feelings. As difficult as this is for me, I restrain myself from writing all over the writers' work. I tend to hold the piece out as a work of literature that is rather sacred territory to the creator.

While I have some ideas, my suggestions take the form of indirect questions. I really do not want to tamper with the authors' intent or style. Yet, I want each student to look at specific areas of their poem. From my own experiences, I know that it is not unusual to revise the same poem several times—and that the focus of revision might change with each attempt. So I don't expect miracles, but I do expect some progress.

What follows is the editorial conferencing remarks I made to each student:

Conference With Michelle Ritter:

(Regarding her poem "Untitled" about her brother)
Dear Michelle:
(This is working—do not fear.)

In view of what you have said about your poem, what do you think you need to develop?

You said you wish to communicate some fear you feel for your brother in terms of his loss. What is it about your brother that causes you to fear for him?

You describe a Daddy—who fills the room and is important to the boy. . .his world even though it is a basement. Perhaps it is more than a basement.

In view of this. . .do you need to take yourself out? Look at your balance; I see some beginnings. How far does your journey take us? Do you want to go farther?

Please send me the final poem if/when you edit.

Gloria Nixon-John

My suggestions were made in hopes that Michelle would take her poem beyond the basement—that it might contain more of her brother's struggle—that I might see the differences in terms of size, and so forth between the boy and Daddy in her revision.

Conference With Renee Nixon:

(Regarding her poem "Something")
Renee:

My favorite image is found in the last three lines where you seem to bring the poem together. Your ending is strong. It makes the reader look up. Based on what you said relative to your poem, you said—to paraphrase

"I sense that the seemingly unimportant things are
significant, but I don't have the capacity to
understand what these somethings mean."

Can you speculate on how they are significant in relation to you?

I wonder if you would look at your poem again and see if any idea—line, group of words, or word—distracts or takes from the feeling you wish to relate.

Does the repetition work in this piece?

Also, feel free to experiment with line length or the shape the poem takes on the page.

Of course, you make the final decisions regarding revision, I hope I've helped.

Love,
Mo

My suggestions were made to get Renee to look at the repetition as well as the mixed diction. And I felt that some of her words detracted from the beauty/flow of the poem. Yet, the repetition may be important to her—I wanted her to read the poem to me—with our next conference, I would ask her to read it aloud for me.

Conference With David Turkel:

Dave:

In view of what you have said about your poems, what changes would you make to clarify intent? At first, the ''her'' (for Cleo, your dog) confused me...later I used it...because I know you have done extensive reading on Whitman, and I know you are aware of his sexual turmoil. Did you want the reader to think on this sexual level? Is the poem balanced? Do you feel you explain too little or too much? Does language ever get in the way?

Now, if you feel you need to revise—do so and return the poem to me.

Love,
Ms. GN-J

My suggestions were made in the hopes that David might hone the language a bit. I sense that description and vocabulary gets in the way at times. It almost seems like a 19th Century style, but knowing David that might be deliberate. I wasn't sure if the dog should be a he or she—and I wondered if David wanted to set up this question about the sex of the dog.

Note that all of my suggestions deal with the poem as a whole—the larger picture that I spoke about earlier. yet, these suggestions direct the students to look at woods and phrases in order to succeed as far as general artistic intent is concerned. Rembember also that the writer ''...is seeking through words to name, compose, and grasp their own (sometimes painful) experience'' (DeMott, 1967, p.31). Keeping DeMott's pioneering remarks in mind will encourage you to praise and suggest rather than correct or mandate certain things form your students.

Also, please note that each poet is ready for different advice regarding rewriting. Therefore, just tossing an editing idea out to a class at large would do little to help target the specific needs of each of these three students.

Later, in the semester or year, I might have the student pull these same poems out to look at things such as line length options/rhythm, use or abuse of repetition, options with regard to closure, etc. A few of the sources I have found helpful in terms of dealing with more specific suggestions for rewriting are: *The Triggering Town* (1979) by Richard Hugo, *Writing Like a Woman* (1983) by Alicia Ostriker; and *For The Good of The Earth and Sun* (1989) by Georgia Heard.

I would also most certainly continue to have all my students examine many classic and contemporary poets, and I would have them respond to the works of these said poets before returning to their own works for another look. In addition, I let my students guide my future lesson planning in order to meet their individual needs as well as the needs of the group at large.

SHARING/CELEBRATING

At this point, I would like to share—rather celebrate—the second draft of each students' poem, poems that I find to be sensitive, insightful, and provocative, poems that I delight in celebrating with you.

His Face

his face is a small struggle
        not to touch the poles with their slithering hooks
a small hopeful triangle
        reflecting the orange life jacket
he is waiting for summer
for the thunder of Daddy
for that first silver flash alongside the boat

waiting as his hands cast timid looping shadows
in the still January air

Michelle Ritter

Notice that Michelle answered her own question. She decided to be the narrator to deal with this piece in third person. In doing so, I think, she has made the piece more clear.

I think it is particularly interesting that she had tightened up the metaphor for face and the metaphor for the noise or activity it related to Daddy.

Note too that she uses adjectives more carefully in her revision, saving a string of them for the end of the poem (timid...looping...still...).

Something

an angry man with a cigarette in his mouth
driving by

it is fall
a rusty car racing a redheaded girl on a bicycle
her bike is faded blue...
her hair is fiery behind her

something
a boy running through the woods
with a plastic machine gun tucked tightly under his arm...

alone here, with my spine on a tree,
staring at something...

about how the wind feels
about how the earth feels
when my bones are perched upon her, something
in the way the trees
fold the wind towards me
while their leaves sing and dance above

Renee Helen Nixon

Notice that Renee has edited out certain words (an occasional "something". . ."an unlit". . ."with a banana seat". . ."butt"). Notice how she used "something" to move the poem along. Her editing decision makes sense to me.

I received this note from David Turkel instead of a revised poem. Notice that his note really tells me what I can help David with at this point. I believe that students usually tell us what their needs are if we provide an environment conducive to freedom of expression.

Dear Ms. GN-J:

With regard to the Whitman piece—I've decided that I like the prose format—it's modest and it fits my impression of the narrator as well as the mode of biography he would employ. Also, I have more respect for the piece and I would like to approach it with a better understanding of typography if I decide to attempt a more specific format.

Thank You
     and
Love,
     Dave

A few years ago I might have thought that David just failed to complete the assignment and that this was a way of dodging an assignment, but I know the student so well through conferencing; and I sense that he is not willing to tamper with this piece because he feels uncomfortable doing so.

I also sense that he loves every word on the page and is not yet ready to let go of any one word.

At this point, I will give David a collection of Raymond Carver's short stories and poems in order to reinforce his feelings about his own prose style. In so doing, I am willing to bet that David will eventually trim his piece a bit. I also might move into my unit of instruction that details with typography as David seems open to suggestions in this area.

IN CONCLUSION

I sometimes think that freeing the minds of students in this decade is the most harowing of all tasks faced by the writing teacher. Many students have difficulty concentrating or meditating and are used to being entertained by the media. It is no wonder that they might have difficulty writing poetry, a form that taps all levels of thinking. Joseph Brodsky (1987), winner of the 1987 Nobel Prize in literature, tells us:

> There are, as we know, three modes of cognition: analytical, intuitive, and the mode that was known to the biblical prophets, revelation. The distinction of poetry from other forms of literature lies in that it uses all three of them at once (gravitating primarily toward the second and the third).

Brodsky goes on to describe poetry writing as "'an extraordinary acceleration of conscious of thinking of comprehending the universe.''

Make no mistake, it is not easy to create strategies that help students learn to focus and maintain some sense of balance in a form of writing that is by nature highly cerebral and spiritual. Doing so requires personal involvement with poetry writing on the part of the teacher. Doing so requires letting go of the concept of teacher as corrector. Doing so mandates hours of individual conferencing. And this magic must all come together in an environment that provides guidance, encouragement, as well as freedom of expression.

REFERENCES

Brodsky, J. (1987). From his acceptance speech for the 1987 Nobel Prize in Literature. Stockholm.

DeMott. B. (1967). Reading writing, reality, unreality. . . *The Educational Record.* The American Council of Education.

Dunn, S. (1985). From his lecture at The 1985 Aspen Writers' Conference.

Lity, W. & McGowan, C. (Eds.). (1986). *A review of the collected works of William Carlos Williams.* New York: New Directions.

Macrorie, K. (1974). *A vulnerable teacher.* Rochelle Park, NJ: Hayden Book Company.

Pinsky, R. (1988). *Poetry and the world.* New York: Ecco Press.

Romano, T. (1987). *Clearing the way: Working with teenage writers.* Portsmouth, NH: Heinemann Educational Books.

SELECTED BIBLIOGRAPHY

Heard, G. (1989). *For the good of the earth and sun: Teaching poetry.* Portsmouth, NH: Heinemann Educational Books.

The title is a bit deceptive as this work deals with teaching about reading and writing as well as teaching poetry. Georgia's approach is open and free. She celebrates poetry with her students. She helps students tap their experiences for the poetry they have tucked deep within.

Hugo, R. (1979). *The triggering town: Lectures and essays on poetry and writing.* New York: W.W. Norton & Company.

Hugo offers up his way of writing in a sincere attempt to help others find their own way of writing poetry later on. He contends that writers' problems are not literary but rather psychological. He provides many samples and many edited lines.

Ostriker, A. (1983). *Writing like a woman: Poets on poetry.* Ann Arbor, MI: The University of Michigan Press.

This book suggests to women that they write from freedom and courage, that they write exactly as they think. She traces the history of holding back on the intimate feminine experiences for fear of ridicule and scorn. Alicia shows all women writers how to be taken seriously.

Anne-Marie Oomen offers us a unique approach to poetry writing with adolescents; a way, perhaps, which helps dispel the ideal that poetry writing need be a lonely, solitary endeavor. Teenagers are social by definition and through her quilting metaphor Oomen invites her students to explore, together, *intensely meaningful topics: first kisses and loves, vulnerability, those held dear, mood swings, all the "stuff" that amazes. Always with a weaving away from or toward their own writing or the literature they admire, Oomen's students are lead through six methods for approaching poetry. The reader will quickly see the idea of quilting needn't stop with poetry, nor be used with teens alone. Anne-Marie's chapter will remind you, somewhat, of Leonora Smith's in that it taps the inventive process afresh. They differ though. Smith taps the unknown to elicit the known, while Oomen taps the known in an attempt to discover.*

CHAPTER 13
INSPIRATION THROUGH COLLABORATION

By Anne-Marie Oomen

PART A: POEMS

Folding Sheets

Not the smell,
bleach and borax,
at least not just the smell,
when the towels snap in air
like broken wire.
Nor is it just his neatly stacked
Fruit of the Looms with
your Satin Balis.
It is not even the dryer heat
or summer sun warmth
coming into your chin
from the ropes of laundry
in your arms

In the end, it is folding the sheets.
Because to do it well
there must be two of you—
another.
They come when you call:
parent, sibling spouse, child.
They come easily,
answering the soft call,
dry percale spreading in your arms,
great sails opening in rooms
of your hands,
a readiness to hold,
walking toward each other,
looking into each other's eyes,
folding the night at both ends.

Anne-Marie Oomen

Ladies Before Gents

A torn weathered hand
moves along the brocade
lifted from the chest
of catarrh air and peptic time.
Ribald cigarette smoke and phlegm
covered skin.
Macramé.
Disease.
Stockings droop, eyelids,
cataracts.
Wine from a heavy silver teaspoon.
The omniscient radio. Clocks. Terrible
shoes.
Mortar bowels, morphine,
the rattle of inclement laughter.
Hip pointers, liver spots, emery board
tongue. That which was an elbow, face, woman.
Facsimile. Nemesis. Jezabel.
A dream in exile.
A young prince forsaken.
A waltz in crinoline with
lost slippers on a wet summer lawn.
The huge sin of kissing.
The sheen of braided hair in sunlight.
Waves. Cambric. Mist.

Ray Nargis

PART B: LITERARY QUILTING:
HOW IT WORKS

Literary quilting is a writing strategy which uses the metaphor of quilting to teach young writers—in particular, high school students—to respond to and write from their own literature, their own creations. It is writing tied by topic, image, structure, or experience. In a literary quilt, writers collect pieces of writing into a whole, creating a block of writings. By building on these blocks, an entire quilt of associated writing can be prepared. The following scene exemplifies how literary quilting helped select the poems in part A.

On my faded pine deck, Ray and I paced restlessly, surrounded by pages of poetry which threatened to fly in the summer wind. We'd weighted the poems with garden stones and coffee cups but the mixed sound of rustling paper and our hollow steps reflected our indecision.

"How do we choose?" Ray asked.

Our task, to select the poems to be published in our chapbook, *Moniker*, had begun in delight, but had been ambushed by uncertainty. Which ones? Did we choose by chronology, quality, subject, theme, or style? Finally I suggested we quilt the pieces.

"Quilt?" Ray asked.

"It's a metaphor Sally Ketchum and I used when we wrote *Drunkard's Path* (1987). We imagined our pieces of writing as quilt pieces which were stitched into a whole."

"Neither you nor Sally sews." He raised an eyebrow.

"We didn't need to. We quilted with words. You might read something in one of my poems that leads to an idea you've explored in one of your poems. So those poems are linked by idea, stitched by theme so to speak. Or one of my images might be one that you've also explored. We could build from that, writing from that image. Quilting is a new name for an old process—finding writing connections. Sally calls it a literary quilt."

From that inspiration, we chose the two poems above, poems linked by imagery (both poems use fabric) and subject (both poems explore endings). The other poems in *Moniker* (1988) reflect similar quilting because the poems are linked by image, or structure, or theme, or any number of literary connections. Our poems are, in essence, stitched together to form a whole literary quilt.

When Sally Ketchum first coined the term, literary quilting, we were writing very freely together, weaving openly from one's poems or short stories to the other's poems or short stories, deliberately exploring each other's written grist, and borrowing like sisters (to speak of the literary cup of sugar). That term, literary quilting, freshened and clarified our approach, aptly identifying our process of writing to, from, and about each other's work our process of connecting. But the process itself seems universal, and I suspect, consciously or unconsciously, happens to many writers. After all, we are all part of a rich and varied soup of experience, and it seems natural that we taste from each other's cup. How many poets have borrowed e.e. cummings free verse techniques? What are children doing when they parody rhymes like "Roses are red, Violets are blue. . .?" Of how many retellings can you think for Cinderella? And currently, how many writers build their writing from the written inspiration offered by other writers? Just as folksinger Ralph McTell builds his lovely song, "The Ferryman" from Hesse's *Siddartha* (1983), Douglas R. Hofstader constructs his scholarly Pulitzer prizewinner *Godel, Escher, Bach: An Eternal Golden Braid* (1989) from multi-leveled connections between art and science, music and philosophy. Certainly among those writing about writing, there is much blending and stirring. For example, Rosemary Deen and Marie Ponsot have borrowed the superstructure of the fable for their initial lesson in *Beat Not the Poor Desk* (1982). Nancie Atwell's *In the Middle* (1987) and Toby Fulwiler's *The Journal Book* (1987) explore variations on the theme of responding and borrowing. This "connection consciousness" among writers is also reflected in contemporary research, including Rosenblatt's *Reader, Text, and Poem* (1978). The resulting "writer's tapestry" of influences may have lead many writers to claim there should be no such thing as copyrights.

However, to my surprise and delight, the process that we had called literary quilting reflected more than history and research, and could grace more than *Drunkard's Path* or *Moniker*. It could be stitched into the classroom, especially into the teaching of poetry, like good thread slipping into a golden needle.

PROCESS: A QUILT HAPPENING

Literary quilting in my classroom did not happen all at once, nor did I identify all the literary quilting techniques immediately. Some came about spontaneously when Sally and I shared our writing with students. Some were invented deliberately when we saw this rich metaphor begin to work in the classroom. Our students discovered some. I suspect many other strategies exist to help students connect with and inspire each other as writers, but I return again and again to six strategies for literary quilting.

1. Group Quilt: A quilting bee with words—single piece, multi-authored
2. Single author quilts: The Lone Pioneer
3. Quilting in pairs: The Tie that Binds—paired authors for a single piece
4. The Quilt Block: Writing on Theme—Collecting scraps: Accidental Organization—Quilting on a new word

5. The Literary Quilt: The Class Quilting Bee—Ten of Hearts, a chapbook
6. Quilt as Reaction (Inside the Quilt)

GROUP QUILT: A QUILTING BEE WITH WORDS

A quilting bee of words happens when a class writes a list on an assigned topic, using the quilt metaphor. It works like brainstorming in that the pieces of the project—(the quilt)—are collected from everyone and the initial result is a rough list. For example, when my creative writing class was learning about the writing process, we wrote (quilted) the introduction to our creative writing anthology, *When the Ink Dries*. I had worked with the metaphor by inviting students to imagine they were contributing a piece to a quilt, represented by a word or short phrase. I asked students to list two or three words or phrases which described creative writing students in various phases of the writing processs. "What do we do when we prewrite or draft or edit?" As the list expanded, students piggybacked ideas. The lesson was noisy and fun. Later, when my student editor decided to include something about the writing process in the introduction, she reordered this list-quilt to describe the various stages of the writing process. Following are two excerpts from the introduction of the anthology:

A Creative Writing Student

risks
writes
laughs
chatters from embarrassment
writes
argues vehemently
writes
gets silly
writes
thinks
revises
dreams, delves, dares
alliterates
is rarely bored
draws
writes
thinks
revises
edits
publishes
gets scared
writes some more

When We Revise We

read it to someone
scratch it out
cry, maybe
cut it
rethink
rebuild
cut again
doodle
rebuild
ask questions
play with m & m's (organize by color?)
argue
"But that's the best part."
paste it back together
fall in love with our first drafts
fall out of love with our first drafts
fall in love again

From When the Ink Dries

As you can see from the list, the topic (ironicaly, the process itself) kept us on track, and the idea of everyone offering only a few words allowed us to feel less intimidated by the blackboard, more like a community. Working on this "bee of words," we organized the list on the board, copied the list, thought about it, returned later to think and play with it. My student editor ordered the final draft. Interestingly, this anthology captured us our first Michigan Youth Arts Writing Award.

SINGLE AUTHOR QUILTS: THE LONE PIONEER

For the introduction of our anthology, the group quilt succeeded and may work well for any single project which can be graced by multiple authorship. However, some students may enjoy writing alone on a single theme: that is, writing their own quilts. And some projects may simply need a single author. Sally and I had been talking about writing from single words, specifically quilt words, by playing with different meanings and views of one word. Sally noticed that some students were picking up on the idea and writing about words in a similar way. The following quilting exercise developed from her observation.

I gave students a list of random nouns, "word pieces" I called them, from which they chose one or two, then brainstormed or clustered from that word. I offered students the option of using these lists as starters for short poems, written in a series, and I allowed for lots of word play and puns. The final results were often rich. For example, one word-piece, "dirt," produced the following single author literary quilt.

DIRT 1

"Gimme the dirt;
I wanna hear it all.
The god awful truth,
the low-down, no good word.
Who did what?
    To Whom?
Gimme the dirt;
I wanna hear it all."

DIRT 2

Life grows
strong and green,
slices
rich soil,
to reach blue
skies.

DIRT 3

Pornography,
dark and demonic,
it hurts deep inside.
Loud and violent,
it abuses the eye.
Ignorant and ugly,
it tears the truth apart.

DIRT 4

Prom night
in the dark
silk and lace
swishes and swirls
about slender, stockinged ankles
in the morning light
on a stark wood floor
a gown
lies in a heap.
Dirty White.

DIRT 5

Below your feet
miles down
permanence in the round.

Kate Husband

Kate writes from a single pun idea, but her poems are linked, thematically patched into a small "quilt," creating an interesting cumulative effect. The dirt poems once again exemplify how the literary quilt can be greater than the sum of its pieces.

QUILTING IN PAIRS: THE TIE THAT BINDS

When Sally and I wrote *Drunkard's Path* we wrote lavishly and easily, allowing inspiration to come from images or ideas in each other's poems and from our past experience. For example, we wrote an herbal quilt which consisted of 36 short poems, all related to herbs. As we wrote, we shared this quilt with our classes and I invited them to write as Sally and I had—in pairs—with unexpected results.

Two students, Rachel and Sandy, used this pairing strategy while attending Project Close-up in Washington D.C. When Sandy and Rachel visited the Vietnam memorial, they found the name of a soldier whose death date matched their mutual birthdays. The young man had died two weeks before his discharge date. Moved by the experience, they made a rubbing of the young man's name, Richard E. Marks, and on the bus ride home began writing to each other about their feelings. The resulting two-voiced essay/poem became an additional model for students who wanted to write together. Because students were writing to each other, they provided an audience neither threatening nor obscure, but instead familiar and clear. In the following two parts from a total of six alternating parts, Rachel's voice is first, Sandy's follows.

TO RICHARD E. MARKS
I visited a black wall. It was enormous.
People stood, some crying, representing only a minute
fraction of the people whose names are carved in stone.
Black and smooth, the wall reflected the faces
of people who walked by.
My face in the wall.

I am seventeen. That couldn't be my reflection
on that wall. Or could it? The average age
of those who died was nineteen. Some were younger;
some were older. War does not discriminate; it consumes
people of all ages.

Rachel Velliquette and Sandy Messing

The emotional content of this paired quilt appealed to my students but the structural idea of stitching reactions together was equally as inspirational, occasionally creating fun as well as reflective pieces. I invited students to continue writing in pairs on topics of their own choice or inspired by journal entries. Two students, Andy and David, borrowed Rachel and Sandy's idea and wrote an eight piece literary block about moods. The difference was this: Even though they did publish the pieces as a quilt, each of the short ''moods'' could also stand alone. Another option.

THE QUILT BLOCK: WRITING ON THEME

Any number of wise artistic choices transforms good quilts into works of art. A patchwork quilt becomes a work of art through pattern and color, as well as stitching and fabric. The art of quilting is further enriched by the number of quilters working on a quilt. After working individual quilt blocks alone, quilters often come together to work the whole quilt in a community format. While writing *Drunkard's Path*. Sally and I found that parallel ideas may apply to literary quilts. Imagine many authors writing on a theme with the intention of making the various writings part of a whole: that is, a whole literary quilt linked by theme, or content, or other literary devices, or combinations of all these things. Michael Ondaatje's *Collected Works of Billy the Kid* (1970) is a very good example. I know now that other good writers have done similar things throughout history; but as Sally and I grasped this concept in our own writing, we shared it with students, inviting them to explore the idea. They went one better by discovering a number of literary quilts for themselves.

Collecting Scraps: Accidental Organization In quilt lore, many examples exist of patchwork quilts made from scraps of clothing, household linens, or the last rags of hand-me-down clothing. Rarely did quilters plan a quilt, then visit the nearest ''Sew and Go'' to purchase lenghts of calicoes or today's ''old fashioned'' prints. Quilters of the past often patched a hodgepodge of scraps, ingeniously coordinating the colors or fabric from whatever was available, finally creating a holistic quilt by accident more than by plan. Just as Sally's and my writing process had paralleled the quilter's ingenuity and accidental putting together, a similar accident occurred for the student editors of our creative writing anthology.

When the students selected the order for the writings in the anthology, they pointed out that by gathering all the grandparent/mentor poems into one section, they could pattern a kind of literary quilt they had not done before. In other words, they collected the ''scraps'' of writing and pieced them together, deliberately linking those with common themes into sections. After they found the first group of writings with a common theme, looking for other categories followed naturally. Collecting writing into thematic sections may not be a momentous breakthrough, but the student editors discovered it for themselves, relating it to the quilting metaphor without prodding. In this case I suspect their realization was aided by the vocabulary of the quilting metaphor, already established in our classrooms. Here are two of the pieces they included in the ''Wrinkles of Time,'' section of the anthology honoring their grandparents and mentors:

OPENER

When I was a young boy, my grandfather would come to my house every year on
the last Saturday in April. This was the "opener" of trout season, and he would
take me fishing in his little creek behind his house. My grandfather was too old
to really fish, but I still remember the time he spent with me. We did not fish for
long, maybe an hour or so. Then we would go up to the house, maybe play a few
games of checkers or cards. We would eat lunch and sit around and talk. These talks
really helped me, made me feel more important, more mature, as if I was his best
friend, as if I was the same age as him. This would happen every year, in the same
way. We never really caught any fish. In fact, I think the fishing was the least important part of the day. But it was an excuse for me and grandpa to be together.
Good fishing meant not catching a thing, so we would have the day to ourselves.

Chuck McPhearson

GREAT GRANDMA KNUST

Great Grandma Knust
Constantly urged me to eat more
Of her boiled, mashed, or
Raw sugared potatoes.

She weaved colored rugs
From ripped up rags
On her loom
While telling me how she had to walk
Two miles to school in winter
When she was my age.
She would put a hot potato in her pocket
To keep her warm.

Her hands are cold now.
Nothing is left of her.
I think of her
In the midst of cold, hard, earth.
I remember her feeding the crows.

Genny Scram

As in most writing classes, the results and quality of writing are mixed. But
the experience revealed students collecting thematic pieces to make a whole. They
perceived it as a whole, seeking individual pieces that would "fit."

Quilting on a New Word: I do not teach a formal vocabulary list in creative
writing but new words come up in the context of class work. I ask students to
write them down and respond to the definitions, redefining, rewriting or expanding in their journals. When submissions for the anthology came in, the student
editors developed this "new word" quilting device. They spotted a number of
short writing pieces based on newly learned words, including one of my own,
ironically titled "Neologism." They suggested we go back to the students who

had written on new words, show them the examples of what other students had written, and ask them to write new pieces from the same words, thereby eliciting new "blocks." These in turn could be published as a whole quilt, all related to new words. If it sounds a little complicated, picture a blocked patchwork quilt. Each of the blocks represents a patch of "new word" writings. Frankly, I was skeptical but when students put them together, the texture of the new word collections pleased me in a way I hadn't expected. Here are some examples of the word, vulnerability, which the editing group blocked together.

VULNERABILITY

Vulnerability burns within.
Everyone has it; it's no sin.
What's that? You say you don't?

Then why do you care about what you wear
and the way you wear your hair?
Vulnerability burns within.

Julie Stolowski

Vulnerability is being effected by the elements
    Vulnerability to me also means being exposed.
    It is being open and manipulated.
    It is like being a puppet.
    Vulnerability.

Jason Miller

THE LITERARY QUILT: THE CLASS QUILTING BEE

This literary quilting experiment worked differently from the others and culminates the quilting metaphor. During the year Sally and I wrote *Drunkard's Path*, the quilting metaphor had become firmly "tied" in our minds and in the minds of my students. We understood the value of writing in pairs and groups, and we often used the metaphor-born quilting strategies. We had invented and played with various ways of writing to each other, and they had discovered organizational devices stemming from the quilt metaphor. We were ready to try something different.

In this case, I set out to create a chapbook with some of my advanced creative writing students. I wanted to do something separate from the creative writing anthology—a special collection for them. For this quilt I wanted to be more involved and more deliberate in the planning. Most of all, I wanted to write the project with them.

I thought about conversations with students about their growing up experiences. I remembered experiences from my own growing up, especially the "firsts" in life. I decided to write three short poems on the theme of first kisses. For my audience, I chose younger students than the advanced creative writing students with whom I wanted to write. I wasn't sure why I made this adjustment but after I started getting results I realized that by aiming my own writing toward a younger audience, I had given my students permission to be more experienced than their audiences, offering them superiority in an otherwise risky topic. I wrote "You Know" and "Away Game." As I wrote I discovered the chapbook would be called the *Ten of Hearts* and would include ten poems about early romantic experiences—like first kisses. Here are two poems that I introduced to my students.

YOU KNOW

The maple at the end of our old road
grew a branch with a knot like a sweet mouth.
I am twelve and just thinking about kissing.
I didn't want to be a real big fool.
So like hens lay practice eggs before that
big event, I practiced on my own hand,
kissing where my thumb and first finger make,
you know, a mouth. (If you draw lips and eyes
on your hand, you can drive teachers crazy.)
But kissing my hand was still kissing me,
not like kissing another anything.
My mom said life isn't the kind of thing
you get to practice. I think she's wrong.

Looking up, I see a way. I climb that tree,
brush the knot real clean, get perched real comfy,
put my skinny arms around that big branch,
kiss my heart out. I kiss pretty good now.
I owe it to that maple knot. You know?

AWAY GAME

He asked me to go to the "away game."
My friends said we'd have such a
nice long bus ride. They laughed.

They were like mom's back yard flowers
in a good wind. They leaned and bounced.
I 'member 'cuz they looked at me,
as bright and silly as mom's flowers.

On the way home
he kisses me.
On the mouth.
Wasn't it supposed to be like that?
On the mouth.
He kisses me like
in the movies.
On the mouth.

But it isn't sweet
On the mouth.
It hurts my lips;
I don't like it.
On the mouth.
I push his mouth away.

He breathes on the bus window
and starts to draw pictures.
He draws pictures in his breath
all the way home.

I just keep seeing the other girls
their bouncing colors,
their bouncing flower faces,
talking about the nice long bus ride.

I shared my early drafts with students. While looking at my poems, we talked about form. Though all of my poems for *Ten of Hearts* are free verse, and are written in what Winston Weathers (Romano, 1987 p. 58) calls alternative style, they are not without form or structure. I pointed out that "You Know" has a ten syllable line, a first step I use to introduce iambic pentameter. "You Know" is not written in iambic pentameter, just ten syllable lines. As an experiment, I asked students to divide a favorite journal entry into ten syllable lines, adjusting as necessary, just to get a feel for line length. From there I pointed out places where they had used iambs accidentally. I did not ask them to revise these pieces (though some did). I also pointed out that "Away Game" shifts tenses in the long second verse, and uses fragmented sentences (Romano, pp. 58–62). Students noticed that the verses often break poem narrative into organic parts, an example of form building from content. I suspect they became involved so easily because they were working with my writing, not some distant textbook piece.

Last, I explained my idea and I invited them to write the chapbook, *Ten of Hearts*, by quilting with me. One of them said about the chapbook, "It's like a community quilt." Furthermore, I was surprised at their willingness to be frank about the subject. Following is Bill Zak's poem for *Ten of Hearts* about early romantic experience.

BLINDING

Sunny day. Lying in the
shade of the picnic table.
My wet eyes,
a giant prism distorting my sight.
She got prettier as the light
got brighter.
Lips must have been magnetic
because I wasn't sure what
I was doing.

Now I know why people
sit when they propose
to marry. If I had
stood when I kissed her,
right then
my knees would've
buckled under.

Bill Zak

The truth rings in that one. Following each of the next two student poems are their journal entries. These entries reveal the inner workings of quilting with each other and with me.

THE OLD GROUP GATHERED AROUND THE BONFIRE

The old group gathered around the bonfire
I tossed woodchips into the flames
watching you through smoke.
You sent a message through your cousin.

Would I kiss you?

I shook my head.
NO.

Half my face hid behind my hair.
The other side turned red
from hot flames.

You threw down the woodchips and
stalked into the blackness
of tall pine trees and night.
I left too,
climbing a small hill.
I sat in the darkness,
hugging my knees.
I watch the light below
highlighting the faces of the group.
Your cousin disappeared,
following your direction.
My cousin joined me on the hill.
"I wouldn't have minded kissing him," I said.
I hugged my knees tighter.

Nancy Bruxvoort

In her journal Nancy wrote, "When I read 'Away Game,' it reminded me of all the ridiculous situations dealing with first loves. I began to think of my own personal experiences which I had found ridiculous. I remembered one which stuck in my mind more than anything else. . .The tone in 'Away Game' set the tone for my memories. It also helped me cluster my ideas.'' This is quilting at its best. Nancy is allowing my writing to give her ideas, and she is aware of the interplay occurring in tone as well as theme.

I THINK OF YOU AND ME

I think of you and me,
how we were when
I sold ice cream
ten to three all day in the summer.
At sunset every other night
in your car
three times we'd kiss,
a peck
on the lips,
a long wet one
as the sky slowly faded from auburn
to a dull black/brown,
and the stars I could still see
in the morning
if I squinted real hard
as coffee spilled over my newspaper funnies
and grown up ego.

Lisa Beckwith

In this poem, Lisa found her idea by allowing Nancy's work to trigger a tie to her own ideas. In her journal she wrote, ''Nancy and Sheila's poems seemed to perfectly describe a typical childhood love but each poem is as distinctive as the authors are distinctive. So in response I tried to capture my personal experiences with young love as they had. Writing helps me understand myself and others (like my sister) better.'' Lisa's poem was triggered by Nancy's poem, and one by Sheila [not shown]. The journal entries reveal how comfortably they allow each other's writing to influence their own. I think the quilt metaphor gave them permission to be experimental with the topic and each others' ideas.

QUILTING AS REACTION

The next phase of the project was impulsive. I read the poems my advanced students had written to my sophmore writing students. I approached them by saying I needed to know if we'd written what we hoped to write. I asked them to tell me the story of each poem, reminding them that poetry is often narrative. Then I asked them to write a reaction in any way they wanted. In this exercise students gave me some of the best reaction writing I have encountered in my teaching. To be honest, many of these younger students were not willing to talk freely about kisses, and of course, some of their kiss stories are not ''good'' experiences. A few were "grossed out" by the idea of kissing a tree (in "You Know"). But almost all of them, in the privacy of their journals, wrote—not always about the poems, but about the subject. Here are examples of student's reaction to the poems in *Ten of Hearts*. Keep in mind that many of these students have been labeled poor writers. I have left spelling and punctuation intact in both of the following responses.

> Love can make you do weird things. Especially when you are young. Young kids pick on you and tease you when they like you. You know they do. You probably do it too, or at least have done it. You know what I mean.
>
> Young kids call someone a name or laugh at them. Kids hit each other when they like each other. They throw sand or snow, they call each other names and chase each other as if they don't like them at all.
>
> I remember I liked a girl named Sara. She was the preacher's daughter at our church. At school she would ignore us when we would pick on her. We would call her names & tease her and be really rude to her.
>
> She finally caught on and she started writing me notes. In the notes she said that she like me and would sit in the window of her house across the road from my house and stare at my house wishing I would come over or call her. I wrote back of course and said whatever went along with her notes.
>
> I stopped teasing her and eventually we started going together. She lived across the road so we were always together. Then it ended. She moved away. It was hard at first but after a while I got over it. She visits church once in a while but we are just friends and we never say anything about what we used to do. It is better that way.
>
> *Jim Bottle*

The sincerity and directness of this piece stunned me. When I asked Jim to talk to me about the piece, he was reticent at first. He finally said he wrote it because he liked Nancy's poem, "The Old Group Gathered Around the Bonfire." He said that he liked the way the ending seemed real to him, and he remembered how sad he had been over the memory Nancy's poem had triggered. He said that because she wrote about endings, he could. I suspect Jim never would have written his reaction unless we had given him permission through quilting with his classmates. In the following, Geoff wrote a quilt response from my poem, "You Know." He had asked me if I had really practiced kissing a tree. When I admitted that I had, he wrote the following:

> Well a kiss is like the first time you ride a bike. You do not know what the heck you are doing. But like they say practice makes perfect. And now I can ride a bike pretty good and I won't get into kissing!
>
> *Geof Grenchek*

Later, Geoff returned to this reaction and revised it into a poem for the anthology.

The following piece was written by a young man who, along with his brothers, had a "bad" reputation among my students. When I first met him, I didn't expect him to write much, (my first mistake) let alone hand in the writing. It took me a while to sort out his tortured script but it was worth it.

> "People say I'm cold and cruel. I except what they say, and act like it, but that not how I really am. They relate me to my brothers. Even though I have a tottaly diffent attitude towards everything than theirs. So when they see me they say "Oh! that kid is cruel, his brothers beat people up." Emotions scare me, they make me dizzy and somewhat deathly sick. For example we did this play in fourth hour. With a husband & Wife, with emotion talking. I was the husband, and I had to say I love You to the wife. Right after I said that I couldn't hardly stand, or even talk. People say look at all the violent things you do, their can't be another side. I play football because it's a channel thru which my only real emotion is expressed. I try to change, but people look at me different when I do. I am afraid what people will do and how they'll react, when I change. I do care for people, and there is love in me. But the fire behind isn't powerful enough yet."

> *Troy Burfiend*

When I talked to Troy about the piece I asked him how he had decided to write it. He said that he wanted to write something different. The irony is that in quilting his defiance, he revealed a true and universal voice, one which I suspect he would not have revealed without other student writers to help him define himself by contrast.

CONCLUSION: WHY QUILT?

My sophomores teased me when I read the poems for *Ten of Hearts* because I had not signed my own poems. I made light of my authorship and they called me on it, claiming I wasn't practicing what I preached. I was embarrassed; I blushed and they laughed—a group of writers trying to be better, laughing at the way we discount and defend ourselves. Ultimately, I think literary quilting, in both method and metaphor, helped all of us find ways of lowering our defenses, ways of connecting as writers, ways of finding the literature and each other in the responses and connections we made. For students the following seemed true:

1. Students' anxiety about writing tended to be reduced because they could write with and to each other.
2. Students learned to write from their own literature.
3. Students tended to inspire and motivate each other when they write in literary quilts.
4. Students tended to find some natural organizational devices when whey wrote literary quilts.

About literary quilting as a metaphor—teaching writing strategies through metaphor is not a new idea. I suspect that teachers regularly discover these kinds of metaphors and that many unexplored advantages exist to teaching with metaphor. Tom Romano uses food as a metaphor in one of his chapters in *Clearing the Way* (1987, pp. 51–58). Certainly, those teachers who are interested may find other metaphors with which to teach the same strategies, but the quilt metaphor seemed to work well with our students for two reasons: It had sprung from the writing Sally and I were actually doing, and it was a metaphor to which they could relate. I think the quilt metaphor is a convenience, a device that worked because it was culturally rich for our students here in the Midwest and because Sally and I were sharing it. The corollary is that any metaphor which is both culturally rich, rich enough in image and form, and to which both teacher and student can bring familiarity, or even great love, would work. Perhaps you have ideas of your own.

REFERENCES

Atwell, N. (1987). *In the middle: Writing, reading, and learning with adolescents.* Portsmouth, NH: Boynton/Cook.

Deen, R. & Ponsot, M. (1982) *Beat not the poor desk: Writing: What to teach, how to teach it, and why.* pp. 11–26. Upper Montclair, NJ: Boynton/Cook.

Hesse, H. (1983). *Siddartha.* Cutchogue, NY: Buccaneer.

Hofstader, D. (1989). *Godel, Escher, Bach: An eternal golden braid.* New York: Random House.

Kechum, S. & Oomen, A. (1987). *Drunkard's path.* (Self-published manuscript.) Williamsburg, MI.

McTell, R. (1970). The Ferryman. *The Ferryman.* Warner Communications, K56296. (Note: Out of Print. Copyright may be held by Fantasy Records, Berkeley, CA.)

Ondaatje, M. (1970). *Collected works of Billy the Kid.* Toronto, Canada: University of Toronto Press.

Oomen, A. & Nargis, R. (1988). *Moniker.* Williamsburg, MI: Split Ivorie Performances and Publications.

Paston, L. (1981). Unbreakable codes. In R. Lachson (Ed.), *Acts of mind: Conversations with contemporary poets.* University, AL: University of Alabama Press.

Romano, T. (1987). *Clearing the way: Working with teenage writers.* Portsmouth, NH: Heinemann Educational Books.

Romano, T. (1988). Breaking the rules of style. *English Journal 77,* 58–62.

Rosenblatt, L. (1978). *The reader, the text, the poem: Transactional theory of literary work.* Urbana, IL: National Council of Teachers of English

Safford, C. & Bishop, R. (1985). *America's quilts and coverlets.* New York, NY: Bonanza Books.

SELECTED BIBLIOGRAPHY

Books

Atwell, N. (1987). *In the middle: Writing, reading, and learning with adolescents.* Portsmouth, NH: Boynton/Cook.

Lots of good stuff about journals. The dialogue journals are easily adapted to quilting exercises.

Deen, R. & Ponsot, M. (1982) *The common sense: What to write, how to write it, and why.* pp. 11–26. Upper Montclair, NJ: Boynton/Cook.

The student's version of their first text. Indispensable how-to's. Their practice of asking students to read work aloud inspires literary quilting.

Fulwiler, T. (Ed.) (1987). *The journal book.* Portsmouth, NH: Heineman Educational Books.

I used many examples of response journals suggested in his text for the final quilting project, *Ten of Hearts.*

Goldberg, N. (1986). *Writing down the bones: Freeing the writer within.* Boston, MA: Shambhala.

Great material on getting started and strengthening sentences. Though this book is not related directly to quilting, I find I use her material when my students and I get "stuck." Good technique for breaking "writer's block."

Kirby, D. & Liner, T. (1981) *Inside out: Developmental strategies for teaching writing.* Upper Montclair, NJ: Boynton Cook.

Material on students working together and on journal anthologies. Chapter six, "Writing Poetry," offers good ways to respond to the writing of poetry. I found myself using it a lot while we quilted.

Stafford, W. (1978). *Writing the Australian crawl: Views on the writer's vocation.* Ann Arbor, MI: University of Michigan Press.

Some gentle analysis of the tolerance we must exercise toward ourselves and our writing. I use this as a personal inspiration for tone in my classroom. It's what allows me to convince students it's OK to write about first kisses.

Articles

Borstein, J. (1989) A writing teacher risks writing. *English Journal 78*, 60–61.

Once again validates that, most of the time, writing teachers could find it helpful to write and to share. In other words, quilt with your students.

Five, C.L. (1988). From workbook to workshop: Increasing children's involvement in the reading process. *New Advocate 1.*(1), 103–113.

Working with connections. Again, quilting, but from reading to writing and back. Her writing reminds me how naturally we quilt and gave me some ideas to explore next time.

Sullivan, A.M. (1989). Liberating the urge to write: From classroom journals to lifelong writing. *English Journal 78*, 55–61.

More good information on journals and their application to other kinds of writing. This article reinforced reaction journals as part of a subtle but effective way of quilting.

Judith Hilla agrees that writing short stories is like scaling an icy rock-face; but, she says, if we were to give people the opportunity to make first drafts too long and too complicated, the task would ease. What refreshing advice from an avid short story writer, since most teachers already know the hard knocks of "too complicated" and "too long." Hilla begins by telling short stories herself, attempting to show her students she needs an underlying structure. Though Hilla deals with all the short story parts, it's characterization that grabs her most. Using story journals, Judie's students see their characters; imagine them moving about; discover through their own writing what others think about them; and more. Frances Temple advocates using journals as a road to discovery, too. In point of fact, if readers look, expressive, discovery writing permeates most of chapters in this book.

CHAPTER 14
WRITING SHORT STORIES

By Judith Hilla

PART A: QUARTERS

Although the sun blazed through the window and the birds sang like crazy, Europa Jones could tell from the frost on the windows that it must be mighty cold outside. Tightening her old winter coat buttons with dental floss, she heard the weather man on the *Today* show say that the temperature would stay below freezing all day. She turned off the TV and put her coat on over her warmest red wool sweater, tugged her fur-trimmed galoshes over her tennis shoes, and looked critically at herself in the hall mirror. She smoothed her gray hair and tied the brown wool babushka under her chin. ''Not warm enough,'' she thought as she stood the coat collar on end and tied a red and green plaid scarf around to hold it up. Her $2.53 she tucked into the deepest pocket of her purse.

Slamming the door shut hard, Europa cautiously made her way down the steps. Since the railing had broken and the landlord hadn't come by with the shovel and the salt, Europa gave up trying to walk on the third step and sat down for a rest. She picked up the newspaper, tucked it under her arm, and used her hands to push herself down to the bottom step. It would not do at all to fall and break something. No one would find her for hours and she might freeze to death or the kids might steal her pocketbook and beat her up.

Europa put her hands in her pockets and walked carefully to the bus stop. No one was outside and she couldn't blame them. Her son, Harold, would tell her she was crazy to come over on such a miserable day. The wind blew the same way the bus was coming from and so Europa tried not to watch for it. But, a habit is a habit, and there is absolutely no way to get a bus to come for you unless you look for it. If you sit on the bench advertising Burger King Combo, reading the newspaper, the bus will never come. But, today, with the freezing snow blowing, it was impossible to read the newspaper anyway.

Straining to look for the bus, Europa saw two kids across the street breaking into a parking meter with a big, red-handled wrench. She did not yell at them and tried to avoid looking over there. If they saw her looking at them, they would run across the street, knock her over the head with that wrench and steal her pocketbook. In this weather, she would never be able to get back to the house fast enough if they were after her. Two big boys. How could she win? The biggest kid, the one with the leather jacket, hit the meter again and again with the wrench, but no money came out. The other kid, the cold one in the blue jean jacket, grabbed the wrench and smashed the meter once. Out came a ton of quarters. They stuffed their pockets full and took off around the corner, fast, when they heard the bus coming.

Europa saw, shining in the snow, some quarters left behind. She could use that money for bus fare tomorrow if her son wouldn't give her any. No. Someone might see her and think she had broken into the parking meter herself.

When the bus came, she forgot the quarters and looked for a seat where she could sit alone and read the paper. "Good morning, Mrs. Jones!" the bus driver said while he waited for her to sit down. "Nothin' good about this mornin'!" She laughed as she sat down in the middle of the bus, near the heater. Europa untied the red and green plaid scarf, unbuttoned the top button of her coat, and opened her newspaper.

She always read the obituaries first. "Death before life," her huband had always said. "God rest his soul." she mumbled to herself. Old Mrs. Winther Brown, who used to live down the street before she went to the home, "passed away suddenly in the night." Was it a stroke or did she just take all of her pills at once? Maybe Harold would know. Romanoff Leopaldski, famous conductor of The Philharmonic Symphonia, "died of cardiac arrest." Used to be just plain old Leo Paldski in high school. "Good Lord! Cecily Townsend!" Europa said outloud. And, here, Cecily thought she would live forever. Now "making her transition" as the paper said. "Memorial service to be held at The Garden of Eternal Rest." Cremated. How in the world would Cecily make her transition without her body? Oh well, a body is more trouble than it's worth most of the time anyhow.

The bus stopped and started, again and again. The rhythm of riding relaxed Europa, reading and thinking about the news of the day, listening only to the bus driver calling out the street names. "Wealthy...Franklin...Hall..." She had until the end of the line, so there was no rush to read the paper. She looked at the movie reviews. Violence and sex, that's all. Too much violence in the world anyway.

When the bus stopped at Hall, Europa was just turning to the business news when she chanced to see two new passengers. Two big boys. "Lordy, Lordy! It's them kids!" she whispered to herself. They sat in the front seat near the driver and she put the newspaper up to cover her face. She peeked out to look again. The leather jacket and the blue jean jacket. It's them alright. She forgot all about looking at Harold's ad in the paper and to see if IBM went up or down. She could only think of the horrible things those kids would do to her if they saw her face. Maybe they even knew where she lived. Maybe they would break into her house and steal her jewelry and her silverware. Europa ducked down behind the old man and woman in front of her. She put the newspaper down on the seat and turned up her coat collar. She buttoned all the buttons and tied the red and green plaid scarf around so that it covered the whole bottom of her face. She put on the babushka so that it hung over her forehead and made a kind of shadow. Europa knew the eyes were a give-away and that's why the Lone Ranger wore his mask over his eyes, but she couldn't very well manage that with no scissors to cut the eye holes.

With the collar and scarf in place, Europa felt more secure. She dared to peek around the old man's wrinkled neck long enough to see that they were counting the quarters. They still had a good pile of 'em. Once they put the money away, blue jean jacket took the wrench out from inside his coat and held it by the red handle. "Red like blood," she thought, "my blood if they find out who I am." Leather jacket took the wrench and hit it again and again against his palm. Practicing for another parking meter or maybe for me! What in the heck are they talking about? More robberies and murders?

Once, they looked her way, but she ducked down. Did they see me? Lord knows, if they recognize me, they'll knock me down in the snow, steal my pocketbook and murder me with the wrench. "52nd Streeet," droned the bus driver. They were dividing up the quarters. At least they put the wrench away. They knew how to hide their weapons. How many old ladies had already bludgeoned senseless? She wanted to yell out, "Help! Police!" She wanted to make a citizen's arrest but they would probably get their gang members to kill her if she reported them.

"68th Street. End of the line. Your stop, Mrs. Jones!" the bus driver shouted out. But, Europa did not rush to the front of the bus. She hid, for a minute, bundled up behind the newspaper. When everyone else had gone, Europa hissed, "Hey you! C'mere!" Once Europa saw the bus driver heading her way, she looked the length of the bus to see it empty and stood up. "I just wanted you near in case I needed protection from those kids with the quarters, but they're gone so I guess it's safe to get off. Did you see which way they went? If I can just get to my son's house, I pray to God he'll take care of me."

"No, sorry, Mrs. Jones," the bus driver said as he helped her get off the bus. "I didn't pay any attention to those kids."

"Ya' gotta' do what ya' gotta' do," she mumbled as she ducked into the grocery store next to the bus stop. "Seen any mean lookin' kids with a lot of quarters?" she asked the clerk.

"Nope," he said. "Most kids are in school today."

"Well, be on your watch for two big boys. One wearin' a leather jacket and the other one in a skimpy blue jean jacket carrying a big wrench they plan to use as a murder weapon." She bought some nice, black Russian rye for Harold's lunch.

Outside, she pulled her scarf around her face again and rounded the corner quickly, ducking into every doorway, every shadow. At the corner, Europa stopped, breathless, looking up and down the street. She saw a couple of big boys in the park, but they were too far away to tell if they were the robbers. She passed the mailman and some ladies out on their porches waiting for the mail, shaking their throw rugs. One old man, barely moving against the wind, walked a big Doberman Pinscher. "That's just what I need," Europa said to herself. "A big, mean dog to keep them kids far away from me." Those robber kids would probably get the dog to be their friend with some raw meat, then kill it with the wrench after they murder me. She dashed erratically from tree to tree. Good old trees to hide behind in this neighborhood.

She could see from down the block that Harold's car wasn't in front of the house. Maybe it's in the garage. Europa was a bit alarmed when she saw that his sign, "Jones Insurance," was not lighted. Maybe he's asleep. She knocked on the door. She knocked on the front window. No answer. She went around to the back door and knocked. No answer. What if them kids live around here? They could really get me here with nobody around. She went to the neighbor's and knocked as hard as she could. No answer.

Europa sat down on Harold's front steps and wrote a note. "Hi Honey, Where in the hell are you? I came all this way and now I have to wait an hour to take the bus home and this bread will freeze. Where is my money? Love Always, Mama." She tucked the note under the door. Then, she felt like crying but she didn't because the tears would freeze on her face and then she'd be terribly chapped.

On the bus again, she kept her collar up just to be safe and read the newspaper. "Ways to Cure Your Winter Blues." It was too bad they didn't suggest staying home so your mother would know where you are. "Parking Meters Vandalized Downtown." There was no mention of the wrench or the kids, but it did say that it costs $500 to fix a parking meter. They would probably take the money out of the senior citizens' fund. Take from the old, give to the young! Oh well, maybe they would have a silent observer number on TV. She could describe the kids without telling her name.

Once she got off the bus, Europa waited until the bus was out of sight before she crossed the street to see if there were any quarters left near the broken parking meter. No one was around and, besides, who would think an old lady was breaking into parking meters anyway? Besides, she didn't think she could do it without a wrench.

The quarters were now covered with new snow, so she pulled out her rat-tail comb, knelt down on the sidewalk, and dug until she found ten quarters. "That way I can take the bus to Harold's tomorrow if he doesn't bring my money today." Europa mumbled to herself. She walked home on the look-out for the leather jacket and the blue jean jacket or any other big boys around looking for parking meters or old ladies to knock off.

The steps were still icy and the railing was still broken, so Europa had to hang her pocketbook around her neck and crawl up to the front door. She would be happy when spring came. Skiers and Eskimos are the only people crazy enough to like snow. Anyway, there was a note on the door. People shouldn't leave notes on doors. That way robbers will know that no one is home. They'll hide in your house and wait 'till you come in and then jump out and kill you with a knife or a wrench.

Inside, Europa took off the red and green plaid scarf and hung it in the closet. She took the quarters out of her coat pocket and counted $2.50. Maybe she could give half to the senior citizens' fund to pay for the parking meters. She put her coat on the hanger with the scarf and looked in the hall mirror to puff up her hair. Her feet began to warm up after she took off her galoshes and tennis shoes. She put on her black velvet slippers and knew she was safe at home, at last.

In the kitchen, Europa started the tea kettle and sat down at the table to read the note. "Ma! Where in the hell are you? I wanted to take you out to lunch and give you your money. I put the money under the cookie jar. Lock your door to be safe. It was unlocked when I got here. Call me right away so I know you are o.k. Love, Harold."

PART B: WRITING SHORT STORIES

Every short story is a fresh assault
upon unmapped and probably dangerous
country. . .One is always a novice,
proceeding by intuition and rightly
fearing the worst. . .one is tempted
to settle for a goal closer to hand,
a green meadow to lie down in, rather
than an icy rock-face to scale.

Brenden Gill

Although students have many stories to tell, it is most difficult for them to write as gracefully and colorfully as the tale is told. For the students, writing a short story is almost always like scaling that icy rock-face. This is probably because once they get around to putting the tale on paper, it becomes much more complicated and long and they are too worried about being wrong. As I sat down at a writers' retreat two summers ago to write a story about Europa Jones, I knew that I had set up a difficult task for myself. I have always been in awe of really great short story writers who are published in *The New Yorker*, who make every detail count, and who explain the universe in a single symbol. The whole task seemed overwhelming to me, but as I sat down at my typewriter and mulled over the character of Europa Jones, I became so familiar with her that she seemed to be a next-door neighbor and I knew that I would be able to tell her story. To begin with a name, to begin with a character, to begin with a situation and a season, is the root of all stories and I determined that students could also learn, as I had, that scaling the rock-face can be fun!

Here are some techniques I have used to keep students happy and interested in their stories from inception through final drafts. I first taught these lessons at a private high school, where highly motivated students had elected to attend extra-curricular classes. More recently I taught writing short stories in alternative high school classes, where at-risk students wrote well in spite of their very limited writing skills and great fear of writing.

I first teach the short story in an abbreviated fashion. It is important to teach form quickly and to get the students writing as soon as possible to eliminate fear of the short story. The basic structure of the short story may be taught in one or two class periods, depending on the prior knowledge of the students. I use the usual sequence—exposition, rising action, climax and conclusion.

INTERNALIZING STRUCTURE QUICKLY!

First, I explain the process and tell a story using the basic short story structure. The story that I have used most successfully is about a boy, named after someone in the class, who instantly falls in love with a beautiful new girl during the exposition. He plots, with increasing tension, during the rising action to attract her attention. Finally, at the climax, he introduces himself to her. Whether she says something positive or negative is the response of the class just dying to shout out her words! The class is also eager to invent the conclusion. This type of presentation causes the class to actually feel the rhythm and tension of a short story and to learn the structure as well. I have found that students are able to internalize the plot structure of the short story very quickly if they are not deterred by long and complicated examples.

Finally, we look for structure in some very short stories. A good source is the Scholastic *Voice* magazine because it contains very short—usually one page—stories, most written by students. In one class period, it is possible to cover two or three of these stories, discuss the structure in each and allow the students to rewrite parts that seem weak, such as the conclusion. My goal is to get five or six stories to use for reference in explaining point of view, conflict, motivation, symbolism and theme without losing the students' initiative to write their own stories.

KEEPING A STORY JOURNAL

During the time it takes me to teach the elements of the short story, I have the students keep a story journal. At any time during the class, they are free to jot down ideas in list form and then, at the end of the class, I give them ten minutes to elaborate on one or two of them. Here is an example of such a list written during a lesson by Todd.

    car accident during snow storm
    deer season
    war story
    death of my grandfather

At the end of the class, Todd wrote:
"Walking in the wilderness is the best part of deer season."
Later, he incorporated this into his story "Wesley and the War."
Many writing exercises focusing on the lessons can also be included into the story journal. Since the students are thinking constantly but are unaccustomed to putting down ideas on paper, if you give them license to do this, they have a multitude of ideas by the end of one week's story lessons.

I usually have students volunteer to read what they have written to the class. If they are reluctant, I ask if I can read it. This is crucial in students' gaining confidence in the validity of their own ideas and writing during the first week of short story. Peer acceptance is a very effective tool in gaining the impetus to write stories.

As the week progresses, their ideas in the story journal should get more complicated and may begin to develop into one or two paragraph stories. I try to check the journal every other day and add encouraging comments. Todd wrote the following about "A Stolen Car and a Stolen Soul" by Byran Woolley to explain what the character will do after the story is over:

> "Bruce could get his soul back by searching and possibly finding his car or he could start all over and try to build another car. He would be more happy if he could get his old car back because he put all the time into it and it also contained the tools his father gave him and he collected."

I commented, "Good ideas. There is usually more than one option in any situation."

CAPTURING CHARACTER

The next set of lessons in the short story series involves characterization. Because I feel strongly that truly good short stories come out of character rather than plot, I advise my students to know as much as possible about the main character before actually plotting the story. Often, in exploring the character, the plot will evolve naturally, as it did for me with Europa Jones. I knew her paranoia, her determination, her love for her son long before I sent her out on a winter's day to get her money from Harold.

Focus is the first problem in characterization and I try to give students a little boost at the beginning by letting them pick from pictures I have cut from magazines and begin to write about that person. A concrete image is a great motivator. Todd chose a picture of a modern man in Civil War costume and started to write about his character. This led to looking up the Civil War in a history book and talking to the history teacher because he wanted to learn more background information. Todd began:

> "Wesly Jones was born in 1842 on a small farm in Ohio. He was the oldest in his family. He had a great love for walking in the forest."

I also give students a copy of "Nine Methods of Characterization" from *Writing Creatively* by J.N. Hook (1967). I encourage the students to start with number one but to move on to others if they get bored or stuck. Often, they happily discover themselves writing very quickly, adding characters, and formulating plot, almost by accident. It is amazing that one venue or another will probably click in and the story will start rolling. Todd said "The story "just took over" and wrote itself." Here are Hook's methods:

1. Tell about the character
2. Describe the character and his(her) surroundings

3. Show the character in action
4. Let the character talk
5. Reveal the character's thoughts
6. Show what others say to the character
7. Show what others say about the character
8. Show the reactions of others to the character
9. Show the character's reactions to others

I also give them my own list of questions to guide the students in getting to know about their characters.

1. When did the character live?
2. Where did the character grow up and where does the character live now?
3. What does the character look like?
4. Where does the character work or go to school?
5. How old is the character?
6. What does the character do in his/her spare time?
7. What does the character believe in?

Once the students know all about the character and have explored dialogue and interaction with other characters, they have no problem contriving believable plots.

Another helper, once the students are steadily grounded in character, is to make articles available about writing fiction. Most recently I used "Hot To Plot" by Mary Kittredge from October, 1989, *Writer's Digest*. The article is about discovering the character's fatal flaw and then putting him into a situation where he is challenged to change his ways or face being defeated by his problem.

Duane remarked after reading this article, "Now I know what I'm doing!" and began to write most energeticaly. Todd decided to challenge Wesly Jones, a pacifist, with the Civil War. He wrote:

"Wes finally gave in and enlisted.
Two weeks later he had a gun in
his hand, a knife at his side,
and a spiffy new Union uniform..."

FINALIZING THE DRAFT

If at all possible, I try to arrange for students to write at typewriters or computers. At the private high school, I was able to use the typing room for writing class. This enabled students to write very quickly and to complete several drafts before they were satisfied with their stories. These students had less fear of wasting paper and more productive rewriting than I have ever seen. Todd, whose "Wesly and the War" was written this fall, moved to a computer for his final draft and added a myriad of details, strengthened his verbs, and eliminated passive voice.

He told me, "The computer just took over and I forgot about my problems." Todd was able to see his story happening during the final draft stage. He invented several twists of plot and elucidated various uncertain areas of his story once he got to the computer. Todd writes here about the death of Sam, Wes's best friend,

> "As Sam fell to the ground, blood ran down his neck, turning his uniform a dark red. Panic suddenly took over Wes' body. He ran to the north wall when he found himself rolling across the ground. He had tripped over another fallen soldier."

It is amazing the amount of work students can do at a computer or typewriter when they have their stories pretty well plotted out in their heads and it is even more amazing how many new ideas occur at the keyboard. For example, if Todd had written entirely by hand, I doubt that he would have finished his story in time to hand it in.

PUBLICATION!

Once the stories are completed, I publish them with whatever method I have at hand. If the stories have been typed, this saves me a great deal of work. If they are handwritten, I often can find an ally in the typing or computer teacher who will assign this job to advanced students for extra credit. Often, students illustrate their stories and enjoy putting the published copies together.

When they see their published work, when their friends in other classes are amazed with their stories, when their parents happily discover the writer in the family, all the pain and fear involved in scaling the icy rock face of short story writing are forgotten and they are very pleased with themselves, indeed.

REFERENCES

Gill, B. (1975). *Here at the New Yorker.* New York: Random House.
Hook, J.N. (1967). *Writing creatively.* Boston: D.C. Heath.
Kitteredge, M. (1989, October). Hot to plot! *Writer's Digest* pp. 26–29.
Woolley, B. (1978, October 16). A stolen car and a stolen soul. *Scholastic Voice.*

SELECTED BIBLIOGRAPHY

Cowden, R. (Ed.). (1954). *The writer and his craft: Twenty lectures for the young writer.* Ann Arbor, MI: University of Michigan Press.

> I found especially interesting "Writing as Design" by Zona Gale which deals with the relationship between reality and fiction.

Martin, S. (1977). *Cruel shoes.* New York: G.P. Putnam's Sons.

> These very short stories are by the comedian, Steve Martin. These stories are ridiculous and shocking enough to pose a challenge for even the most savvy students.

Macroirie, K. (1968). *Writing to be read*. New York: Hayden.

This high school writing text is my favorite. Macroire's technique of using student writing to teach students about writing is a winner. "Tightening" is perhaps the most valuable chapter in this text based on writing from experience. Since Macroire was once my undergraduate teacher, I have both learned and taught his techniques with success and pleasure.

McCullough, D.W. (1980). *People, books & book people*. New York: Harmony Books.

David McCullough presents a wonderful spectrum of writing and writers. Students are always interested in how famous writers write; this book provides excellent anecdotes.

Scholastic Scope—For samples and ordering information, write:
Scholastic Inc.
2931 East McCarty St.
Johnson City, MO 65102

In this fascinating chapter on writing fairy tales, **Carol Steele** *shows us how writing serves to "get past being stuck." After writing tales herself, as well as with many children, Steele believes ". . .fairy tales offer psychological road maps to aid the child's develop-ment." She begins, as does Hilla, with models both* **told** *and read. I highlight "told" because children are fascinated by adults who know stories by heart. Perhaps it is the eye contact, or maybe it has to do with respect-ing the human memory: Our capacity to store lengthy passages of language we both admire and* **need** *as human beings. Steele gives us a way into fairy tales not known to many Westerners: the six dramatic roles uncovered by the French drama critic, Souriau. Not at all like the story grammars many educators eschew, the "forces" Souriau has identified help Steele and her students label, and then manipulate, the tacit knowl-edge people have of the motives and conflicts that propel all stories. The reader will find Souriau's roles a useful addition to Asher's play writing chapter, Temple's historical fiction, Hilla's short stories, The Roops's "fac"tion, even Hayes's editorials*

CHAPTER 15
WRITING FAIRY TALES: CREATING MYTHS AND POSSIBILITIES

By Carol Steele

PART A: THE GATE TO THE CASTLE

Once upon a time there was a very special castle. It was smaller than other castles, but graceful and appealing with a dancing brook beside the wall. Into the wall was set a large scrolled gate, and above the gateway was an ornate arch with the words NAUGHT SAVE WHAT IS ASKED. People had once wondered at the meaning of the motto, but in time the ivy thickened around it and it was forgotten.

Anyone in the village could have told a newcomer that the castle was inhabited. There were stories of riches and rumors of magic connected with that castle. The resident of the castle was generous to those who made requests at the gate, but no one in the whole valley had ever been inside the castle or had a real conversa-tion with its inhabitant. So the rumors remained just rumors.

The tradespeople made deliveries regularly at the gate. Whenever they rang the bell, the resident came, swathed in a voluminous grey cape. The cape had a deep hood that scarcely allowed a glimpse of the face inside. Each visitor received prompt and exact payment, and a clear and steady voice remained in the memory of all those who came. But no social invitations were ever extended.

One day a wandering beggar came to the castle gate. He pulled the bell cord and waited. Soon the gate swung open. The hooded figure stood just inside.

"I came in answer to the bell," said the calm voice. "Was it you who summoned me?"

"Yes, if you please," said the beggar. "I am so tired and hungry. I came to ask for. . ."

"For what, gentle traveler?" asked the resident.

"For bread, please, to ease this grawing hunger." whispered the beggar.

The resident stood a moment as if waiting for the beggar to continue.

"You want bread?"

The begger noded and hung his head.

The hooded figure returned in a moment with the heartiest loaf of bread ever seen by the beggar.

"I have brought what you asked for," said the resident. "I wish you Godspeed."

The beggar murmured his thanks and turned toward the road. As the gate swung shut, he was already gnawing on the loaf of bread and feeling his strength return.

Some days later, a miserly man from the village made his way toward the castle. He had listened for a long time to the rumors of magic within the castle. Since there was nothing extraordinary about the castle itself, he had come to believe that if there was magic, it must reside in the strange cloak worn by the resident. The man was resolved to gain some magic for his own.

He had decided to pretend he thought the cape quite ordinary, and after he pulled the bell cord, he fidgeted until the gate swung open. Then he smiled a too-sweet smile and began to whine his request.

"Begging your pardon, but I came seeking a cape to last me through the winter. You and I are the same size. If I could have your cloak, I would pay you tuppence. After all, you have used it for many years."

As he said this, the crafty man could scarcely keep from laughing. He thought he was doing a splendid job of hiding his real purpose.

The resident listened, then waited to see if the man was finished.

"You came to ask for this cloak—an old cloak that will last you through the winter?"

"Oh, yes," said the man solemnly.

"Very well, you shall have what you ask for," said the resident, stepping back into the shadows and laying the cloak carefully over the scrollwork.

The man threws the cloak quickly over his shoulders. It still felt warm. For just a moment, he thought he saw a swirl of color before his eyes like a field of fluttering butterflies. But as quickly as the sensation came, it was gone. As he walked, he looked down at the gray cape and noticed for the first time that the hem was ragged and the sleves were beginning to fray. He tried every magic word and incantation he had ever heard, but nothing happened. At last he stomped into the village, furious to have spent a precious tuppence on a useless old cloak with barely a season's wear left in it.

Days passed. One evening, as the shadows began to lengthen, a shepherd came up the hillside toward the castle, circling the wall to reach the road that lead toward the gate. As he climbed, he stopped occasionally to look before moving on to another vantage point, where he paused again. It took a long time for him to reach the gate.

He stood with his head thrown back and his feet set wide apart while he surveyed each graceful spire and parapet. Finally his hand stretched toward the bell cord.

"I came in answer to the bell," said the calm voice. "Was it you who summoned me?"

"Yes," said the shepherd quietly. Then his steady gaze moved from the hooded figure to the brook, the ivy, the grassy courtyard just inside the scrolled gates. A single white flower bloomed beside the pathway. When he looked back up at the resident he was smiling.

"What is it you came to ask for?" asked the calm voice.

"I wanted to see this place and know who lived here, who cared for the castle that I have loved." said the shepherd.

"That you have loved?" The hooded figure stood quietly, head cocked to one side as if listening carefully.

"Yes, since I was a boy. I tend sheep on the mountains far across the valley, always in view of the castle. In sunlight the gracefulness of the spires makes them almost seem to dance. When fog fills the valley, the castle's silhouette is a mysterious promise. At sunset the windows gleam gold. During the long nights, the windows beam a starlight of their own.

"I always knew that once in my life I had to come near it, so I could set it all forever in my memory."

The calm voice responded. "You have eyes that truly see, and a heart that has learned love. Life's magic lies therein. All may be yours, for loving has made it yours already. Perhaps you will want to stay forever."

With those words the resident pushed back her hood. Smiling, she opened wide the scrolled gate and welcomed the shepherd inside.

The glow of sunset washed the courtyard with a golden light. A butterfly hovered over the motto, NAUGHT SAVE WHAT IS ASKED, then settled on the flower by the path. Laughter mingled with the babbling of the brook as the two residents glided into the castle.

PART B: WRITING FAIRY TALES

My first fairy tale grew out of an on-again, off-again relationship during my twenties. One Sunday afternoon I sat thinking about it and decided I was a worthwhile person, in spite of not being appreciated by the person I was then dating. When I stumbled on this ''He doesn't realize what he's missing'' attitude, I felt better, but I kept thinking and realized that in a larger sense each of us defines what we believe life can give us, and our beliefs determine what we receive. Suddenly I wanted very badly to clothe this idea in story.

This lead me to write the story at the beginning of this chapter, in which each character receives only that which he is capable of appreciating and asking for. Once started on fairy tales, I was hooked.

Recently I was moved to write a story for my daughter when I saw her discouragement at being passed over year after year in class elections. I wanted her to understand that her abilities were more important than the opinions of others, so I fashioned a fairy tale around the idea. Before my students wrote fairy tales, I read them stories I had written and shared the story behind each story.

My fairy tales come from a clear sense of the truth I am trying to illustrate. Before I write, I play around with possible scenarios that would illustrate the truth. I feel I am asking my subconscious mind to provide the pictures I need. Curiously, it rarely takes long in actual minutes—a couple of idle minutes one day, a sense of waiting two days later—but may be spread over days or weeks. An image begins to form which makes the point. I can't remember having to scrap one of these ideas: Once they have formed, they are well-suited to my goal.

Story ideas do have to be fleshed out, however. They emerge from my mind as a clear sense of direction and character, usually with a beginning and an end, but not as finished products. For instance, while writing the first draft of Second Best Princess, the story for my daughter, I wrote seven pages and suddenly realized I had veered off the course the tale needed to take. I went back to page four and took a different route, toward an end that was compatible with my sense of the story. My students seemed both interested and reassured to hear the discovery method that I use.

TEACHING FAIRY TALES

When my son was five, I finished my first draft of Second Best Princess, the story for my daughter.

"Come and listen, Allan," I said, "I'm going to read this story I wrote for Noel."

When he was settled, I began, "Once upon a time. . ."

"Oh," he interrupted, "it's a fairy tale!"

I was amazed that he knew what a fairy tale was, yet he could categorize an example of the genre immediately. This is the kind of familiarity I want young writers to develop.

With a class, I spend time recalling familiar tales, retelling them or inviting students to act them out. I also introduce less familiar tales to expand their range of understanding. According to Bruno Bettelheim, it is important that children hear the original tale, not a highly abridged or watered down version. Fortunately, this is easily arranged. When I brought in illustrated children's books as examples of fairy tales, my 16- to 20-year-old vocational education students begged me to read aloud, which is exactly what I had hoped they would do, but I thought it best to create a situation in which they might request it, rather than give them the opportunity to resist my suggestion.

But hearing fairy tales and looking at illustrations is not enough to reveal the process of creation. I have found Etienne Souriau's dramatic roles to be very helpful for class discussions of stories, and as an approach to writing. Souriau's six roles are each symbolized by a sign from the zodiac. While these new categories may seem odd at first, they open the door quickly to lively discussions.

FIGURE 15-1. Souriau's Dramatic Roles

Lion Force	♌	The hero: The character around which the action centers. He or she desires something.
Sun	☉	The desired object: This role can be identified by asking who or what the Lion Force wants.
Mars	♂	The rival: Anyone or anything trying to stop the Lion Force from getting what he wants.
The Moon	☽	The helper: Several helpers may exist, helping the Lion Force or Mars or any other character.
The Earth	⊕	The receiver of bounty: Lion Force may want the bounty for himself or for someone else.
Libra	♎	The judge: Any character who determines whether the Lion Force receives bounty.

I make a bright card for each role, including the name and symbol and hand the cards in the classroom. Then we begin to talk about how these roles are played out in specific stories, for instance, "The Three Little Pigs." Invariably someone claims ignorance of the story, so I quickly retell it.

Who is the Lion Force, or main character, I then ask. The three little pigs, someone volunteers, because they want something—homes and safety. Making their way in the world is their Sun. If we're lucky, someone protests that the smart pig who built with bricks is really more important than the others. This leads us to the idea that all three pigs play the role of Lion Force at the beginning of the story, but later on they are differentiated. The smart pig is a helper or Moon to the other two. Souriau emphasized that characters can share roles, play several roles, or move from role one to another as the story unfolds.

What does the Lion Force want? In the case of the pigs, they want to build houses and be safe. Survival and success are the Sun, or desired object.

Who tries to stop the Lion Force from getting what he wants? The wolf, of course, so he is Mars, the rival.

Does anybody have a helper? In time of danger, both the foolish pigs run to their more prudent brother and he plays the role of Moon, or helper.

Who receives the bounty? This concept needs elaboration for many students. The Lion Force may be trying to obtain the desired object for himself, or for another. The pigs all hope to live. When they outwit the wolf, they are Earth, the receiver of bounty. The bounty here is survival.

Who (or what) decides if the Lion Force gets the desired object? The kettle of water boiling on the fire seems to arbitrate the final outcome, thus playing the role of Libra.

Over a period of several days, we discuss these roles as they are played in a variety of stories and films. My students seem to catch on quickest if I let them identify the dramatic roles in movie videos they have all seen, especially horror stories. But soon they can identify the roles easily in "Snow White," "Beauty and the Beast," or any fairy tale.

We've had fun with this, identifying a number of fairy tales that the class knows well, writing their titles on slips of paper and having each group draw a title from the hat. Then each group writes a short synopsis, identifies all six roles in their tale on a worksheet and reports back to the class. There is general consensus on these interpretations, but also enough differing opinions from listeners to keep our conversations lively.

BACKGROUND INFORMATION

Defining fairy tales is difficult. In spite of their name, most fairy tales do not have fairies in them, although many have a magical or fantastical element. While students need not know all about fairy tales, it is helpful for the teacher to have a complete grasp of the genre. As the class progresses, you will be able to decide what information they need to have, or share in conferences certain information that is pertinent to some students but not to others.

In Nagy's *Teaching Vocabulary to Improve Reading Comprehension* (1988), I found a way to compare and contrast fables and fairy tales through the use of a Venn diagram. As I looked over the features of these two genres, I had the sensation of recognizing information that I knew, but could not have stated as clearly.

FIGURE 15-2.

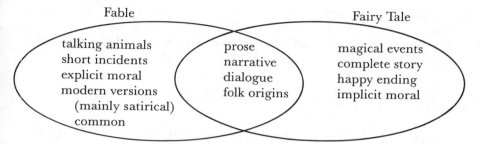

Then it occurred to me that much of the material on fairy tales that I read referred to their mythic qualities, yet pointed out their differences from myths. I found it useful to construct a Venn diagram of my own to compare and contrast the features of myths and fairy tales:

FIGURE 15-3.

Myth

superhuman hero
tragic ending
pessimistic

symbolic
rites of passage
express inner
conflicts

Fairy Tale

"Everyman"
happy ending
optimistic
nameless characters
are common

Bruno Bettelheim (1976) devotes a great deal of attention to the power of fairy tales. Here is what he says:

> The myth presents its themes in a majestic way; it carries spiritual force; and the divine is present and is experienced in the form of superhuman heroes who make constant demands on mere mortals. Much as we, the mortals, may strive to be like these heroes, we will remain always and obviously inferior to them.
>
> The figures and events of fairy tales also personify and illustrate inner conflicts, but they suggest ever so subtly how these conflicts may be solved, and what the next steps in the development of a higher humanity might be. The fairy tale is presented in a simple, homely way; no demands are ever made of the listener. This prevents even the smallest child from feeling compelled to act in specific ways, and he is never made to feel inferior. Far from making demands, the fairy tale reassures, gives hope for the future, and holds our the promise of a happy ending. That is why Lewis Carroll called it a "love-gift"—a term hardly applicable to a myth...
>
> To decide whether a story is a fairy tale or something entirely different, one might ask whether it could rightly be called a love-gift to a child.

According to Joseph Campbell (1988), "a fairy tale is the child's myth. There are proper myths for proper times of life. As you grow older, you need a sturdier mythology." He asserts that "all of these dragon killings and threshold crossings have to do with getting past being stuck."

Bettelheim and Campbell's statements suggest that fairy tales offer psychological road maps to aid the child's development.

WRITING THE TALE

A day or two before students are to begin writing, I announce to the class that they will be writing fairy tales of their own; I believe the subconscious mind goes to work on the challenge during the interim. We studied fables and discussed morals before we began reading and recalling fairy tales, so the idea of the meaning or Truth of a story was not new. When I read "Gate to the Castle" to them, and told about the situation that led to its being written, some of the students protested that the story didn't have anything to do with my boyfriend and me. Others argued that it did, and began to explicate their understanding of it. This seemed to open some minds to the possibilities of symbolism without teaching it directly. And throughout the semester we had tried to make our personal narratives strong and true, so finding a truth to clothe in story didn't seem to be a problem for them as they prepared to write.

On the day we start writing, I ask them to write a quick synopsis of what their proposed story will be. I give them ten minutes to write down a title which they may change later, and two or three sentences about the story they will write. Here is what Michelle's (age 17) looked like:

PROPOSED TITLE: Lase, the Princess
SYNOPSIS: A young girl falls in love with a handsome prince. But is it real?

Some writers spill out a synopsis and are ready to begin writing the first scene. Others are stuck. For them, Souriau's now-familiar questions will help. Who would you like to write about? What is his or her Sun? Who is Mars, the rival? Are there any helpers? With these assists, students are usually writing in a matter of minutes.

It takes a lot of time for the writer to commit the story to the page. Michelle's case is a good example. We began writing our fairy tales on Halloween morning; Michelle left her synopsis on her desk and procrastinated, peeling back a poster to use the mirror behind it to complete her Halloween makeup.

"I'm *thinking*, Mrs. Steele!" She responded to my proddings to get started. Looking back now, I'm sure she *was* thinking, although she also admitted that she only started the story so I would leave her alone. She had no real faith that she would be able to produce a fairy tale.

The next day at the end of writing time, I asked if anyone would like to read what they had written so far. Michelle volunteered:

> She was a beautiful maiden from England, who every day did nothing but sit in her room after school and look out the window. She was an unhappy young lady. Her name, Lase. The name fit her too, for she wore a dress made of white lace with a creamy white background and a lace ribbon to tie her hair. White was her favorite color. . .
>
> Lase had teddy bears of all sorts, but only one was her favorite. A big white bear with coal black eyes. Every day after school she would rush to her room, throw her books on the table and sit near the window with her favorite teddy, Star. Star was the perfect name for this teddy, it was a special gift to Lase. It seemed that every time she looked at the teddy it would have a look as if it had something to say.

This opening page brought murmurs of appreciation from her peers who commented that it "sounded just like a book." They immediately wanted to know what was going to happen next. Michelle refused to answer; actually she hadn't yet gotten a clear idea of how the story would unfold.

But a week later, glowing with pride, she stood up to read her completed tale. Here is how it ended:

> Then the brightness went away. Lase was no longer holding the hand of the prince, but the paw of a white teddy bear. It was Star. As she gazed into his eyes, she saw a tear form in its eye.
>
> Lase was stunned. She didn't know what to do. Then a voice came from nowhere and said, "He forgot to tell you. . . he could not be kissed until the two of you were married." The voice began to laugh and disappeared.
>
> "Zeno! Zeno!" Lase cried out. "Where are you Zeno?"
>
> A big wind formed in the air, then Zeno appeared with a white rose in his mouth. He turned to Lase and said, "Cry into the rose and let the tears fall upon Star's eyes and the prince will be free. Lase did as the pegasus said to do. In a flash of light the prince returned.
>
> "See, you do love me," Saint said. "your love is true too. Will you stay and love me forever?"
>
> "Yes, I will love you forever and a day."
>
> Lase and the prince stayed together and lived happily in love.

At the conclusion she received a round of spontaneous applause from her classmates. There was general rejoicing that one from their own ranks had created this piece. Then, to encourage those who were still struggling to finish, Michelle explained that she never knew for sure where the story would go next, but each morning there was a new part in her mind, ready to be written. "Just keep writing," she said.

The elation we feel at completing a story is one thing that keeps us coming back to writing. But my experience as a writer has shown me that producing a draft is only the first step, a fact that I share with my student colleagues. I must delete unnecessary material and streamline my sentences. "The Gate to the Castle" shrank from 1400 words to less than 1100 words before I submitted it to *Cricket Magazine*. During the time it spent ''resting'' in my drawer, I gained enough objectivity to see I was wordy and repetitive in the last part of the story. I often delete 20 to 30% of the rough draft on the way to my final story.

I must also check out reader response because, invariably, something that is crystal clear to me as the writer, has been imperfectly captured on paper and leaves the reader confused. When I sent in my polished manuscript, it was as good as I could make it. It was accepted for publication, but the Assistant Editor, Kim Shively, had questions:

> ''Several of our readers wondered just what the shepherd does to deserve this happy ending? His speech is nice, but does it reveal everything? It doesn't seem as if the shepherd has any choice in the matter. What if he is unhappy in the castle? How does the woman feel about him? Basically, the last episode seems incomplete and overly romantic. Perhaps you could rethink the ending a bit, though you don't have to try to answer each of our questions individually.''

This feedback surprised me since the story was totally clear in my mind, but it made me realize I had missed getting some of my ideas into the reader's mind via my words.

I went back and made several changes in the shepherd's remarks, and added a sentence for the resident: ''Perhaps you will want to stay forever.'' I was pleased with the revision and so was Kim, although in the editing process, she changed a few other phrases and words to make the story read smoother. Hearing about these changes makes students more open to the revision stage, even though their percentage of change is usually smaller than mine.

Before long we are ready to publish. I push hard to encourage students to illustrate their fairy tales, even though teenagers are old enough to find this idea repugnant when I first mention it. Still, when they hear they can recruit an illustrator if necessary, they usually agree. The resulting books are very satisfying to writers and readers alike.

Our final activity was a trip to third grade classroom where my teenagers read to the children and left their books for the classroom library. Then we listened while they read to us some of the books they had written. It was a day of shining faces.

OTHER IMPLICATIONS

I believe that students' satisfaction with their fairy tales is more than just pride of ownership, because there are very personal patterns in what they write about. Students from second grade through adult can write fairy tales which satisfy both writer and reader, and may help the writer in ''getting past being stuck'' on issues in their own lives.

My students are in their middle to late teens; they often write stories about issues which I know they are grappling with, not because they are told to, but because their deepest concerns are addressed in the enchanted worlds they create.

Becky, for instance, spent time in foster care as a child and plans to become a social worker. Her story was about Mickie, a girl whose mother had died and whose only friend was a stuffed bear named Rags. Mickie resisted her father's attempts to bring her aunt into the family, fearing she too would leave Mickie, until Rags showed her the Slide of Time in a dream, and convinced her it was time for her to make other friends.

Michelle, who was quoted above, was sitting in class one day when her boyfriend came striding in and demanded his ring back. We suffered with her as she pulled the ring off and handed it to him. Michelle's princess, Lase, fell in love but felt confused and doubtful about whether the prince could be trusted, and whether his love was true. It was.

Another student whom I'll call Dan is a 17-year-old constantly in motion and often in trouble, so his nickname of Chaos seems appropriate. He wrote about a hero named Kayoski who battled a witch to bring peace back to the village.

In the light of my students' use of fairy tales to grapple with the challenge of growing up, and their ability to find happy endings to keep hope alive, I believe that fairy tale writing is educational in a far deeper sense than most other assignments.

References:

Campbell, J. (1988. *The power of myth*. New York: Doubleday.

Bettelheim, B. (1976). *The uses of enchantment: The meaning and importance of fairy tales*. New York: Vintage Books.

Nagy, W.E. (1988). *Teaching vocabulary to improve reading comprehension*. Newark, DE: International Reading Association.

Nathan, R., Temple, F., Juntunen, K. & Temple, C. (1989). *Classroom strategies that work: An elementary teacher's guide to process writing*. Portsmouth, NH: Heinemann Educational Books.

Shively, K. (1989). Personal communications.

Temple, C., Nathan, R., Burris, N. & Temple, F. (1988). *The beginnings of writing*. (2nd ed.). Boston: Allyn and Bacon, Inc.

*Sandy Asher moves from child's play to writing plays
with the same fluidity as the chiding between her two
main characters, Sir Galupshus and Sandy Cactus,
in* **A Song Of Sixpence**. *She's a pro who knows
how to handle beginners, whether they're children in
her classroom or teachers learning to become coaches,
ultimately "directors." The reader starts slowly, just
characters is situations, but the action rises quickly as
Sandy shows children how to introduce conflict, write
dialogue, build toward a climax. As in the Hayes and
Steele chapters,* **The Elements of Playwriting**
*works with the whole by elucidating its parts in a clear
and straightforward fashion.*

CHAPTER 16
THE
ELEMENTS OF
PLAYWRITING

By Sandy Asher

PART A: EXCERPT FROM *A SONG OF SIXPENCE*

When blackbirds nip the noses of King Hempleworth's servants, the servants
quit. The king sends his faithful knight, Sir Galupshus, to the four corners of
his kingdom to find a remedy for the nipping birds. This scene takes place at
the Southern Border, a desert. Near a beach umbrella, SANDY CACTUS swings
a floppy beach hat and chants sweetly.

SANDY: Bat, bat, come under my hat And I'll give you a slice of bacon. And
when I bake, I'll give you a cake If I am not mistaken.

(Swoops hat down, looks inside) Nothing! Tricky little critter. (Chants, more
threateningly)

Bat, bat, come under my hat And I'll give you a slice of bacon. And
when I bake, I'll give you a cake If I am not mistaken.

(Swings hat, looks inside) Still nothing! Phooey! (Angry now) Bat, bat, come
under my hat . . .

(KNIGHT enters crawling and dragging his horse—the kind on a stick. Both
KNIGHT and HORSE wear sunglasses)

KNIGHT: Water! Water!

SANDY: Water? On the desert? There's no water on the desert. If there were
water, it wouldn't be a desert, would it?

KNIGHT: You mean you haven't any water?

SANDY: Well, that's an entirely different question. Sure, I've got water. It's the desert that doesn't have any water. This is the desert. All this sand, got it? I'm a person—Sandy Cactus is the name.

KNIGHT: Could I have some water?

SANDY: Well, now, that's a third question. What do we have thus far? Fact: The desert does not have water. Fact: I do have water. Question: Could you have some water?

KNIGHT: Please?

SANDY: Why not? There you are.

KNIGHT: Oh, thank you.

SANDY: Think nothing of it. Think, instead, of the answers to our three questions. In summary, No, Yes, and Why not? Isn't that fascinating?

KNIGHT: Not very.

SANDY: My dear man, you must continually challenge your mind, or in this climate it would very soon evapoarate, dry up, blow away. Poof! You wouldn't want to lose your mind, would you?

KNIGHT: I'm not sure I already haven't.

SANDY: Think fast. If you can think, you've still got it.

KNIGHT: What shall I think about?

SANDY: Look around you. Ask a question. Seek an answer. Those are the laws of survival here.

KNIGHT: Well, uh, what were you doing with that hat?

SANDY: Good question. I was chasing bats.

KNIGHT: Chasing bats? In the desert?

SANDY: Of course. Any fool can chase bats in a cave. But to chase them in the desert, now there's a challenge worthy of my attention.

KNIGHT: Have you ever caught one?

SANDY: Never.

KNIGHT: Then why do you go on with it?

SANDY: Don't you see? It's the perfect challenge. Fact: I must keep my mind active. Fact: There are no bats in the desert. Fact: No matter how long I chase bats in the desert, I shall never catch one. Therefore: I will always be challenged and never lose my mind.

KNIGHT: (snickering) No, but you might get a little batty.

SANDY: I don't get it.

KNIGHT: Never mind. I suppose you're wondering what I'm doing here.

SANDY: No, I hadn't wondered yet. But that's very good. A new question to ponder. I'll give it a try. Say, fellow, what are you doing here?

KNIGHT: I'm here to deliver a proclamation from King Hempleworth.

SANDY: Never heard of him.

KNIGHT: But he's your king.

SANDY: Didn't know I had a king.

KNIGHT: Where have you been all your life?

SANDY: Right here.

KNIGHT: Don't you ever go anywhere?

SANDY: What for? Plenty of questions to ask right here. Plenty of answers, too. Then there are the bats, of course. They keep me busy.

KNIGHT: Of course.

SANDY: But it's good to know there are other places with other questions. Think of it: a whole world full of untried questions. Gee. I'd like to try one or two. Just for the fun of it.

KNIGHT: Go on.

SANDY: All right. Who's this King Hempleworth? And what does he want? And what's a king, anyway? And . . .

KNIGHT: Wait a minute. One at a time!

SANDY: I'm sory. I got quite carried away. A whole world of questions. It's very exciting, you know.

KNIGHT: Yes, well. King Hempleworth is in charge of this whole country and he has a problems and he'd like your help.

SANDY: Seeking an answer, is he? Oh, I like him already. What's his question?

KNIGHT: His question is, what can he do about the blackbirds that are nipping the noses of his servants?

SANDY: Oh, that's a beaut! It's got real style.

KNIGHT: Any suggestions?

SANDY: Let me see. Fact: Blackbirds are nipping the noses of his servants. Question: What to do about it? Answer: Get servants without noses.

KNIGHT: There are no servants without noses.

SANDY: Hmmmmm. Well, let me think again. Fact: Blackbirds are . . . hmmmmm. Blackbirds, noses, servants. Can't get rid of noses. Don't want to get rid of servants. Therefore: Must get rid of blackbirds! There you have it, get rid of the blackbirds.

KNIGHT: Yes, but how?

SANDY: Ah, a new question. Lovely! Fact: Have blackbirds. Fact: Must get rid of them. Question: How? Answer: Capture them.

KNIGHT: In what?

SANDY: Oh, you are good at this, very good. Fact: Must capture blackbirds. Question: How? Answer: In your hats!

KNIGHT: Our hats?

SANDY: Of course. If it works for bats, it'll work for blackbirds.

KNIGHT: But it doesn't work for bats. You've never caught one.

SANDY: A mere technicality. Your challenge is not so great as mine. I have no bats. But you DO have blackbirds.

PART B: THE PLAY'S THE THING

They don't call it a "play" for nothing. Sure, they also call it "drama," "comedy," "tragedy," "thee-ay-ter," and less flattering names as well. But a play by any other name is still a play, and closely related to the work children do, which is also called "play."

Playwright and professor Sam Smiley calls his very serious and grown-up book *Playwriting: The Structure of Action* (1971). And isn't that exactly what children do when they play Let's Pretend? "You be the students," one will say, "and I'll be the teacher. You pretend you didn't do your homework last night and you come in crying. And I'll make you sit in the corner."

Roles are assumed, action is structured, and learning occurs—about the use of language, the logical progression of ideas, the consequences of behavior, role-playing and group dynamics. Disagreements break out, roles are reassigned, action is restructured, and more is learned.

"The play's the thing," Hamlet said, "wherein I'll catch the conscience of the king." A dramatic scene performed by living, breathing actors cannot be denied. It's hard to ignore and even harder to forget. Play, plays, and playwriting also capture the conscience, the imagination, the *attention* of students of all ages.

"Ask questions," Sandy Cactus says in the excerpt from my play, *A Song of Sixpence.* "Seek answers." He's pretty silly about it, but he has a point, and I get students to create plays by asking lots of questions. They seek—and find—plenty of answers, through the very natural process they call "play" and I call "playwriting."

A SECOND GRADE PLAY

Often, the writing is done only verbally, but the basics of structured action remain the same. A playwright's first task is to introduce the characters and their situation to the audience. I show several hand puppets to a small group of second graders. "What kind of story can we tell about these characters?" I ask. In context, they grasp the meaning of the word "characters" and begin assigning (or grabbing) roles: "I want to be the dog!" "I'm the lion. Rrrrrroarrrr!"

And on we go until everyone has a puppet. (There are more puppets than children.)

"The girl and the dog are friends," someone decides.

"Okay," I agree. "What do they say to each other?"

The girl puppet is jiggled in the direction of the dog puppet. "Hi," she says. "Hi," he replies.

"What's your name?"

"Shawn."

Shawn? I think. Odd name for a dog. But mine is not to question why. Mine is to keep the tape recorder running.

"Do you want to play?" the little girl asks.

"Yes," says Shawn, the dog.

"Let's go over here."

We are creating dialogue! We're introducing characters and their situation. But we are doing it by mouth and tape recorder, because a second grader's mind goes so much faster than his or her pencil. (Actually, we're doing what all actors do, amateur and professional, child and adult, when they improvise, an important writing and acting skill.)

Obviously, the child playing the little girl is a stronger influence on our play then Shawn, the dog. But that's fine. He's moving right along with the flow she's creating. And he's challenging her to work harder.

The little girl, whom we later discover is named Lily, soon meets a rabbit, a mouse, and a pig, and they begin to play. (A play within a play!) Since our space is a corner of the classroom, not a puppet stage, the children dance themselves as well as their puppets around, each assuming the puppet's personality.

The playwright's next challenge is to introduce *conflict*. Conflict is the heart of drama. The characters must have a problem to solve, or the play has no *plot*. "What kind of trouble can these friends get into?" I ask.

The lion has been waiting in the wings for just this opportunity. He roars and chases the other puppets, who scream and run away. That's fun, and good stage action, for a while. When it shows no signs of progress, I pop the next question: "What happens after they get away from the lion?" (Clever me. I can see that the boy playing the lion has nothing but a good long chase in mind, so I give him his moment in the spotlight, but a moment only, not an hour.)

"They've all run off in different directions," someone points out.

"They're lost," another adds.

More conflict! A new problem to solve. Exactly what we need. The action is escalating. To be in trouble together is bad; to be in trouble alone is even worse. With any luck at all, we're building toward a climax. (Keep an eye on the tape, I remind myself.) Enter the witch.

With a wave of her magic wand, the witch turns everyone into statues and then hauls them off to her castle. No dialogue; she simply tells us what she's doing and then does it. That's fine. She's added a wonderful new dramatic twist to our tale—and she's managed to gather all our characters back into one location.

Except we have a problem. I point it out, again in the form of a question: "If everyone is a statue, who will rescue them from the witch?"

Time to rewrite. Lily and Shawn hide and do not get turned into statues, we decide.

LILY: "Oh! Look what's happened!"

SHAWN: "What are we going to do?"

The others remain frozen, which is entirely appropriate. Lily and Shawn are our protagonists and therefore the ones who must solve the problem through their own choices and actions. This is simply good storytelling. These second graders seem to know it instinctively.

LILY: "Well, in the story book, *The Wizard of Oz*, the little girl poured water on the witch and she melted."

SHAWN: "But this isn't *The Wizard of Oz*!"

LILY: "Oh, who cares?"

(Yeah! I think, silently cheering our feisty heroine.)

"We've still got a problem," Shawn points out, not one to be denied—and a long way from his monosyllabic responses at the beginning of our play.

LILY: What?

SHAWN: We'll have to find a way to turn back the statues. We'll have to find her wand and see if it works.

LILY: Well, we can just look for it. Let's go get some water.

Dialogue is abandoned as they explain that they find water and pour it on the witch. True to tradition, she melts. They then search for the wand and pretend the cat (an unused puppet) is lying on it. Lily says she has to pull his tail to get him to move.

SHAWN: I've got the wand! I've got the wand!

LILY: Since you got the wand, turn them back into themselves.

Shawn waves the wand. The others turn back into themselves. Without any prompting from me, everyone cheers and we know our play has come to an end. That night, I transcribe the tape into a written script for them, adding a narrator to handle some of what was said not as dialogue but as they moved about, thinking things through and making choices. For instance:

> Narrator: it took them a while to find the wand because the cat had it. He was lying on it, and in order to get it, Lily had to pull the cat's tail.

Had I had more time with them, I would have played back the tape, and then encouraged them to work out the narrator's role themselves, or better yet, add dialogue and action that eliminates the need for a narrator by getting the information across to the audience directly. "What might Lily and Shawn say about the cat and the wand?" I'd ask. And perhaps I'd get something like this:

> "Look! There's the wand! The cat is sitting on it!"
> "We'll have to pull her tail to get her off."
> "You pull. I'll grab the wand!"
> "Okay! One, two, three, GO!"
> "Meow. . ."

But because I had only one short classroom visit to work with these youngsters, this was the end of my playwriting adventure with them. They were obviously naturals at it. I've rarely found a group that wasn't, whatever their ages or tested abilities.

No matter who is writing a play, a second grader, a colledge student, or a professional in the field, the basic elements are the same: *Through structured action, a clearly-defined main character overcomes increasingly difficult obstacles to solve a pressing problem or reach an important goal.*

With older students, and in my books *Where Do You Get Your Ideas?* (1987) and *Wild Words! How to Train Them to Tell Stories* (1988), I discuss each of these elements of story-telling. I give examples from works familiar to them: Who is the main character in the movie "E.T." (E.T.) What is his problem? (He needs to get home.) What obstacles stand in his way? (He can't make contact with home. People want to capture him and study him. He doesn't want to leave his earthling friends.) And so on.

I also point out the similarities and differences between storywriting and playwriting. Basically, the need for character, problem, and solution are the same. But in a play, everything has to be shown to the audience through dialogue and action. Everything has to be performed by flesh-and-blood human beings within the confines and limits of a stage. Unlike readers, audience members can't stop the play and reread it if they get confused, so it's best to stay with a small cast and only one or two settings, especially in a short play.

This last bit of advice helps give the play the classic unities of time, place, and action (unities learned and then often abandoned by experienced playwrights). It also eliminates the youthful tendency to write ten minutes of costume and set changes for every twenty seconds of dialogue. One might blame the brisk and exuberant leaps through time and space on watching too much television, but I can remember doing the same thing in my early attempts at playwriting, *circa* second grade.

Whatever the cause of this common mistake, I point out to all but the very youngest playwriting hopefuls that writing for the stage is different from writing for radio, TV, movies, or the printed page. The limitations in time, place, and action should be recognized and accepted as challenges to the imagination. With the very youngest, I use the gentle prodding of my questions to keep things on track. I hope they'll get a feel for what works on stage by doing it; I know discussing it won't get us far.

The younger or weaker the students I'm working with, the more active part I play in the writing (or talking onto tape) of a script. My questions guide them through the process, which we keep light, fun, and progressing quickly to a satisfying conclusion: a play that makes a dramatic sense and is obviously based on their own contributions.

With many of these younger or weaker students, I bring in stories that easily adapt into plays. (Carol Korty's *Writing Your Own Plays: Creating, Adapting, Improvising* (1986) has valuable advice on this.) I look for stories told mainly through dialogue and action—the kind of action that can be performed on a stage. "Stone Soup" and "Chicken Little" are examples of stories I've used with good results. The basic character, plot, and even some dialogue are already in place, but the students are encouraged to improvise beyond the given test. Professional playwrights do this, too, of course; *A Song of Sixpence* (1988) is the nursery rhyme plus a large dose of "What would happen if. . .?"

I've found that elementary and junior high students are strong candidates for creating good plays orally, through improvisation. This is a valid playwriting procedure. Words on a page, even those written by professionals, need to get "on their feet" to prove themselves stageworthy. Older students can be coaxed into improvisation—and enjoy it once in—but by senior high and college, those without theater training and/or high motivation prefer writing scripts down first, individually or in groups of two or three, and then reading them aloud. I believe in keeping writers comfortable, and so adapt my approach to the prevailing mood.

If possible, I present those working orally with a typewritten version of their script afterward. I've often seen youngsters start immediately on "my next play," imitating in notebooks the standard format of the typed first play even though I haven't said a word about that. Those working directly on paper get a simple format to follow, an excerpt like the one from *A Song of Sixpence*.

WORKING WITH OLDER STUDENTS

One of my most gratifying teaching experiences involved the opportunity to work on plays with 15 junior high students for an hour and a half a day over a week's time. Here's how the work was divided:

Day 1: After reading them short samples of several different kinds of plays, I divided them into groups of five and gave them ten minutes to decide what kind they wanted to write: realism, mystery, fantasy, whatever. Enthusiastic as they were, they could have generated endless ideas, and never settle on one. Reporting back after ten minutes meant a commitment, once and for all. In the time left, we discussed the similarities between storywriting and playwriting: the need for character, problem, solution.

Day 2: Our discussion continued into the differences between storytelling and playwriting: the reliance on dialogue and action, the limitations of the stage. We also talked about theme. Our choices about what to show on stage have to do with the point we're trying to make. It's often helpful in deciding what our plays are about to summarize them in one sentence: Pride goes before a fall—*Macbeth*.

Armed with ideas and ways to structure action, they got to work. They talked their characters and plot through, assigned roles and improvised dialogue and action. They tape recorded, listened, revised. (After a while, they felt familiar enough with the material to find the taperecording more trouble than it was worth.)

Day 3: The first half of the session was devoted to more rehearsal of the plays in individual groups. The three "first drafts" (acted out, not written) were then performed for the entire group. Comments and questions were offered. The three groups of five met to discuss their next steps.

Day 4: Costumes and props were brought from home or made on site. The plays were revised, refined, rehearsed.

Day 5: The "finished" plays were performed for the entire group. We had one detective story, one knights-on-a-quest fantasy, one realistic piece about a bag lady, and a great deal of excitement about the entire process.

ME: Were the plays perfect?
THEM: No.
ME: Were they fun?
THEM: Yeah!
ME: Did you learn something?
THEM: Sure! A lot!
ME: Do you want to do it again?
THEM: Yes! Now? Can we? When?

Unfortunately, our time together was up. But I know for a fact that several of them went on writing plays on their own, because it was fun. And I know they learned more each time. Because that's the way children *do* learn. The *play's* the thing.

REFERENCES

Asher, S.F. (1988). *A song of sixpence.* Orem, UT: Encore Peformance Publishing Company.
Asher, S.F. (1987). *Where do you get your ideas?.* New York: Walker and Company.
Asher, S.F. (1989). *Wild words! How to train them to tell stories.* New York: Walker and Company.
Korty, C. (1986). *Writing your own plays: Creating, adapting, improvising.* New York: Scribner.
Smiley, S. (1971). *Playwriting: The structure of action.* Englewood Cliffs, NJ: Prentice-Hall.

SELECTED BIBLIOGRAPHY

In addition to Carol Korty's book (mentioned above), I've found two worthwhile books about playwriting that speak directly to the young playwright, upper elementary school and older:

Tchudi, S. & Tchudi, S. (1982). *Putting on a play, a guide to writing and producing neighborhood drama.* New York: Scribner's.
McCaslin, N. (1975). *Act now! Plays and ways to make them.* Chatham, NY: S.G. Phillips.

Teachers working with young playwrights may refer to Sam Smiley's book or a number of other general books on playwriting published by *Writers' Digest* and *The Writer.* Creative drama techniques are useful with all age groups for building confidence, flexibility, and "stage sense," and for practicing improvisation. Explore:

Kase-Polisini, J. (1988). *The creative drama book: Three approaches.* New Orleans: Anchorage Press.
McCaslin, N. (1988). *Creative dramatics in the classroom.* New York: Longman, Inc.

For an excellent source of stories to dramatize (100 of them, grouped by age levels), see Ward, W. *Stories to dramatize.* New Orleans: Anchorage Press.

Larry Hayes believes editorial writing might be the centerpiece of a high school or colllege writing program: Their shapes vary widely; the form, essentially persuasive, makes use of every other type of discourse, narration, description, and exposition; and stylistically the writer's got the upper hand. What better forum for the teenager, where the goal is to persuade and where the voice counts. After defining editorials, Hayes explains each part of the form and provides alternative approaches. His easy style (reminiscent of E. B. White) coupled with his wide background as an editorial writer for the Journal-Gazette in Fort Wayne, Indiana, give his chapter an authenticity teachers yearn for. As with many other authors in **Writers In The Classroom** *(e.g., Nixon-John, Steinberg, Roop, Janosz, Steele, Hilla), reading and analyzing the form before writing, in this case editorials, proves integral to his teaching style.*

CHAPTER 17
EDITORIAL WRITING: DEVELOPING VOICE AND CLARITY

By Larry Hayes

PART A: BLACK HISTORY, OUR HISTORY

You've heard of a child having self image problems? Consider this account by the eminent black psychologist, Kenneth Clark:

"I remember one child in Arkansas, a little boy. . . When I asked him the key question—which doll is most like you?—he looked up and smiled, laughed, and pointed to the brown doll, and said, 'That's a nigger. I'm a nigger.' "

It was in the early 1950s that Clark was showing brown and white dolls to black children. Almost invariably, growing up in segregated neighborhoods and inferior, segregated schools, those children would tell him the white doll was "nice" and the brown doll was "bad." When Clark asked the children which doll was most like them, the children said the bad doll.

NAACP attorneys introduced Clark's research in Brown vs. Board of Education. It was the centerpiece of evidence that segregation engendered feelings of inferiority in black children. Writing for a unanimous court, Chief Justice Earl Warren cited the research as compelling proof that separate was not equal.

One month out of the year doesn't do justice to Black History. It's not enough to celebrate the achievements and recall the tribulations of blacks. It's a story worthy of retelling throughout the year, in our classrooms, in the halls of our great universities and in the inner sanctums of our homes.

It is not some marginal story that happened incidental to the frontier's expansion, the Industrial Age and modern society's advances. Black history is inextricably intertwined with the lives of all of us and our immigrant ancestors.

Yet the story is unique. Blacks were our only slaves, shackled, whipped, deprived of education, degraded in a thousand ways. There was no fugitive slave law enacted against the Irish, German or Italian immigrants to punish them for fleeing their masters.

There were no Jim Crow laws to force native Americans to ride the back of the bus or Swedish immigrants to drink at segregated water fountains or to use segregated restrooms.

Even after the civil rights movement crushed legal segregation, blacks have had to contend with discrimination at every turn. It separates teenagers at school dances. It causes white bank depositors to hesitate at the black teller's window.

We've abandoned our central cities to poor blacks, where they've become the principal victims of the dope dealers, the muggers and the slumlords.

To learn of black history is to recover the whole story of these private tragedies. To learn that history is to begin to make the connections between the Kunta Kintes who came here on the slaver sailing ships and the pregnant black teen-age girl in the tenement house. To learn the history is to help the rest of us connect with our hopes, fears and dreams of our black neighbors and fellow workers.

There are so many places to begin. With Nat Turner, the slave who led a rebellion. With the George Wallace, standing defiantly in the schoolhouse door in 1963, proclaiming ''segregation forever.''

With United Nations ambassador, Ralph Bunche. With the bombing of the 16th Street Baptist Church in Birmingham. With Andrew Young, now mayor of Atlanta. With the lynching of a black man in Marion, Ind. With A. Philip Randolph, founder of the Brotherhood of Sleeping Car Porters.

Or begin black history with Lincoln's Emancipation Proclamation, Jan. 1, 1863. With Rosa Parks, the woman who was too bone weary to give up her seat on a bus in Montgomery. With a young preacher's ''I have a dream'' speech at the Lincoln Memorial in 1963.

It doesn't matter where you start. Be forewarned, however. The terrain of our national psyche is rock-strewn and jagged.

There is injustice. There is struggle. There is tragedy.

But because so many black Americans have been tested to such extremes, blacks often are the exemplars of the human spirit. Medgar Evers. Sojourner Truth. Roy Wilkins. Autherine Lucy. Fannie Lou Hamer. They appeared on the scene like giants. We must never forget them.

In fact, in every field of human endeavor, if most conspicuously in athletics and music, American blacks win international applause. Scientists, poets, novelists, painters. They're all part of black history, too.

Yet the black child struggles to be visible as a person and not the ''bad'' doll in Kenneth Clark's experiment. And the question remains today, what is that child's identity—black American, Negro, African-American, and so forth?

Can that child someday find an unconditional, unequivocal, respectful niche? That's up to all of us, to really see that child, to strip away the stereotypes, the race prejudice, and fears. The whole story can be found in black history, our history.

PART B: HOW TO TEACH EDITORIAL WRITING

It was just a few days after Iranian students took American hostages at the U.S. Embassy in Tehran. Journalist-historian Garry Wills was the guest lecturer that evening at Indiana-Purdue University, Fort Wayne. I was driving him to a reception, and I happened to mention that I sometimes teach writing at the university.

"How can you teach anyone how to write?" Wills asked.

He was not being facetious but went on to make the point that you can teach grammar and that's about it.

I replied with what's the only honest answer: Teaching writing isn't easy.

And in the case of editorial writing, I've wondered myself if the form can be taught at all. I've tried out a number of talented, seasoned reporters for editorial writing positions. Often they flounder with a form that asks them to make judgments.

John Alexander, editorial page editor of the *Greensboro (NC) News & Record*, says, "Some people just can't pull the trigger—can't make up their minds."

Most of the skills that are central to editorial writing can be learned. In fact, I've come to believe that editorial writing could the centerpiece of a writing program in high school or in college, and it would be tremendously satisfying for students and instructors alike.

Preparing and writing editorials takes students beyond one-word and one-sentence answers. It gets student thinking analytically on events and issues they care about. When the last draft is written, when it's read by students and the teacher, there's no need for a quiz. Everyone knows real learning has happened.

JUST WHAT IS AN EDITORIAL ANYWAY?

"Black history, our history," the unsigned essay printed here, is an editorial. Take my word for it. People who read a lot of editorials probably would recognize the piece as such. But I've never found even a simple definition that would cover all the cases where people would say, "Well, here's an example of editorial writing." But I'm sure many readers have an intuitive sense when they're reading editorial comment and not straight news. Certainly professional editorialists have some notions.

Gil Cranberg, George W. Gallup professor of journalism at the University of Iowa and formerly editorial page editor of the *Des Moines Register and Tribune*, says he considers an editorial simply an essay, and an essay can be about anything.

So far, so good. Cranberg's definition distinguishes an editorial from narrative writing and from poetry. It also tells us an editorial isn't bound by a formal structure.

But take it another step. Alexander says. "Editorials can do a lot of other things, but their first role is to persuade." Newspaper and magazine editorial writers would agree.

After that element of persuasion, the form is wide open. Some editorials are very direct: "Congressman Winklebottom should be defeated in his bid for reelection." An editorial that opens that way would move briskly from one complaint to the next.

Some editorials are written to advance a proposed situation. They open by saying why rebuilding a bridge at the old site is too costly, then present the reasons that an alternative site is cheaper and more feasible.

Editorials can be written in dialogue. Consider this on the occasion of the 200th anniversary of George Washington's inauguration:

> . . . Do we expect too much of our leaders in this generation?
>
> I was honest and true. . . I respected the religious and political opinions of others. . . I don't think that's too much to ask of a president. I just assumed it was expected.

Editorials can be funny. Serious editorials can include humor. Others thunder with the wrath of God. So you'll find editorials that express outrage when children die of hunger. Other editorials groan in dismay over a mayor's misuse of campaign funds.

Keep in mind that when we're talking about newspaper, journal or magazine editorials we usually mean the management's statement about the events and issues of the day, from lotteries to elections, from civil wars to wars on poverty.

WHO WRITES EDITORIALS?

At smaller papers, the editor or even a reporter might write an editorial about the local drive for a bond issue to pay for a new library building.

At the larger dailies, with a circulation of 30,000 or more, there's probably an editorial page editor or a full-time writer who is responsible for the editorials.

As a rule, editorials are not signed. The reason: The editorial states the opinion of the newspaper as an institution in the community, and not the personal opinion of one individual, such as you find in a newspaper column today.

But let's not be too narrow with the definitions. If you look at an editorial as basically a statement of opinion, then a letter to the editor qualifies as an editorial. Of course, using the expression to refer to different elements on the editorial page can lead to confusion. As in:

> "How dare you print such an editorial attacking the library board!"
>
> "But madam, our editorial today was on the latest Star Wars proposal. You must mean Mr. Jones' letter."

There's also the signed column. Many of us recognize the names of James Reston, David Broder, Evans and Novak—just a few of the scores of syndicated columnists.

Many newspapers will also publish signed columns by their own, in-house writers. Often newspapers and magazines will invite readers to submit guest columns, which qualify as editorial comment. The "My Turn" column each week in *Newsweek* is a good example.

Editorials, letters to the editor and signed columns all have a lot in common. They state opinion. They appeal to reason. But they may also appeal to emotion.

HOW TO GET A CLASS STARTED

One of the first things to do when you're introducing students to editorial writing is ask them to bring examples of editorials they liked and those they didn't like to class.

It's the best way to help students see the different form editorials can take and how editorial writers can choose from different writing styles. "Black history, our history" is intentionally personal, and yet it conveys a spirit of dignity throughout.

I should mention, too, that most journals of opinion such as *The Nation, The New Republic* and *National Review* carry editorials with each issue, always near the front. Such editorials echo the current thinking of those associated with the same political, social or theological philosophy as that of the journal.

Church letters, newsletters circulated by special interest groups like the National Organization of Women, Common Cause and People for the American Way and even pamphlets put out by the local fire department on fire safety carry editorials.

Again, "My Turn" in *Newsweek* serves as an example. Students will readily identify how the writer makes a clear statement of the main point early in the piece. They'll see right off how the writer signifies an attitude of passion, anger or approval toward the subject.

When students make these observations, they're not only discovering for themselves the nature and variety of editorials. They're beginning to develop ways of judging them.

In that connection, I think it's well for the teacher to point out that when a publication runs an editorial, the reader is probably safe assuming that this is the way the publication wants to present itself to readers.

So to read an editorial isn't just to know the mind of the writer; it's often to know the heart and soul of the institution.

Now let me return to answer Wills more fully. I believe that people can learn to write better. And I'm talking about more than grammatical correctness. I have in mind style and form. Furthermore, I believe it helps to have other people talk about their writing. This is the kind of teaching one does with writing. It applies to editorial writing.

How The Pros Help Each Other

At the annual meeting of the National Conference of Editorial Writers, about 200 of the country's editorial writers spend one day ''critiquing'' each other's work with the idea of improving it.

I've attended maybe a dozen of the sessions over the years, and they're marked by candid, even brutal criticism. Sometimes, editorials give too much background. They don't come to the point. Or, they're lacking in imagination. Or, they don't back up arguments with facts.

In the long run, such NCEW critiques have had good results. Today, editorials in daily newspapers are better researched, more forceful, more persuasive. No question about it.

Phil Haslanger, editorial page editor of the Madison (WI) *Capital Times*, notes that ''No one is born an editorial writer. But there are collections of editorials one can learn from. . .There are principles of persuasion.''

Like most editorial writers, Haslanger didn't take a course or have formal training. ''I learned from the editors around me.''

There's no formula for the ''good'' editorial. There's no one-two-three step method of teaching editorial writing. Think of it, rather, as a collaborative effort that involves the teacher, the student and his or her peers—all engaged in the editing and rewriting that shape the final editorial.

A newspaper editorial can carry a lot of weight. That's worth reminding students. Because here's a form that almost anyone can learn how to use and it can be put to the service of a good cause.

For one thing, a lot of people look to the newspaper for leadership. They believe that the newspaper is an impartial witness to events and, therefore, more objective. Besides, people are just naturally interested in what others think, and expect to use those opinions in forming their own.

I can think of many instances where just putting out some information in an editorial brought about a change. So when I wrote about the need for better regulation of ice cream vendors selling popsicles and fudge bars in the neighborhood, I simply cited the obvious hazard and how other communities regulated the vendors. I wasn't surprised when our city council decided that it was time for new rules.

Some of our editorial endorsements have helped elect candidates to public office. My paper has campaigned for a ban on corporal punishment in schools, and the city school board, prompted by the editorials, banned the practice. We campaigned for years to get the district's elementary schools desegregated. That process is now well underway.

I've seen our proposals for emergency medical services picked up by public officials and then become part of the system. I cite these examples to make the point—editorials matter a lot. I've had students take one local topic and find examples of the newspapers' editorials on that topic to see if the editorials seemed to have some impact. It can be exciting for students to discover that the editorials set the agenda, then steered the course of the community debate. Usually, letters to the editor will be part of it, too.

Editorials such as "Black history, our history" aren't likely to produce tangible results. They can help sensitize people to an issue. Generally, it's hard to show a direct cause and effect relationship. Here's what I'm talking about: It's rare that the newspaper will call for the mayor to resign one day, and then he does it the next. It is clear the newspaper is playing a role in the debate.

What you've got with such a basic introduction to editorial writing is a bonus—a lesson in how the political process works. In fact, I've found that students are eager to do extra follow up on the issue. They interview council members, business leaders or parents involved in a controversy.

The student gets an experience that cuts across several disciplines and an appreciation for our system that could never be gotten out of a textbook.

Students will discover for themselves that many editorials don't presume to shake the world. They're content to provoke people to think or to see a fresh side.

I once wrote an editorial that described how the last sandlot baseball game used to mark the end of summer and how organized sports for kids had taken some of the magic out of summer. Only one person remarked on the piece. It was a school board president, who said the editorial got him to recall fondly his days as a boy playing sandlot baseball.

GOOD WRITING EQUALS GOOD EDITORIALS

I think what you're trying to achieve with an editorial is often what marks all good writing—a voice that rings true and enough facts and logic to drive the point home. And clarity above all else.

But there are some other things that will help, too. Consider this editorial that urges kids to wear bicycle helmets: "For most kids, a bike is an essential. But, unfortunately, most kids think bicycle helmets are something only nerds wear." The lead here gets the reader's attention. With one word, "unfortunately," it signals the editorial position, what it intends to persuade the reader of.

That's not always necessary, or even desirable.

I regard the *New Yorker* magazine's "Notes and Comment" as model editorials. Yet they often begin with a languid setting of the scene, as in this example, which takes up the subject of AIDS: "Surgeon General C. Everett Koop recently stepped down as the top guardian of the nation's health. Dr. Koop's exit from government service was a remarkably quiet one, considering all the hullabaloo that surrounded his tenure."

The passage is clean as a whisker, no rhetorical crumbs cluttering the paragraph. It's a seductive lead. It makes us wonder, "Yeah, what about that hullabaloo?" and we're reading on to find the answer.

Here's another lead that creates the air of a mystery. This is from Fort Wayne (IN) *Journal-Gazette*, and reprinted in the clippings of the Educational Excellence Network. "The picture from Concord, NH, of Lou Cartier Jr. being put into an ambulance made the front page of *Education Week*."

"That's a little strange," you say to yourself. Then you read how this boy was fatally shot by the police after he had held two students at gunpoint. And you read that Lou was a school dropout angry with the world.

An editorial can go straight to the point, the way this one does: "Some readers took deep offense at Dan Lynch's political cartoon, which appeared on this page Thursday. But Lynch's critics miss the point."

An Easter Sunday editorial I wrote in 1987 began very broadly: "What a season this has been for putting religion on the front page." Such leads often are very much a product of trial and error. The research, the developing of a point or a statement doesn't end when you sit down at the typewriter or word processor. It continues as you write the lead, often until you're finished with the first draft and look back to see what you've said.

The point is this: People who are just getting the feel of editorial writing need to be given a lot of latitude about the way they start. But every good editorial has a good lead. It's no sin to return to the lead after the rest of the piece is drafted.

A good editorial has some logical order to it. Keep this option in mind, though. Editorials can meander lazily evoking a mood, as in this editorial by *The Journal-Gazette's* Evan Davis:

> The view from the south bank of the Wabash is striking, there on Bluffton's downtown bluffs. It's the site where the new Bluffton-Wells County Public Library might have gone, to solve the library's space problem. It looks across to a greenway and downstream to a handy bend in the river and a row of old houses.

There is a logical structure here. The writer is setting the stage for the controversy. Then he notes that the controversy over the library could continue. At last, he declares, "The board has a reasonable alternative." The rest of the piece develops the case for the alternative, a new rather than a renovated library.

In some editorials, the logical structure leaps out at you, often right from the start. Consider "5 good reasons to settle," an editorial I wrote to push the school board and a parents group into a desegregation settlement: "Here is the case for Fort Wayne Community Schools settling the desegregation lawsuit out of court and avoiding a trial."

The editorial builds its argument as systematically as a legal brief, moving from the most specific and least important outcome of a trial—the cost in dollars and cents—to the most important outcome—the harm that would come to many individuals.

THE QUEST FOR CLARITY

When I'm teaching this kind of writing, I don't encourage students to make outlines. The outline may assure logical structure. But a lot of students have trouble with the outline. Those who follow it often follow it slavishly, with predictable results.

Better to write out a few main points that the editorial writer wants to make. Those can be rearranged in the actual writing of the draft or shifted around later.

Professional editorialists develop their own system. Many won't even write anything down, believing that it cramps their style. Editorials are rarely long, so it's not hard to stick to the subject without having a written plan.

Other writers,—I'm an example—will make a list of the points and perhaps items of fact to refer to for the spelling of proper names or for precise statistics. Even then, making a plan will depend on how complex the issue is—such as the capital gains tax debate or subsidies for the steel industry. Making a plan also depends on how much the writer knows and how clear he or she is about the position.

Van Cavett, former opinion page editor with the *Louisville Courier-Journal* and now at the *Morning Call* in Allenstown, PA, applies this easy test to see if it at least makes a point: Can you think of a headline that captures the essence of the editorial?

Cavett says if the headline test fails, the editorial probably doesn't have a clear point, and the writer has some rewriting to do.

The second thing to ask is whether the editorial adequately builds the case. In other words, does the argument back up the point so that a reasonable person is likely to agree?

One thing often omitted in a persuasive-type editorial is a fair examination of opposing arguments. "Always make a good case for the other side," T.G. Burks, a University of Cincinnati philosophy professor, used to tell his logic students.

The place to deal with the other side is high up, right after the lead paragraph. And the reason this belongs in an editorial is two-fold:

First, you've forced yourself to grapple with the most difficult problems in your own position. For the thing that persuades the other side is usually the weakest part of your argument. Answering it right off shows confidence.

Second, you establish your fairness with your reader almost immediately.

Let's go back to the editorial that defends Dan Lynch's NRA cartoon. The third paragraph begins: "Critics of the cartoon cried foul. They said it's outrageous and clearly unfair to imply, as Lynch does in the cartoon, that the NRA is responsible. . ."

Note that the editorial states the other side's case in the strongest terms. That's the best way to show that you're being fair and straightforward.

It doesn't follow that if you're showing fairness that you have to pull your own punches when you get to your side of the argument. Note as I pick up the defense of the NRA cartoon: "Fine. The NRA didn't pull the trigger. But who is responsible for the fact that somebody as troubled and dangerous as Patrick Purdy can get his hands so easily on such a semi-automatic assault weapon?"

There's no doubt about where the paper stands and its reasons.

I would only add this reminder. The timid editorial, the piece that pretends to be fair but is only being cautious, doesn't persuade.

WHAT MAKES A GOOD EDITORIAL?

This brings me to the heart of good editorial writing: Research.

The writer must know what he or she is talking about or else the statement of opinion is merely an exercise in self-indulgence. For the editorial, "Black history, our history," I read several accounts of the way civil rights attorneys drew upon social science to prove to the Supreme Court that segregation harmed black children.

There was a time when editorial writers at daily newspapers did little if any research, when they had no contact with the news reporters, when they merely parroted the old party line. For many newspapers, that day has passed, thank goodness.

A good editorial writer must first be a good reporter. That is, someone who reads the auditor's report on the council's sloppy bookkeeping or drives to the nearby city to hear firsthand the arguments for and against building a new library.

For students, this part of the task might appear at first the most formidible. Calling people for interviews can seem like a lot of bother for students used to doing little more than paraphasing information from an encyclopedia or textbook. My experience is that true reporting quickly makes the project more interesting.

When, say, a student has actually interviewed a physician who performs abortions or the homeless mother at the shelter, that student is on the way to becoming an authority on that little part of a very big and complex issue.

The piece won't write itself. But it's less a chore. And most of us get real pleasure from seeing our efforts at research take shape and form. Teachers may justly consider the research one of the most powerful motivating tools and should never give it short shrift.

But how do you get students to do research?

I define research very broadly. It can be reading up on the subject. It can be calling somebody who's engaged in a controversy. It can be going for a walk through a run-down neighborhood that the writer wants the city to rebuild.

I define research to include students talking with fellow students. I've often paired students and urged them just to discuss a topic they think they might want to write about.

At larger newspapers, an editorial board meetings regularly to carry on this very kind of discussion. Whether it's professionals or students, the process usually broadens the writer's perspective. It can reveal the writer's true feelings about the subject. It can show the writer what still must be learned.

Teachers with a knack for Socratic dialogue can help the class think through an issue. It can be an exciting exchange, between teacher and student. If it's before the entire class, other students likely will jump into the discussion. The effect is to create interest in editorial writing.

"So John, you'd like to write an editorial about heavy-metal music."

"You think it gets a bad rap?"

"Can you give me a for instance?"

"Is there another way of interpreting your father's remark?"

Such questioning demonstrates the process of research, opening up lines of inquiry into uncharted territory. Back and forth the talk goes, as you lead the student to explore the topic and to develop a clear point of view.

Here's another class exercise that helps students to establish a point of view. Invite them to observe their surroundings, then write down what they see, hear, smell and feel.

The student will write down things like the dusty chalkboard, the initials carved of a neighbor's desk, a student's khaki jacket, the hum of the ventilating system, the tangy smell of somebody's shaving lotion.

Then ask the class to turn the observations into judgments: "The chalkboard needs cleaning; the initials are poorly carved; the jacket needs a good cleaning." And so forth.

The exercise brings out the sharp difference between fact and opinion but also the difference between news and editorial comment. Further, it tips the student off about how to develop an argument.

Ask the student, "What makes the chalkboard dirty?" "Why do you say the initials are poorly carved."

Then the student will say something like, "The chalkboard has lots of writing on it. And it has posters cluttering up one end. And much of the writing is smudgy."

What the student has just done is to line up the logic of the argument that supports the premise—the judgment he or she has made on the observation. Following this kind of exercise, my students found it easy to write a simple, straightforward editorial.

WHEN TO PLUNGE IN

If you've spent a few class hours exploring the editorial form, your students are ready to plunge into the writing. If you wait for everyone to have the concept pat, you'll never get to the really serious work.

I like students to do some writing in class. I put them into writing groups. What I'm after is a spirit of colleagiality whereby students act as both audience and editor.

The idea is for students to feel free to interrupt each other at any point to ask what every writer wants to know: "How does this sound?"

When students become comfortable with listening to others' work, asking for and getting suggestions on revision, there'll be lots more rewriting throughout. Which is precisely what you want.

Students will spot each other's clumsy, vague sentences. They'll detect weak arguments. They'll find abstract points that need to be made concrete with word pictures. Even professional editorial writers often forget that a vivid metaphor can help a reader "see" the point.

Consider the use of this extended metaphor in an editorial that links the July 4 American celebration of freedom with the Tiananmen Square prodemocracy demonstration in China: ''We're left with one haunting image above all, of a lone young man standing in front of a column of tanks. When the lead tank moves to the left, he moves to the left, blocking its way. When the tank moves to the right, he moves there, too—a checkmate of military might with moral power.''

The writers' group can also act as an editorial board to select one of the best pieces a member has written and send that as a letter to the editor or guest editorial to the daily newspaper or the student publication. I always try to get the broadest possible audience for student writers. And most editorial page editors are happy to print thoughtfully written pieces.

No student should ever be made to feel, ''Well, I'm only a student and my opinion isn't worth much.'' To the contrary, assuming the teacher has seen to it that the student has done the interviewing and other legwork, the student will have something of real value to contribute on a public issue. What style it lacks can be overcome with honest work and a tone of sincerity.

As always, students will fret about the length. As they should be reminded by looking at sample editorials, an editorial can be just a few sentences or can run to 600 or 700 words, for the heavier pieces in, say, *The New York Times*. I point out that this is a much more manageable length than a term paper and helps students develop some thinking skills that the term paper doesn't.

On the selection of topics, your best sources are the daily newspaper and the weekly news magazines. The articles, even the briefest ones, provide the student writer with the basic facts and should suggest things that deserve further investigation.

Let's say the county jail has had its first escape. The man has been caught. But it was scary piece of news to have a dangerous man at large even for a day or two.

Ask students, ''What's the main issue here?''

Good editorial writing begins with identifying that. Some students might say that the main issue is catching the escaped convict. Others may be reminded that crime is on the upswing. Those are interesting things to explore. But not in an editorial that's meant to respond to the news event.

The main issue here is security at the county jail. Is it lax? Who's responsible? How many escapes over what period of time is it realistic for such a jail to expect? What kind of security problems do other communities have? If security has gaps, what will it take to fill them? How much money? Will it mean more personnel better trained?

It's important for the teacher to lead the class in freewheeling discussions of all the marks of a good editorial throughout the time of writing and revising. The discussions will help students have a clear idea of what they're trying to accomplish.

When the early drafts are completed, the discussions will help students evaluate their own work and that of others in their writers' group. Of course, the discussions will let everyone know how the teacher plans to evaluate the editorials.

FINISHING TOUCHES

I want to suggest here some tips on writing conclusions. It's common—I speak from 16 years' experience—for the writer's interest to flag toward the end of the piece.

Here's what happens. The problem has been clearly identified. The research suporting the point has been marshalled. The writer has huffed and puffed throughout. Then it's time to send the piece to the copy editor or hand it in to the instructor. It's at this point that the editorial writer's mind becomes mysteriously flooded with cliches: "It's time for the council to get moving on this." "We all must bear the burden." "So it's three cheers for Councilman Burns." "We hope this episode is the last we'll hear of the subject."

The reader is left with an unsatisfied feeling. The reader may even be wondering whether the writer truly knows what he or she is talking about.

Better for the writer to take extra care with the conclusion.

The first thing is to go back and look closely at the first paragraph. That reminds the writer of the editorial's main point. Needless to say, the conclusion should somehow restate or echo that.

Take the closing words of an editorial by Elma Sabo of *The Journal-Gazette* on the need to put devices on playground equipment so the physically handicapped children can use the equipment: "But until the special device is reality, the Turnstone Center and the parks department could join together in granting more access to the already existing playground for disabled kids."

Sabo's conclusion doesn't stir emotions. But it sums up the basic point of the editorial and then proposes an interim solution.

A conclusion to an editorial that does appeal to emotion is this one: "Abortion is none of the government's business. It's the woman's business. It is her decision. Turning back would be a profound tragedy."

Here's a conclusion to an editorial that tackles the slaughter of marine life through the use of large nets that sea life that's not being sought for food:

"What's needed is worldwide willingness to ban practices that harm our shared resource. Otherwise, the oceans may no longer have much to share."

I regard this a strong conclusion, even sobering. It is not, given the case the writer sets forth, melodramatic.

In "Black history, our history," the conclusion attempts to make the challenge of overcoming racism a personal challenge: "That's up to us, to really see that child, to strip away the stereotypes, the race prejudice, the fears. . ."

Here's the way I wrapped up an editorial that set forth the qualities my newspaper wants to see in a new school superintendent: "The point is this. The school board can afford to be picky."

Short, snappy conclusions like this carry punch. The reader is left with something specific to think about.

If my first conclusion doesn't seem to match the emotional force of the rest of the editorial, I may write three or four endings. Often it's just a matter of changing a couple of words or phrases to get the effect I'm after.

In the example I just cited, I might have started with something like, "The school board should be very selective." I regard that as too formal, almost academic. My audience isn't a computer programmer devising software that checks spelling. It's a guy having a second cup of coffee over the breakfast table. "Very selective" won't stay with him. "Picky will."

But no matter what part of the editorial the student is working on, rewriting and reworking pay big dividends. Because of that, I recommend that you assign no more than one editorial for any two-week period. That gives the student plenty of time for interviewing and other research and for making numerous revisions. At the same time, you're showing the student that the writing process is just as important as the final product.

Maybe in the case of editorial writing, the process is more important. With the finished copy, the student gets only a grade and, perhaps, some deserved praise. With the process, the student is learning how to make some sense out of a crazy world.

REFERENCES

Rystor, K. (1983). *The why, who and how of the editorial page*, New York: Random House.
Stonechipher, H. (1979). *Editorial and persuasive writing: Opinion functions of the news media*, Hastings House.
The Masthead (Fall, 1986). The quarterly journal of The National Conference of Editorial Writers, *38*(3).

Frances Temple strongly believes in combining *make-believe and research in social studies: "Empathy and curiosity work in tandem and increase the demand for each other." Historical fiction begins in journals in Temple's room, where children imagine and write; imagine, research, and write; or respond, analyze, and write. Key, however, to successful journal writing, where children find their voices and the voices of their imagined characters, is the environment Temple and her children create. Sandy Asher's, "The Elements of Playwriting," is as much a part of Temple's chapter as her own. Props matter, as does the playfulness of both teachers.*

CHAPTER 18
HISTORICAL FICTION: THE INTERPLAY OF MAKE-BELIEVE AND RESEARCH

Frances Temple

PART A: AN EXCERPT FROM *THE SONG OF BEDU HALIMA*

Halima drew her knees up to her chin and sat encircling her ankles with her hands. The shapeliness of her feet pleased her. The singsong of the storyteller's voice lulled her, as did the soft glow of lanterns on the dark wall of the tent, on the embroidered cushions and on the faces of the women and children who listened. Halima played with her ankle bangles, her mind drifting from the story.

"There was, there was not . . ."

The wind sighed outside the tent, blowing the desert sand in swirls, trying to find a crack through which to drive sand into the tent. Halima smiled in the darkness. She dreamed of her cousin, Atiyah, her betrothed, he of the clear eyes and winged brow, he of the quick wit and ready laugh. She pulled a large pillow toward her and curled her arm on it playing with a tassle, pillowing her head. The better to sleep, the better to dream.

She was awakened by a hand firmly grasping her ankle. The tent was dark, the grip strong.

"Hush cousin, quiet! I must talk with you!"

How easy it was to daydream of Atiyah when she was kept strictly apart from him in the women's tent. What a different matter altogether to have him there next to her, shaking her foot in the night. Girls of the Beni Khalid found with their lovers before the marriage ceremony were put to death, and rightly so, to protect the honor of the tribe.

"Atiyah, we must not . . ." (but as she spoke she wondered—Atiyah's own name meant the Gift of God: could gifts of God be refused?). When he pulled on her hand she followed him, crawling under the tent side, and sat next to him on the side away from the wind, where no one could hear them through the thick, black felt.

"Do not think that I would risk you so, my Halima, for a matter of small importance. You know that you are worth more to me than sight or breath." Halima's heart pounded in her ears so that it was hard for her to hear what her cousin said next. "I have come to say goodbye; I have been sent away." His voice was low, urgent, and, she noted ruefully, happy with excitement.

"Our uncle Saladeen is riding towards our tents. Your father does not wish his path to cross mine. Essafeh called me just after Saladeen's messenger came to him. He said, "Go, Atiyah. Go, raid the Shummari, or hunt lizards in the desert, that I may say you are gone. Stay away until the moon has waxed and waned again.""

"Why, Atiyah?" asked Halima.

"Eeh!" continued Atiyah, holding up his hand, "Why, Essafeh? I asked him." Atiyah's face flashed a grin as he recounted Essafeh's reply, and Halima smiled at his imitation of her father's familiar gesture, one hand over his heart, and of her father's gruff voice.

" 'Because, Atiyah, because my wife Miriam had a dream! Ask no questions, nephew and son of my heart. Just go!' And so of course, though no more enlightened than a Saluki hound, I am going."

Atiyah turned serious again. He held Halima's hands and gazed into her face. His face was dark in the hurrying moonshadows, his eyes almond shaped and almost black, the whites bright, his teeth like hailstones. "Halima," he said at last, "by the next moon, perhaps a cloud will have burst, and we will dance in the desert again."

"We will draw water-rings in the wadi," said Halima, low, falling into a chilhood game of poetry making.

"And scatter rainbows with the droplets."

"We will gather flowers in the desert."

"And chorus with the singing of the frogs."

"We. . ." She bit her lip. As usual, she was the first to run out of words. She was full of anxiety for him, as always when he went on a raid, for he threw himself into danger with the fearless concentration of a hawk. "I must leave tonight," he said, "while the wind is blowing enough to cover my trail. No one must notice that I have gone, until it cannot help but be noticed."

Halima clung to his hands, feeling their strong bones, feeling time as precious as jewels flowing through her fingers like sand. She touched his hands to her lips, and then to her forehead.

"Go, then," she said, "and may Allah smooth your homeward path." Summoning her courage, she let go of his hands. In one quick movement, he rose and left.

Halima sat alone, listening to the moan of the wind, watching the clouds scudding across the moon. She watched to see Atiyah ride off, but she saw nothing, only the swift gray moonshadows of the clouds, moving like skittish ghosts across the dunes, all flowing away from her. She sat until the tears came. She sat until the crying was over. She crawled back into the tent and slept.

"Up, girl! We have guests coming!" The hand, shaking her hip this time, could only be her mother's. The tent side was pulled up. Sunlight poured in. The wind had died, the sky was clear blue. The sands glittered, traceless, warming fast.

The sudden crackle of burning thornbrush, the slow warm smell of smouldering camel dung told her someone else had lit the morning cook-fires and she had overslept. She hastened to pull herself together, washing with the wet cloth her mother handed her. Wake-up sounds: the slapping of bread dough, and now the rhythmic tattoo of the coffee-grinders, her brothers, who made a dance of beating the beans in the tall mortar before the tent door, singing and throwing the pestle down TA TOOM TA TA TOOM! releasing the fine smell of crushed beans. How could she have slept? Inside the tent, dark in contrast to the bright outside, copper pots hung on the center poles caught the light and gleamed. From among the scattered pillows, the tousled heads of her little cousins and siblings rose like dark mops, like the sudden blooming of flowers after a desert rain. Goats and sheep bleated nearby, some impatient to be milked.

It all seemed so ordinary.

Maybe it was a dream I had, thought Halima, hopefully, and Atiyah will laugh when I tell him. But it had not been a dream, as she well knew.

"Why must we feast Uncle Saladeen? *You* do not like him. *I* do not like him. He is coming to hurt us. So why?" Halima's little sister Nazreen questioned her mother, as the three of them stood together, the mother combing and plaiting the little girl's long hair, Halima poking in a box, finding beads to adorn the ends of the plaits. Halima knew what the answer would be before her mother spoke, but she noticed the careful flatness in her mother's voice, and knew that she too was afraid.

"Because we are the Beni Khalid, Nazreen, and no one ever goes hungry from our tents."

"Saladeen minds, doesn't he, that Father is called Essafeh, the Welcomer, whereas he is only called Saladeen, the Scourge. It makes him angry with us, doesn't it, Mother?"

"Shhh, Nazreen. Saladeen is a worthy name. We will not speak ill of a guest."

The coffee-grinders' work was almost finished, and their sounds had announced to all the tents that there would be guests and feasting in the tents of Essafeh, and that, as always, all were invited.

Still, chores had to be done. Halima was out milking the goats when Saladeen and his men, tall astride their camels, their head-cloths snapping in the breeze like banners, came into sight over the crest of a dune. Saladeen. Saladeen. How often she had heard that name spoken, hissed between her mother's locked teeth. Their was some bitterness in her mother when she spoke that name, an old story, some disagreement between Saladeen and Essafeh that ran deep. It had not concerned Halima much until today, until now that the disagreement threatened Atiyah, took him away from her.

She stripped the last rich milk from the goat's udder, patted her roughly on her bony rump, and moved on to the next. In a pit behind the tents, a whole camel was being roasted. She had heard its death-cry earlier, and its throat had been slit to prepare the feast. A great sacrifice, and one considered noble among the Beni Khalid. Its hair would go to make her robes, to make the black tents bigger. Yet it seemed unreal that this camel, whom she had first seen drooping his eyelid above the campfire, smiling at the stories, should be turned to mere meat and cloth with the thrust of a knife. She shivered.

"Cha-aa! I am worse than a baby!" she told herself, finishing the last goat and sending her on her way. She rose, 'tall as a sugarcane and as sweet,' Atiyah had said to please her, though he knew she'd know it was a phrase he'd heard in the old stories. She carefully lifted the bowl full of milk to her head, conscious of her height and grace. She settled the bowl on her head-cloth, and, supporting it lightly with her finger-tips, glided back to the tent. From within the guest tent, she was noticed by Saladeen's companions, who watched closely until she was out of sight. Halima felt the strange men's eyes upon her, but she did not look that way. Outside the zenana, the women's tent, she helped her mother scour the long metal platters with sand, to that they would shine for the feast. She set some milk out to sour, and some she mixed with dried dates, to sweeten it for drinking, and this she kept in the shade to cool. She took down the copper bowls from the tent-posts, and filled them with dried dates and nuts from the storage sack.

"Where is Atiyah?" her mother asked. "I did not see him go to greet his uncle." Halima looked at her mother, as she stood, her hands full of bread dough, her face impassive. Did she know? Did she wonder if Halima knew? Halima let out a sigh. "Nor did I, Mother."

Halima stood before the men in the greeting-tent, where she had meant to pass unnoticed. Saladeen called for her, and her father had had no choice but to call for her as well, in his guest's name. Saladeen stood before her, his face like wood, his eyes reddened, unreadable. He ran the side of his finger along her arm, from elbow to shoulder, as if, thought Halima, she were an eggplant from the oasis, a fruit he was testing for ripeness. Halima's skin flinched involuntarily but she held her head high, her neck arched like a gazelle caught before a hunter.

"So this is my beautiful niece Halima, betrothed to my nephew Atiyah, the Gift of God." Saladeen's heavy voice was filled with unpleasant irony. "You are to be proud, my brother."

Halima's father Essafeh nodded politely.

"And the noble Atiyah himself, why has he not come to greet his uncle?"

"He went with a party of young men to the south, to search for some missing stock. They left just before your messenger came to us," said Halima's father.

"AHAHH!" grunted Saladeen, and his grunt was like that of an angry beast.

Halima held out the kettle of water and hand-cloth, so that the guest might wash before eating.

PART B: IN THE CLASSROOM

We interrupt this story to bring you back to work, writing teachers!

I write historical fiction because it satisfies my wish both to *imagine* more richly, and to *know* more specifically. To me writing is just like reading only more strenuous. Not only must I think my way into a situation, but I have to understand it well enough to rebuild it in words, to draw others in. Historical fiction is like any fiction, with the added dimension that you need to do much of the research outside of your own self and surroundings.

Historical fiction combines make-believe and research.

MAKE-BELIEVE

The capacity for make-believe is one of the most delightful raw powers that a child brings to school when he starts his formal education. Occasionally we teachers, in our zeal to follow the dictum "Get children to write from their own experience," overlook the make-believe side of children's lives. Teaching whole language carries a responsibility to think holistically: We have only to watch preschoolers at play to be reminded that their experience as princesses, rescuers, race-car drivers, are as real to them as supper at McDonald's, and potentially even more fun to write about.

The capacity for make-believe doesn't die out with schooling, or with the development of logical thinking. Much of it is channeled into the willingness to participate in fiction, to identify with certain characters. The same child who by power of imagination transforms the school jungle-gym into a blazing apartment house, and then overcomes all her fear to rush through fire to rescue a stranded cat, will, at age fifty, so fully participate in a novel that she will come from it more experienced, deepened or renewed.

Within the capacity for make-believe is embedded the ability to discern story, to find that which is powerful, moving, and universal.

RESEARCH

Research skills are one of the many skills people are supposed to acquire in school. Some aspects vary with available technology. I use the card catalogue, but prefer sometimes to wander in the stacks. I am slowly learning to use ERIC and other computer search services, as the need arises, for my books. Research is not all done with books or microfiche. It entails calling people up, asking questions, world-watching. Teaching children to make use of book sources, people sources, and observation is part of our job.

THE MERGER

Empathy is mostly cultivated through imagination. Knowledge is mostly build through research. But empathy is the motive for increasing knowledge, and knowledge increases empathy. If, for example, we know nothing about Arab culture, we won't much care when bombs are dropped on Libya. If we know Halima, we'll have somebody on the ground. And later, a reason to read the papers, or to turn to books for insights into history, to look up old poetry, to read the Old Testament and the Koran.

Both as teacher and as writer of historical fiction, I find myself confronting the same principle: The child who is informed cares, and his caring motivates a search for more knowledge. Imagination and knowledge work in tandem.

ACTIVITIES

As a teacher you may be looking for specific ways to bring historical fiction into the classroom. Like the nomad peddlar I come into your tent and spread my wares on your carpet, hoping that among them you will find something you need, something you want. Buyer beware. Select and adapt. I teach first and second grade. After school I sometimes work with a mixed-age gang (10–15-year-olds) in theater and writing. My ideas are culled from these groups. I can only assume that they will work well for middle grades, and be adapted for use with adults.

If you are a beginning teacher, bear in mind two ranges as you choose. One runs from the concrete to the abstract: Young children will benefit from props, masks, bits of costume, artifacts, spaces for physical make-believe. Older children and adults are more adept at manipulating ideas. The other concerns the balance between fantasy and fact. The younger child will get engrossed in make-believe, full of emotion and empathy; he may shun facts. As people age, this balance sometimes shifts to the opposite extreme.

A word of caution, too, about assignments. Some students find their voices and take off on their own ideas with no guidance. Others benefit from prompts, some from vague open-ended assignments. Some prolific writers get bogged down midstream, apply assigned tasks to their work, and float clear. Some children find their own voices and discover their native wit in response to assignments. My general approach is: Try everything, force nothing.

Making an Authentic, Mind-Stretching Setting for Make-Believe   The novel *Halima*, the first pages of which open this chapter, is based on half-pages of writing I was able to do during writing workshop in my primary class. We were studying North Africa and Islam. We learned some things by rote: names of countries in North Africa, names of foods and animals. We memorized and discussed the five pillars of Islam: alms, prayer, study, fasting, pilgrimage. We furnished the classroom with whatever props and resources I could find: pictures of nomads in the desert, of ancient cities and forts, UNESCO paper-dolls from the Mid-East, a starscope, books about camels, deserts, oases. Someone lent a black sheet, an old oriental carpet, and we rigged a Bedouin tent that took up a third of the classroom. Everyday, we sat in the tent and read Arab folktales.

In the midst of all this, writing workshop went on as usual, forty-five minutes of free writing every day, with no assignments given.

I would guess that about a third of the writing generated during that time had to do with North Africa. Examples:

AMINA WET TO THE WEL. SHE MET A BEOUTEFOOL BRD. THE BEOOTEFL BRD SED "FOLLOW ME AND I WEL TAK YOU AKROS THE SKY." SO SHE DID. AND HE DID.
(Written and shared by Daisy, a first grader.)

Eeeee ooooooh! Eeeeeeeh! Ooooooooh! Camel on the moon, camel on the moon, far away in the sky when the moon is right, you will see the lion and the bear. . .Camelon the moon, oooh eeeh!
(Camel-calming song by Alex, a first grader, sung at sharing time.)

Neighbor (approaching the tent): Salaam Aleikoum, Djuha! Can I borrow your donkey?
Djuha: Oh, my best frind, my very good friend, I would like to help you, but my donkey is not here today.
Donkey (behind the tent): HEE! Hawhaw HEE! HEE! Hawhaw HEE!
Neighbor: Oh! I am blessed with good fortune! Your donkey is here after all, Djuha!
Djuha: What? We have been friends for so many years that our beards are white with age, yet you believe a donkey, and you don't believe ME!?
(Scene from a play improvised by 3 second-graders based on a Bedouin folktale.)

Stock-Taking   On the second page of *Halima*, she wakes up and sees what is around her. The reader sees it too, and begins to identify with Halima. Because of what the writer writes, the reader hears what Halima hears. This is stock-taking.

Exercises in stock-taking can be done verbally, in the here and now:

■ Teacher: Close your eyes. Be perfectly quiet for a minute. . .O.K. One at a time, what did you hear? Did you imagine seeing anything? When you opened your eyes, what was there?

With a little more stage-setting, exercises can be used to ease children into a setting:

- Teacher: After days of difficult travel across the rocky desert, you arrive at a small oasis. The people who live nearby wish to welcome and comfort you. They come, bringing gifts. What do they bring? (There is a shepherds' song along these lines in *Amahl and the Night Visitors*.)
- Teacher, to one student: In your story, Miriam and Fatima meet at the well, in the evening. How can you make the the reader be there? Perhaps here, before Miriam and Fatima begin talking, you could put something in. . .Which one arrived first? While she waited, what did she see, hear, smell?
- Teacher, to two boys who have been working on a camel report: Try this: A caravan arrives and Ahmed tries to help water the camels. See if you can put the reader in Ahmed's place. What does he do, moment by moment? Does he make any mistakes?

Journal-Keeping   Why might your historical alter-ego be needing to keep a journal? This is a key question you need to answer if you are writing a story in this genre. Why does the hero of *I Capture the Castle* keep a journal? Why did Lawrence of Arabia?

You and your students can play with setting up reasons. Example: You are a spy, and have been parachuted into the desert to lead the villagers of Ouadi Kouf away before the arrival of Turkish enemies. You write down every landmark.

Letters   Letters are similar, but you have to answer two questions: why are you writing, and to whom? Examples of set-ups:

- You have fallen ill at the oasis. Is there someone you could write to, to tell where you are and what has happened?
- Let's suppose you have done something stupid and landed in jail. You are charged with something more serious than the crime you actually committed. Write to your father or the governor and expain the situation. See if you can get a short story rolling beginning with this letter.

Ways of Thinking, Ways of Talking.   One of the pleasures of writing *Halima* was to read through Arab folktales and pick out expressions (May Allah smooth your path) and comparisons (sweet as the sugarcane, trembling like a gazelle) which, though they no doubt would sound hackneyed to an Arab reader, are still fresh and poetic to most of us. Exercises, from simply collecting expressions and turns of phrase, to listing topics characters are likely to be discussing, to improvising or writing actual monologue and dialogue can set the wheels of imagination and curiosity rolling. Here are some examples:

- Read an Arab folktale (choose one with plenty of greetings), and write down the greetings people use when they meet and when they part company. Using these or similar greetings, write a short polite dialogue between an old teacher and a student he meets on the street.
- In my story, Abdul, a camel driver, is caught in a blinding storm. I think he would sing to his camel to keep him calm. Can you help me make up the words to his song?

(Alex's camel-calming song was in response to this question, which was given not as an assignment, but as a writer-to-writer cry for help.)

The Search for Structure   What are the historical conflicts in the setting you have chosen to write about? In *Halima* there are conflicts between nomads and settled farmers, conflicts between the legalistic Moslems and the most mystical Sufi Moslems, conflicts between those who want to shape events to their plans and those who wish to live life poetically, accepting it as it unfurls.

Where do your characters stand? What are the personal conflicts? (as between desire and duty, for instance, or between loyalty to one's sister and anxiety over her safety.)

These questions are easier to apply to student work once some models of historical fiction have been discussed in class. No need to start with *War and Peace*. A book as simple as Jay Williams' *Everyone Knows what a Dragon Looks Like* (1976), in which almost all the historical information is provided by the pictures, can serve admirably as a model for analysing plot and conflicts. The simpler the model, the easier it is to use.

Superactions   What is it that Halima, as portrayed in the first chapter, most wants? What does Saladeen want? A superaction is someone's strongest motive at the moment, best expressed as a verb: to dominate, to control, to comfort, to reconcile, to entertain, to distract, and so forth. Halima's, in the first scene, is simply to be with Atiyah. Saladeen's is to control.

To make a given scene vivid, I explore the conflict between superactions. In one of the scenes given from *Halima*, the superactions of two characters are sketched: Saladeen's is to control, to exercise power; Essafeh's is to appease, to make peace.

The idea of superactions yields interesting writing exercises: Examples:

- Analyze *Trouble River* (1969) (or any story) in terms of superactions.
- Brainstorm for a variety of superactions, put them on cards, have pairs of students pull two at random and improvise a scene with dialogue built on the conflict between the two.
- Create a single character in whom two superactions vie for supremacy: for instance, to profit and to be respected.
- Discuss with a group of students the historic conflicts inherent with the times being studied. Then ask them to create a scene with two people who have conflicting superactions that dramatize the historical conflict.

Brotherhoods   By this term, for which I am indebted to Dorothy Heathcote, I mean the ability to universalize a happening or feeling in the story, by thinking of other people who have been in a comparable situation or and the same feelings.

Let me take as an example a scene in *Halima* where Raisulu meets Zenaya in Halima's presence. Raisulu and Zenaya are in the brotherhood of estranged lovers who still feel strong emotional bonds, who would rather fight than have no contact.

In trying to construct words between them I thought of the other couples: Kate and Petrucchio, Titania and Oberon, not to mention real friends. I borrowed words from Oberon, love-hate words ("Ill-met by moonlight, fair Titania"), for their brief dialogue.

In a wide variety of circumstances we have all been in the brotherhood of those who wait anxiously, of those so excited and elated that they cannot sleep, of those who prepare for celebration, of those who feel cheated, and so on.

The device of seeking brotherhoods helps us bring all our human material to the aid of our writing: it is the one that calls our empathy and accuracy of feeling. Examples:

■ Teacher to individual student: In your story, the goatherd has lost a goat, and you say that he is afraid to go back to his father. Let's think for a minute about how he feels. Is he one of the brotherhood of those who live in fear of their parents because their parents are unreasonably cruel, I wonder? Or is he one of those who love their parents and are afraid to disappoint them?. . .

■ Teacher to individual student: Your Fatima is preparing for a dance. She is of the sisterhood of those preparing to celebrate. Can you think of other people in that sisterhood? How do they feel? Does anyone remember the song Maria sings in West Side Story when she is getting ready for the dance? Have you ever watched your brother or sister get ready for a party?

Though the concept of brotherhoods is hard to verbalize, it is one most young children use instinctively. It is an instinct to be cultivated, to be modeled through open-ended self-questioning, perhaps.

One last word about the development a teacher might expect within the genre of historical fiction. It will be new to most of your students no matter what age group you teach.

The youngest children are likely to be long on empathy and short on facts. However, I find that once their empathy is engaged, they become voracious seekers of facts. Look for historical scenes or circumstances that appeal to empathy (slaves trying to escape, miners on strike, Richard the Lion-Hearted locked away in a castle keep). Be prepared with sources of facts that they can dig out themselves, and restrain the urge to choose for them. Instead, write your own story using the sources in the room, and share as a fellow-writer. Expect amazement.

Eeeeeh oooooh! Eeeeeeh! Ooooooooh! Camel on the moon, camel on the moon, far away in the sky when the moon is right, you will see the lion and the bear. . .Camel on the moon, oooh eeeh!

REFERENCES

Bushnaq, I. (1986) *Arab folktales*. New York: Pantheon Books.

Byars, B. (1969). *Trouble River*, New York: Viking.

Menotti, G.C. *Amahl and the night visitors*, recording.

Wagner, B.J. (1986). *Dorothy Heathcote: Drama as a learning medium*, Washington, DC: National Education Association.

Williams, J. (1976). *Everyone knows what a dragon looks like*. New York: Scholastic, Inc.

*Writers of many books for children, **Connie and Peter Roop** bring us a model for teaching scientific writing that is at once refreshing and scientifically sound—not an easy task. By showing children how they capture their readers and how they sculpt their texts, Connie Roop invites her middle school children to do the same. This chapter is not just for science teachers. The adaptability of the Roops' approach will be as apparent to the reader as Frances Temple's use of journals is for writing historical fiction. In addition, while Frances works with elementary children and Connie with middle schoolers, age quickly becomes irrelevant in both chapters.*

CHAPTER 19
THE NATURE
OF WRITING
IN THE
SCIENCE
CLASSROOM

Connie and Peter Roop

PART A: SPRING,
EXCERPT FROM *SEASONS OF THE CRANES*

Winter is leaving the tundra wetlands of Wood Buffalo National Park in northern Canada. The warming sun melts the last snow of the passing season.

Ripples roll across the water of a shallow pond. The raspy croaks of a lone wood frog announce the wakening day. Butterflies whirl over the wetlands. A rambling bear drinks from the pond. In the distance, the branches of a spruce creaks in the wind.

The frog croaks again but its voice is drowned out by the trumpeting call of a whooping crane.

"KER-LEE-OO. KER-LEE-OO."

The call echoes throughout the marsh and nearby woods

"KER-LEE-OO, KER-LEE-OO."

The large white cranes, their wings tipped in black, swing in a wide spiral out of the clear sky. Two more whooping cranes have returned to Wood Buffalo.

The birds, a male and a female, bank and turn gracefully as they approach a possible nesting territory. But they fly on as they see another pair of cranes already established in the pond.

The four birds call back and forth to each other.

The cranes find another nesting site, a pond surrounded by clumps of bulrushes. Fluttering their wings, they glide down and land.

In an age old instinctive pattern the newly mated cranes bow their heads and quickly raise them. Beaks pointed at the sky, they unite in their unique call and announce the return to their spring home.

The whooping cranes immediately begin stalking the marshy wetlands. After their 2,700 mile journey from Texas, they are anxious to start nest building.

They are also very hungry. The long-legged whoopers hunt snails and damselflies. As they search for food, they claim a territory of nearly two square miles for their future family.

After feeding, the cranes preen themselves. They dip their beaks into the still-chilly water and carefully rearrange their white, satiny-soft feathers.

The sun hangs low on the horizon and the cranes prepare for the coming night. The howl of a gray wolf cuts through the air. An early evening breeze passes through the marsh rustling the bulrushes, still brown from winter.

The last rays of the sun silhouette the long-legged cranes. Heads raised, the pair calls again in unison. As the silence of evening settles over the ponds and marshes, the cranes stand close together and sleep.

Morning dawns. Ice has formed on the fringes of the ponds. Diamonds of sunlight flash on the frosty bulrushes. Awake and alert, the cranes call together to the new day.

The cranes feed on snails, leeches, and water bugs, leaving trails of their three-toed tracks on the muddy pond bottom. As they feed, they search for a safe nesting site.

Suddenly, the male crane leaps into the air. He lands, dipping his long neck in front of his mate. He curves his neck back, raising his seven-foot wide wings skyward. He sweeps his feathers through the air.

"KER-LEE-OO," he calls as he begins another round of the cranes' courtship dance.

The female watches her mate as he swags and prances, weaves and bobs for her. Within moments she joins him, matching his movements. Arching her broad wings she chases him into the pond and quickly follows. Together they point their beaks at the sky and trumpet. Their calls echo over the marsh.

Back on shore, the male crouches, then springs five feet into the air. He lands and bends low. Opening his beak, he grabs mud and reeds flinging them as he scurries behind his companion. With skill and grace he leaps over her.

As the days pass, the cranes dance more often. Their dancing is interrupted only by feeding and nestbuilding. Each dance strengthens the bond between the new mates who will remain true to each other for life.

As the days lengthen, the courting becomes more intense. The whoopers eat, preen themselves, dance, rest, and renew their dancing.

Tall bulrushes are trampled, broken, and carried to the nest site. The surrounding bulrushes camouflage the nest. Slowly the cranes build a mound of reeds nearly three feet across. A shallow bowl in the center is left for the eggs.

The first egg is laid. The olive-colored egg, sprinkled with brown spots, is four inches long. The female stays on the nest several hours, scarcely moving. Her mate feeds and preens himself while watching the surrounding marsh. Stretching to his full height of almost five feet, he peers over the tops of the bulrushes watching for predators with his piercing yellow eyes.

The female cries softly, calling him to relieve her. He walks slowly to the nest, pausing between each two steps. He stops twice, once to peck a fresh water clam and again to assure their safety.

The female stands, stretching to her full height. Nearly as tall as her mate, she flaps her wings and steps carefully off the nest.

The male nudges the egg, rolling it over gently with his beak. The female stalks away while the male settles himself on the nest. He twists and turns until the egg rest comfortably beneath him. Feeding and preening, the female takes up the patrol.

A second egg is laid the following morning. The two eggs, twice as long as chicken eggs, lie side by side in the shallow bowl of bulrushes. The cranes continue to exchange duties. With each change the eggs are rolled over so that a healthy chick grows inside.

Late that same day another crane flies over the pond.

''KER-LOO,'' cries the male, rising from the nest.

''KER-LEE-OO,'' comes the answering call from the approaching bird.

The male steps off the nest. The female snuggles protectively over their eggs. Flapping his wide wings, the male moves rapidly away from the nest. He stops when he reaches the edge of their territory.

The incoming crane lands nearby and begins searching for food. The male, angered by the intruder and determined to drive him away, calls again and again.

''KER-LOO. KER-LOO. KER-LOO.''

He flaps his huge wings, spreading his jet black wingtips to appear more fearsome.

The intruder continues to feed but makes no effort to challenge the protective crane. He feeds further away from the nest. When his hunger is satisfied, he spreads his wings, rises skyward, and skims over the pond. Without a mate, he will be unable to claim a territory of his own.

The male crane remains on the ground, his red-capped head motionless.

Now that the intruder has left, he begins patrolling the entire boundary of their territory. He circles the pond, stalks to the edge of the spruce trees, crosses the narrow twisting steam. Occasionally he pauses to spear a frog or snatch a dragonfly.

For the next 30 days the watchful cranes keep the eggs warm as the chicks grow.

A moose wanders through the pond each morning feeding on the tender sedge grasses. The cranes watch her closely. Whenever she feeds too near the nest, the cranes trumpet their call of alarm, and the moose moves off in a different direction.

Black bears, wolves, and lynx are rapidly chased away from the cranes territory. Soaring eagles and swooping great horned owls keep their distance from the ever vigilant cranes knowing their hard, sharp beaks can cause great pain.

Early one morning the cranes hear a weak peeping sound coming from one of the eggs. The peeping continues all that day and into the next. In the early afternoon a tiny beak pokes a hole through the shell. The chick taps and chips at the shell all afternoon. Using the eggtooth on the end of its beak the chick slowly enlarges the hole. By late afternoon the chick knocks away the last of the shell, sheds it watery membrane, and at once, dives under the warm feathers of its mother.

A little later the chick emerges. A warm breeze fluffs her to a reddish ball no bigger than a robin. The newborn crane is so weary from her struggle to hatch that she can stand for only a few minutes.

Night falls. It gets colder but the mother warms her chick and egg through the night. Standing on guard, the father protects his family.

By morning the crane chick is stronger. She takes several wobbly steps on her shaky legs. The male crane watches the chick while warming the second egg. The female leaves her family, poking and probing for food with her long beak. She eats for herself and then returns to the nest with a grasshopper in her beak. She crushes the grasshopper and dangles the morsel in front of her chick. The chick pecks at the bit of food. The female drops the grasshopper onto the ground and the peeping chick pecks again. Tilting her head, she swallows the grasshopper bit by bit.

The second egg hatches that afternoon. It is a male. Like his sister, this chick is out of the nest and wobbling about within 24 hours.

The family abandons the nest the next day.

The crane chicks instinctively peck at everything: sticks, rocks, bugs, each other, even their parents' legs. Only sometimes do they succeed in capturing their own food. Both parents bring them dragonflies, damselflies, and grasshoppers to eat.

The female chick, hatched first, is bigger than her brother. Her parents feed her first. She often fights her brother and steals his food.

As they eat more and more the little cranes grow tremendously fast, sometimes as much as an inch a day.

As the chicks grow taller, the days lengthen. By the time the ruddy sun sets on the last day of spring, the two young cranes stand a foot tall.

Twenty hours of sunlight grace Canada's far northern wilderness that day. Twilight quietly and gently ends the first season of the cranes.

PART B: WRITING IN SCIENCE CLASS

For the past 17 years as a science teacher, I have astonished students by discouraging them from writing reports. Instead, I steered them towards other types of projects: reading literature with a scientific theme, the creation of jokes and riddles based upon science vocabulary, developing classroom debates about scientific controversies such as the extinction of the dinosaurs.

However, it did not occur to me to introduce writing into my science program until after Peter and I had written *Seasons of the Cranes* (1989). By bringing *Seasons of the Cranes* into my classroom, I provided an excellent model for meaningful writing. As William Zinsser point out in his book, *Writing to Learn* (1988), "...writing is learned mainly by imitation."

By imitating the process Peter and I used in writing *Seasons of the Cranes*, I hoped to help my junior high students write well. As Zinsser says, "Clear writing is the logical arrangement of thought; a scientist who thinks clearly can write as well as the best writer."

In *Seasons of the Cranes* our goal was to write the story of a year in the life of a crane family that would appeal to a broad audience of young readers. We first decided upon the seasonal structure of the book before beginning our intense research about Whooping Cranes. Using real incidents in crane behavior, we then created the story of one year in the life of a crane family. While each incident in the book was based on scientific fact, the book as whole was written from the storyteller's viewpoint. We combined the facts of research with the fiction of storytelling.

INTRODUCING *SEASONS OF THE CRANES* TO STUDENTS

To appeal to a wide variety of student learning styles, I introduced the writing project to my class by showing slides while reading excerpts from *Seasons of the Cranes*. Students listened to the language of the text while responding to the visual "information" given by the pictures. They saw how the slides in the book supported as well as added to the information within the text. I discussed using photographs and illustrations as a research source as well as a technique to draw the reader deeper into the text.

As a class, we listed all the information they remembered from each chapter. The students were intrigued by the incubation period for Whooping Cranes. "For the next 30 days the watchful cranes keep the eggs warm as the chicks grow inside.'' accurately and actively describes the incubation period for Whooping Cranes.

A chorus of "Oh's" rippled through the class at the sight of the downy, newborn crane chick.

They were impressed by the seven foot wing span of adult Whooping Cranes.

We discussed how we wove these facts into the fabric of our story. We also discussed how and why they as readers responded to these facts.

MODELING THE WRITING PROCESS

I then shared the writing process. I read from different drafts and, using an overhead projector, discussed the drafting process as we molded the story. I showed them our mistakes and how we revised.

For example, one scientist pointed out that one aspect of our description of the Whooping Crane unison dance was not correct. Sandhill Cranes, not Whooping Cranes, toss plants and mud "painting" themselves while dancing.

Our editor asked us to tighten and to use more poetic and less scientific words within the text. For example, one of our first paragraphs originally read, "Having reaffirmed their life-long bond to each other, the Whooping Cranes immediately begin surveying the marsh wetlands." She suggested we cut "Having reaffirmed their life-long bond to each other, since a similar statement appeared later in the manuscript. She did not like "surveying;" it was too scientific. That paragraph became, "The Whooping Cranes immediately begin stalking the marshy wetlands. After their 2,700 mile journey from Texas, they are anxious to start nest building.''

The photographs available required other changes in the text. The number of cranes invading our crane family's territory was changed to fit the number of cranes in our photograph.

Students learned how we incorporated the input from scientists as well as our editor. They understood how we made the photographs match the text.

The students reacted with surprise and amazement to the drafts.

"Boy, are your drafts messy! You didn't spell every word right either!"

"You changed words and cut whole paragraphs!"

"You wrote the book fifteen different times!"

"Your beautiful book was rejected 20 times!"

I stressed that a first draft is just that, the first time that you try to get all of your ideas and information onto paper. Reshaping and rewriting come next.

In responding to the drafts, I ask them the questions we ask ourselves. Does this sentence make sense? Does this move the story forward? Is this really the way the cranes would have acted or am I giving them human characteristics? Can I shorten this paragraph and say the same thing? Would someone else want to read this and enjoy it? Is my ending strong enough? As I ask these questions, we discuss them by highlighting examples from our drafts.

Here is one example of how we improved one paragraph. Originally it read, "Increasing attention is paid to nest building. Tall grasses are trampled and pulled to a spot well hidden by cattails. Reeds and sedges are used to create a camouflaged nest. Eventually the shallow bowl, nearly three feet across, is ready for the arrival of eggs."

Rewritten this read. "Tall bulrushes are trampled, broken, and carried to the nest site. Slowly the cranes build a mound of reeds nearly three feet across. A shallow bowl in the center is left for the eggs." This more actively and concisely tells about nest building.

By closely examining *Seasons of the Cranes*, I wanted to encourage my students to do the same with their own writing about mice, owls, whales, wolves, and other animals. I believe that for many of my young writers, the process of writing became real when they saw actual drafts and attempted to incorporate my approach into their own writing. I hoped for, but did not expect, that all my students would write well. However, most students *did* experience growth as a writer.

Another advantage of this method is that my students see the importance of revision. By sharing and demonstrating my own writing process, I show my students the necessity of revision. Second, even third drafts, are seen as the natural part of writing, not a punishment that teachers invented to torture students. I also stress that, if they expect to find an interested reader, their writing should be the best it can be. "Why write a story or an article if no one is going to enjoy reading it?" I ask.

TEACHER AS EDITOR

Students then were given the assignment; they were to become "writers on assignment." I was to be their editor. As their editor, I established these guidelines for this writing project. They must write a quality article or story about an animal that illustrated the animal's life cycle through the seasons. Information on the animal's habitat, behavior, number of young, and care of young must be included.

As editor, I set the deadlines. I allotted eight weeks for the project. Within the next two weeks, they had to show me their research materials. A first draft of their manuscript was due two weeks after their research materials were checked. A second draft was due two weeks after that and the final manuscript was to be submitted and published within the next four weeks.

As a writer, I feel it is necessary to provide an adequate time for a writing project. Often we do not give students enough to research, write, react, and revise. This leads to imprecise and uninspired writing. Time for reflecting upon one's writing is critical and I provided this for my students.

I emphasized the writer's vocabulary. I wanted my students to talk and think like writers. Author, manuscript, draft, rewrite, revise, submit, deadline, editing, editor, publication, writer, proofreading were used regularly by me as well as the students. They began to see themselves as real writers with real deadlines who would submit real manuscripts for real publication. Through both our words and our actions in class, we modelled professional writing. It was interesting to me that only one student complained about the multitude drafts required to complete this project.

I left the form open for student choice. They could select any fictional form or nonfiction format for their project. At the end of the project I received poems, short stories, long stories, articles and letters to the editor. Two students (who selected an owl and mouse) had originally hoped to produce a play to demonstrate the interaction between these animals but this proved impractical for them for one student was highly motivated and the other missed her deadlines.

Students were aware that they were expected to share their work with the class, not just me. I mentioned that I hoped their manuscript could be published in other places such as our school newspaper ''Rebel Talk,'' a local magazine, ''Lakesider,'' nature center newsletters, local or national magazines. I reemphasized that they were not writing for me but for reaching a broader audience.

STUDENTS AS WRITERS

After they had decided on their individual animals, we then spent a class period in the school library looking for and selecting material on their animal. At first, most students limited their research to books. By looking at copyright dates, it was easy for them to see that much of the information was not current. They then searched for magazines and periodials for up-to-date information. Students brought in magazines like the *Zoo Books* or *National Geographic* from home and I searched my files for newspaper articles which I had clipped.

Students selected a wide range of animals in a variety of environments. One student, interested in endangered species, wrote about whales. Another selected toads because our class had been given a toad for a classroom pet. A deer hunter selected White-tail deer while another student chose to write about a Water Moccasin.

Individual student writing often generated or reflected strong feelings about the animal. Carolyn, who wrote about whales, not only learned scientific information but her story reflected her concern for the survival of these animals. Her epilogue concluded by saying, ''Whales are an endangered species. If their killing continues, they will become extinct. Extinction is forever. But, if everyone helps, the whales might just survive.''

She followed up this assignment by writing letters in support of international bans on the killing of whales. Her voice will reach beyond my classroom—to our community and our government.

Another student wrote about owls. Her first draft follows. A good start, but it did not fulfill all the criteria in my writing guidelines. Sarah had accurately described some of the activities and habits of owls. Her language reflected the owl's nocturnal habits as in her last stanza, ''As the sun rises with soundless wings, the owl flies back to its den, to sleep until the next moonshine begins, so he can become a night bird again. However, she needed to add more information to her poem. What about an owl's young? How many does it have? Does it build a nest? Does it have any major changes in activity throughout the year? Does it have any natural enemies?

First Draft of Poem by Sarah Ryerson

|First Draft)   Sarah Ryerson

Reference: Owls By, Herbert S. Zim
© 1950 Published Dominion of Canada
Wm. Collins Sons & Co, Canada Ltd.

1) Owls are night birds and hunt in the dark
they capture a mouse scurring away
as they soar over the oark
dangling from their mouth is their prey

2) As you know the owl can turn its head around
which it does now
and without a sound
kills a rabbit with its powerful claws

3) The owl sees another victim for his feast tonight
and like a magic wand
goes into flight
and grabs a duck from the pond

4) Owls swallow small animals whole
when they kill it
they don't eat the bones though
they're thrown up in a ball called a pellet

5) As the sun rises with soundless wings
the owl flies back to its den
to sleep until the next moonshine begins
so he can become a night bird again

By, Sarah Ryerson

She succeeded in her second draft to include the necessary information. Sarah accurately described the activities of an owl. ''Seeing predators and other owls, they fluff up their feathers, and hiss like cats do.''

Second draft of poem.

As the moon rises
the owl's pupils grow wide
no, he is not surprised
and away he glides

Owls are night birds and hunt in the dark
they capture a mouse scurring away
as they soar over the park
from their mouth dangles their prey

Depending upon how much food they catch
a certain number of young
will hatch
and thus live among them

Animals and humans that get too near
will see an owl swoop down
to tell them they shouldn't be here
and then they return to their nest so as not to be found

Owls swallow small animals whole
when they kill it
they don't swallow the bones though
they're thrown up in a ball called a pellet

A thick covering of feathers
on the owl's feet and legs
protect them from predators
like rats, mice and snakes

As you know the owl can turn its head around
which it does now
and without a sound
kills a rabbit with its powerful claws

When owls see predators
or other owls too
they fluff up their feathers
and hiss like cats do

The owl sees another victim for his feast tonight
and like a magic wand
he lifts off and goes into flight
and grabs a duck from the pond

As the sun rises with soundless wings
the owl flies back to its den
to sleep until the next moonshine begins
so he can become a night bird again

by Sarah Ryerson

I am not a poet but did realize many lines were too long, the poem was wordy, and the rhyme was sometimes forced.

Her final draft reflects literary changes. She reduced the length of her lines and eliminated words. Sarah has submitted her poem to a variety of publications.

Final Draft of Sarah's Poem.

As the moon rises
the owl's pupils grow wide
no, he is not surprised
away he glides

Owls, night birds, hunting in the dark
catching a mouse
as they soar over the park
from their mouth dangles their prey

Depending upon food caught
certain numbers of young
will be hatched
to live with the mother

Animals and humans getting near
will see mother owl swoop down
to say go away from here
then returns to the cowering owlets, not to be found

Owls swallow small animals whole
when they kill it
they don't eat bones though
they're thrown up in a pellet

Thick coverings of feathers
on the feet and legs
protect from predators
rats, mice, and snakes

The owl can turn its head around
it does that now,
then without a sound
kills a rabbit with powerful claws

When owls see predators,
other owls too
they fluff their feathers
hissing like cats do

The owl sees another victim tonight
and like a magic wand
lifts off going into flight
grabbing a duck from the pond

As the sun rises with soundless wings
the owl flies back to its den
to sleep until the next moonshine begins
and thus becomes a night bird again

References

Owls
By, Herbert S. Zim
© 1950 Published—Dominion of Canada
Wm. Collins Sons & Co., Canada Ltd.

Owls Zoo Books
By, Timothy Levi Biel
© 1987 Wildlife Education
Printed by Frye and Smith, San Diego

CONCLUSION

It is possible for students to write nonfiction creatively, and imaginatively. To accomplish this goal, students must be given realistic deadlines, assisted in researching the information and writing and rewriting their project. This is a writing project which requires a purpose. A student's writing audience can be the class, school, community, state, or nation.

Through writing nonfiction, we give our students a necessary lifetime skill. No matter what field of study is involved, good writing is essential. As William Zinsser explains, "Whoever the writer and whatever the subject. . .the common thread is a sense of high enjoyment, zest, and wonder." Perhaps, both in learning to write and in writing to learn, they are the only ingredients that really matter." Students need to be able to seek and acquire current, accurate information, to write information in an interesting and convincing format. They learn that through their words they can direct change in their life and their world.

I realized through this writing project that I should share more of our writing with my students. Up to this point in time, I have been reluctant to do so. However, their response was overwhelmingly positive. I am providing a link to the world of writing, a world in which students can actively participate.

REFERENCES

Roop, C. & Roop, P. (1989). *Seasons of the Cranes*. New York: Walker & Co.
Zinsser, W. (1988). *Writing to learn*. New York: Harper & Row.

SELECTED BIBLIOGRAPHY

Clark, R.P. (1988). *Free to write*. Portsmouth, NH: Heineman Educational Books.

This book is an excellent resource for any teacher of writing. It explains how to be a writer and an effective teacher of the writing process. It concludes with a list of resource books on teaching children to write, the writing process, the craft of journalism, and children and literacy.

Roberts, E.M. (1986). *Nonfiction for children*. Cincinnati, OH: Writer's Digest Books.

This book is a valuable resource for both writers and teachers of nonfiction. Using a nuts and bolts approach, Roberts provides background on children's books, the writing process, and getting published.

Kobrin, B. (1988). *Eyeopeners*. New York: Penguin Books.

Kobrin has compiled, categorized, and annotated many of the best nonfiction books available for children. She gives readers ideas how to utilize books in each topic. It is an excellent resource for teachers, librarians, parents, and writers.

In this beautifully written epilogue to **Writers in the Classroom,** *Sheila Cowing reiterates the message, once again, that teachers who teach writing must come to grips with their own literacy. She also makes clear the need to publish children's work in school—even more than in national magazines, where "most submissions will have to be rejected." My hope is that while listening to Sheila Cowing talk about the writer's craft, a craft she knows well, you will leave* **Writers in the Classroom** *with a clearer sense of purpose: a mission to ensure that all students have the opportunity to write, often, and that their teachers publish their work.*

EPILOGUE: Choosing Publication For Children

Sheila Cowing

After the class finishes its wonderful stories and poems, how will the children celebrate them? The teacher who writes with them understands the need to applaud their effort. The act of completion is one kind of celebration, but children are often eager to read their work to each other, soliciting reactions. Showing the created work is part of its purpose.

One writes to be read, and art is a circle of gifts—writer to reader, reader to writer. Young writers and readers like school publishing programs. Whether school publishing means display on a bulletin board, pages bound and graphics applied with a desktop publishing system, or reading the work out loud to a school PTA assembly, feedback is drawn to the creator soon after the work is finished. What a reinforcing moment—when a classmate tells a young writer, "I really loved the storm in your story, you made me feel I was *in* it."

Some children, however, feel that school publishing is not real, but merely an imitation of the world, and therefore, that their writing is not being taken seriously. For these young writers, or for particularly strong writers, teachers may want to consider national magazine publication. Books such as *The Market Guide for Young Writers*, from Betterway, in Crozet, Virginia and *Children's Writers & Illustrators Market* from Writer's Digest Books in Cincinnati, describe national markets for students. If possible, study two sources. Write editors with questions and request copies of magazines; most will be free to educators.

Sealing a manilla envelope around children's poems or stories should be a carefully considered act. A sensitive, creative child may receive much needed reinforcement from publication in a national magazine. But the risk of rejection is large.

253

When Sara, 11, sends her story to a children's magzine such as *Shoe Tree*, or *Stone Soup*, or *Creative Kids*, she has no idea what to expect. Writing has been an intense experience for Sara, one in which she "lost herself." She loves her story, and her teacher suggested it was good enough to publish. Sara worries; how long will she have to wait? When, two months later, a letter finally arrives, it begins. "I'm delighted to inform you," and Sara is excited. Now she worries about the wording of the paragraph she writes for the magazine's contributors' notes.

The editor decides that Sara's story, a mystery featuring Australian animals, would be even more fun illustrated. The editor sends a copy to Mary, whose drawings she has seen and asks her if she'd like to illustrate. It is August and the illustrator has lots of time to work on her black and white creations. When the drawings are done, black and white dingos and koalas live near an Aussie estate where murder has been committed. The editor writes a pleased letter. Story and illustration go to the typesetter and then onto the printer.

Sara's story comes out in the winter issue, seven or eight months after Sara mailed it in. The magazine presents the work with respect and carries short paragraphs about both the author and the illustrator. Sara and Mary feel confirmed in their talent, as all writers and illustrators, all human beings, need to be. They feel special.

And they *are* special. With 3 or 4 64-page issues a year, the magazine can accept roughly 60 poems and stories from among 1000 or more submissions.

Imagine now that Sara submits her story and the editor has no space. Such a story may be accepted for a later issue; often it must be rejected. A story may be refused for a number of reasons that have little to do with its quality or even how it compares with writing by other children. Perhaps the editor already has two animal stories, or five contributions from Michigan; perhaps there is space for a three-page story, and Sara's story is six. Sara receives a form letter, one which encourages, but still a form letter. If the writer is younger than nine, she/he receives a certificate of thanks, one that never even says "sorry" or "unfortunately." As editor of one of the national magazines written and illustrated by children, I question the value of submission each time I mail a rejection letter.

An editor seldom knows when a child is upset by rejection; when she learns, she may write almost frantic personal letters trying to comfort. What this editor wants is not to comfort, but to encourage, even inspire, small writers—while encouraging the needy small writer in herself.

For this editor is first of all a writer, as a child and young adult a "closet writer," keenly aware of the sensitivity of children who attempt art. Many start seriously, copying a master, Wordsworth or Walt Whitman. We substitutue our own words, and "the tops of our heads come off," as Dickinson wrote, when our words flow with the master's rhythm. While we can't submit copies to a magazine, we are learning the form, the way a master of constitutional law must first understand the Magna Carta. We become immersed in the form and the process. To help, our teachers too write; they need to understand how in "the airy nothing" between imagination and paper, words develop color and light—or run to mud.

If the airy nothing attracts a negative response, the chances are good that the magic smears. Critical comment from *anyone*, particularly one who cannot imagine choosing one image over another, may negate not only the story, but its teller's feelings about self.

The process is every bit as fragile as it sounds. Each attempt to say imaginatively is sound, until perforated with suggestions. Revision, re-vision, is an acquired taste. Young writers are not one bit tough, and the creation of art is very difficult. That is why it is essential that adults who work with children writing, write themselves.

The process is both the glory and the problem. Creativity may be impossible to teach; taught mechanically, writing can be boring, or worse, a turn-off. But writing can be taught through the creative process if the teacher has experienced it personally. Pleasure in art must be in process, not in the product, which is why grades, yes, even publication, may not matter. Writing is for the joy or the pain or the fear. Communication? Of course. But the greatest temptation for a writer, one that we abet by urging publication, is a kind of greediness, a *need* to be in print. This need to prove one's worth (or to show off, or to earn confirming dollars) can speed or freeze writing, paralyzing the loose associations of the imagination, until the creative process itself may be destroyed in eagerness to be done and published. Little fine writing results from too much interest in being in print.

Try not to permit students to inflate the idea of publication. Publishing in a children's magazine will not grease a writer's way into *Harpers*. The adult publishing world is extremely competitive and not particulary sensitive to creative sensibility. This is one more reason why teachers who teach children writing should themselves write—to develop their own creative sensibilities, to feel a child's passion for the process. Students may have reasons for writing that are personal and intense, and we must be concerned for these children.

All that said, some children's literary magazines are beautiful, compiled, and edited with great care. Inside their covers, the quality of poems and stories is inspiring for young writers and teachers alike. An intelligent, compassionate editor tries to nurture young writers. Contributors may grow in confidence; in such a magazine the publishing experience may help a child develop a lifetime love of good writing.

CONTRIBUTORS

Ruth Nathan   received her Ph.D. in Reading Education from Oakland University, Rochester, MI. She has been a writing consultant for several Detroit area public schools and is co-director with Keith Stanovich of the reading research team at Oakland University. She is coauthor, with Charles Temple, Frances Temple, and Nancy Burris of *The Beginnings of Writing*, 2nd edition, Allyn and Bacon, 1988.

Sandy Asher   is currently writer-in-residence at Drury College. She received her elementary education certification from Drury College and has done graduate work at the University of Connecticut. Her publications include over a dozen children's books and ten plays. She has a series, *Ballet One*, now in progress with Scholastic.

Terry Blackhawk   teaches high school English and creative writing at Mumford High School in the Detroit Public School system. She is currently engaged in doctoral work on language education at Oakland University. Her poems have been widely published in a number of journals including *Passages North*, *Wayne Literary Review*, *The Louisville Review*, and others.

Roy Peter Clark received his Ph.D. in English from the State University of New York at Stony Brook. He is author of *Free to Write: A Journalist Teaches Young Writers*, Heinemann, 1987, and *Coaching Writers: The Human Side of Editing*, St. Martin's Press, in press. He is Dean of the faculty at the Poynter Institute for Media Studies.

Sheila Cowing is Editor of *Shoe Tree Magazine*, a national magazine of student writing.

Rosemary Deen is Associate Professor at Queen's College, City University of New York. She is the poetry editor for *Commonweal* Magazine. Her current projects include a book on writing about literature and a volume of poetry. Published works include *Beat Not the Poor Desk* (with Marie Ponsot), 1982 and *The Common Sense*, 1985, both published by Boynton Cook/Heinemann.

Larry J. Hayes is the editorial page editor for the Fort Wayne, IN *Journal-Gazette*. He received more than 30 state and national awards for editorial writing and was a finalist for the Pulitzer Prize in 1986. He is at present Chairman of the Ethics Committee, NCEW, and Vice President of the Education Writers' Association.

Judith Hilla is English and Communications Instructor at North Kent Alternative High School in Comstock Park, MI. She devotes much of her time on creative writing and cultural enrichment for at-risk high school students.

Will Hobbs received his M.A. in English from Stanford University and is the author of three young adult novels, all published by Atheneum: *Changes in Latitudes* (1988), *Bearstone* (1989), and *Downriver* (1991). *Bearstone* was voted an ALA Best Book and was also an IRA Teachers' Choices Book as well as a Children's Book Council Notable Book in Social Studies. *Changes in Latitude* is one of four finalists in the U.K. Earthworm Children's Book Award sponsored by Friends of the Earth.

Juliana Janosz   is a fifth grade teacher and teacher of writing to teachers in Walled Lake, MI. She received her degree from Central Michigan University, and has done graduate work at both Michigan State and Oakland University.

Heather Monkmeyer   received her B.S. in Elementary Education from Oakland University. She is currently completing her M.A.T. in Reading and Language Arts and is also a fifth grade teacher in the Walled Lake, MI, Consolidated School District.

Gloria Nixon-John   received her M.A. in Speech Communications and Journalism from Wayne State University and is currently working toward a Ph.D. in Composition Theory and Literature. She teaches in the Troy, MI, School District and also serves as writing consultant to several other districts.

Anne-Marie Oomen   received her M.A. from Western Michigan University. She teaches at Elk Rapids High School, MI. Her poetry has been widely published.

Connie and Peter Roop   both teach in the Appleton (WI) Area School District. Connie received her M.A. in science teaching from Boston College, and Peter received his M.A. in Children's Literature from Simmons College. Together they have written 14 books ranging from historical fiction to science. One of their books, *Keep the Lights Burning, Abbie*, (1985) published by Carolrhoda Books, has been featured on Reading Rainbow.

Leonora Smith   received her Ph.D. from Michigan State University, where she is currently an Assistant Professor in the Department of American Thought and Language. She has two published chapbooks, and her poems have appeared in over a dozen periodicals nationwide.

Photograph by Robert Turney, 607 Division, East Lansing, MI 48823

Carol Steele   received her M.A. in Communications form Wester Michigan University. She teaches in the Grand Rapids Public School system. Her stories have been published in a number of children's magazines, including *Cricket*.

Michael Steinberg   is Professor of American Thought and Language at Michigan State University, where he received his Ph.D. in English. He is author of *The Writer's Way: A Process-to-Product Approach to Composition* (1981), published by Heinemann.

Frances Nolting Temple   is a primary school teacher in Geneva, New York. She received her M.Ed. in Comparative and Community Education from the University of Virginia. She is co-author of *The Beginnings of Writing*, 2nd edition, published by Allyn and Bacon, 1988 and *Classroom Strategies: An Elementary Teacher's Guide to Process Writing*, 1988, published by Heinemann.

Alan Weber received his Ph.D. in English from the University of Illinois. He is currently an Assistant Professor at Central Michigan University. His inservice workshop series deals with writing for critical and creative thinking.

Heidi Wilkins is an elementary school teacher and district writing consultant in the Walled Lake, MI, Consolidated School District. She received her M.A. from Michigan State University.

INDEX

STRATEGIES INDEX